AF552536

A Buddhist Doctrine of Experience

A Buddhist Doctrine of Experience

A New Translation and Interpretation of the Works of Vasubandhu the Yogācārin

THOMAS A. KOCHUMUTTOM

MOTILAL BANARSIDASS PUBLISHERS
PRIVATE LIMITED • DELHI

4th Reprint : Delhi, 2017
First Edition : Delhi, 1982

ISBN: 978-81-208-0662-7

MOTILAL BANARSIDASS
41 U.A. Bungalow Road, Jawahar Nagar, Delhi 110 007
8 Mahalaxmi Chamber, 22 Bhulabhai Desai Road, Mumbai 400 026
203 Royapettah High Road, Mylapore, Chennai 600 004
236, 9th Main III Block, Jayanagar, Bengaluru 560 011
8 Camac Street, Kolkata 700 017
Ashok Rajpath, Patna 800 004
Chowk, Varanasi 221 001

MLBD Cataloging-in-Publication Data
A Buddhist Doctrine of Experience
by Thomas A. Kochumuttom
ISBN: 978-81-208-0662-7
Includes, Abbreviations, Introduction,
Appendix, Bibliography, Index
I. Buddhism, II. Kochumuttom, Thomas A.

Printed in India

by RP Jain at NAB Printing Unit,
A-44, Naraina Industrial Area, Phase I, New Delhi–110028
and published by JP Jain for Motilal Banarsidass Publishers (P) Ltd,
41 U.A. Bungalow Road, Jawahar Nagar, Delhi-110007

FOR MY FATHER

CONTENTS

PREFACE

The name Vasubandhu has been associated generally with two significant events in the history of Buddhism : the composition of *Abhidharma-kośa* on the one hand, and the founding of theYogācāra system on the other. More precisely, Vasubandhu is known as the author of *Abhidharma-kośa*, and also as the one who co-founded the Yogācāra system with his brother Asaṅga. As these two events—the composition of *Abhidharma-kośa* and the founding of the Yogācāra system—represent two different traditions within Buddhism, one begins to wonder if Vasubandhu the author of *Abhidharma-kośa* and Vasubandhu the co-founder of the Yogācāra system really are one and the same person. The traditional answer to this question has been that Vasubandhu the author of *Abhidharma-kośa* was later converted by his brother Asaṅga to the latter's Yogācāra line of thinking. That could very well be the case. But when it comes to deciding how to date Vasubandhu, the problem seems to reappear with a greater complexity. This is because the tradition gives as many as three dates for Vasubandhu : the year 1100 after the *nirvāṇa* of the Buddha given in *The Life of Vasubandhu* by the historian Paramārtha, the Year 900 after the *nirvāṇa* of the Buddha given in the commentary of *Madhyānta-vibhāga* by the same historian and the year 1000 after the *nirvāṇa* of the Buddha given by the Chinese pilgrim Hsüan-tsang. Based on the very few historical clues available from various sources, and taking into account the different ways of reckoning the year of the *nirvāṇa* of the Buddha, many scholars have tried to reconcile these three dates, and to arrive at a probable, if not definite, date for Vasubandhu. The dates so proposed range roughly from the early third century A.D. to the early sixth century A.D.[1] None

---

1. J. Takakusu in his "The Date of Vasubandhu, the Great Buddhist Philosopher", *Indian Studies in Honour of Charles Rickwell Lanman*, (Cambridge Mass. : 1929), pp. 79-88, repeating 'A.D. 420-500' for the date of Vasubandhu which he had proposed as early as 1905, has summarised the findings of different scholars in the meantime.

of them, however, has been universally accepted, although many of the opinions would agree on the fifth century as an approximate period for the life and works of Vasubandhu.

Then in 1951 Professor E. Frauwallner proposed his new theory of 'two Vasubandhus' as a way out of the three conflicting dates mentioned above : the years 900, 1000, and 1100 after the *nirvāṇa* of the Buddha.[2] His basic assumption is that the two dates given by Paramārtha, namely the years 900 and 1100 after the *nirvāṇa* of the Buddha, refer to two different persons, namely Vasubandhu the elder and Vasubandhu the younger respectively. He then argues that the date given by the Chinese pilgrim Hsüan-tsang, namely the year 1000 after the *nirvāṇa* of the Buddha, is the same as the year 1100 after the *nirvāṇa* of the Buddha given by Paramārtha, only they are arrived at by different ways of reckoning the date of the *nirvāṇa* of the Buddha. Thus, for Professor Frauwallner, the traditionally given three dates can be reduced to two, namely 900 and 1000/1100 after the *nirvāṇa* of the Buddha, and these two dates, he further said, correspond respectively to a time prior to 400 A.D. and the period 400—500 A.D. His final conclusion, there fore, is that there have been two Vasubandhus, of whom the elder who lived prior to 400 A.D., co-founded the Yogācāra system with his brother Asaṅga, and the younger who lived between 400—500 A.D., wrote *Abhidharma-kośa.*

The above theory of 'two Vasubandhus', possible as it is, does not seem to have received much support from scholars. On the contrary, P. S. Jaini, for one, on the evidence of the manuscript of *Abhidharma-dīpa* (together with a commentary—the *Vibhāṣā-prabhā-vṛtti*), discovered in 1937, "throws some doubt on Professor Frauwallner's thesis and confirms the older and universal tradition about the conversion of the Kośakāra Vasubandhu to Mahāyāna,"[3] Some of the recent studies,

---

2. E. Frauwallner, *On the Date of the Buddhist Master of the Law Vasubandhu* (Rome : Serie Orientale Roma, III, 1951).

3. P. S. Jaini, "On the Theory of Two Vasubandhus", *Bulletin of the School of Oriental and African Studies,* XXI (1958), p. 49.

notably those by Stefan Anacker[4] and D.N.G. Macleod,[5] also see little point in Frauwallner's theory of 'two Vasubandhus'. What is more, the latter himself is suggested to have later given up this theory.[6]

As far as the present work is concerned, as it is strictly a textual analysis, the questions of Vasubandhu's date and other biographical details are of little importance. I may, however, point out by way of a suggestion that an almost spontaneous transition from *Abhidharma-kośa* to the Yogācāra system is not altogether unwarranted. For instance, the theory of store consciousness (*ālaya-vijñāna*) which is universally recognized as a basic innovation by the Yogācārins, is after all only the "christening" of the theory of the seeds (*bīja*) in the *Abhidharma-kośa*. This latter theory has been given there in answer to questions such as : how are defilements associated with a previous moment of consciousness carried over to the next moment of consciousness ? How does a past deed produce its effect in the future ? How is it possible that a past experience can be recalled in the future ? In answering these questions, all of which concern the continuity between the past, present and future, Vasubandhu the author of *Abhidharma-kośa*, following the Sautrāntika point of view, drew on the imagery of the seed-fruit relationship, and said that the present and future are determined by the seeds left behind by the past : the seeds of the defilements associated with a previous moment of consciousness are carried over to the next moment of consciousness; the seeds of the past deeds produce their fruits in the future; and the seeds of the past experiences enable one to recall those experiences.[7] Then what the Yogācārins later called *ālaya-vijñāna*, is for all practical purposes just the collection of those seeds of the past determining the present and future behaviour of an

---

4. S. Anacker, "Vasubandhu : Three Aspects, A Study of a Buddhist Philosopher" (Ph. D. Dissertation, University of Wisconsin), 1970.

5. D. N. G. Macleod, "A Study of Yogacara Thought : The Integral Philosophy of Buddhism" (Ph. D. Dissertation, University of Dundee), 1978

6. Ibid., p. 29.

7. Ibid., pp. 212 ff.

individual. In other words, the *ālaya-vijñāna* of the Yogācārins is in effect only a collective name for what was described in the *Abhidharma-kośa* as the seeds (*bījas*) of past experience. If so, it is not impossible that the author of *Abhidharma-kośa* himself worked out, on his own or in collaboration with others, the theory of *ālaya-vijñāna* and other allied theories of the Yogācāra system. This sounds still more plausible when one considers that already in writing his commentary on his own *Abhidharma-kośa* he had shown his openness to new doctrines and formulations : although he wrote *Abhidharma-kośa* from the Vaibhāṣika point of view, later finding the Vaibhāṣika position unacceptable he wrote his commentary (*bhāṣya*) on the same *Abhidharma-kośa* from the Sautrāntika point of view. A possible conversion of the author of *Abhidharma-kośa* to the Yogācāra line of thinking is further confirmed by the above mentioned manuscripts of *Abhidharma-dīpa* and the *Vibhāṣā-prabhāvṛtti*, which, as P. S. Jaini has pointed out, cirticize the author of *Abhidharma-kośa* for his leanings towards the Sautrāntika and Mahāyāna positions, and thus 'allude to the conversion of the kośakāra to Mahāyāna Buddhism'.[8]

So much, very briefly, for the personal identity of Vasubandhu. Now, coming to the scope of the present study, it proposes to analyse the following four texts : (i) *Madhyānta-vibhāga-kārikā-bhāṣya*, (ii) *Trisvabhāva-nirdeśa*, (iii) *Triṃśatikā* and (iv) *Viṃśatikā*. These four texts are definitely among the basic works in the Yogācāra tradition, and are generally attributed to Vasubandhu. Whether this Vasubandhu was himself the author of *Abhidharma-kośa* or not, is no concern of mine here. What is important for the present purpose is the fact that these four texts do have, besides a fairly uniform style of language, a single, consistent, underlying system of thought so that one can safely take them as belonging to a single author, who is traditionally called Vasubandhu. To avoid confusion one may call him Vasubandhu the Yogācārin. Moreover, when I refer to the Yogācāra system, I am thinking of it particularly as it is presented in those four texts, which may or may not correspond to the Yogācāra system as it is presented in the other works of

8. P. S. Jaini, op. cit., p. 51.

the same school. However, considering the very high degree of systematization and comprehensiveness of those texts, one may reasonably take them as representing the orthodox form of the Yogācāra system. What is significant about this particular set of texts is that it gives a complete picture of the Yogācāra system.

The present work consists mainly of a new translation and interpretation of the texts under reference. I have taken the utmost care to make the translation literal and uniform throughout. However, I am aware that there are some minor instances where I had to give up this rule of 'literalism' and uniformity, either for the sake of clarity or convenience. For example, the Sanskrit terms *ākāra*, *prakāra* and *bhāva* have all been translated by the single English term 'form'; similarly the single Sanskrit term *abhāva* has been translated differently as 'unreality' and 'non-existence'. But for these and similar minor instances, I have all through this work insisted on the rule of 'literalism' and uniformity, at the same time, however, trying to avoid clumsy or far-fetched English expressions and constructions. I hope to have succeeded in this attempt at least as far as the key terms and concepts are concerned. To help the reader I have always made a point of reproducing the original texts in transliteration, by way of footnotes, on the same pages as their translation occurs, even when it meant repeating some of the previous notes. Again, I have spared no efforts in giving the corresponding English or Sanskrit expressions, as the case may be, within brackets in the body of the work. All these devices are expected to help the reader locate the original passage or expression with the minimum possible effort. Futher, for a continuous reading of the texts, I have added an appendix giving the complete translation of them at a stretch, at the same time referring back to the pages where the respective passages are interpreted and explained.

Incidentally, my translation, new as it is, is not the first for those texts. They have already been translated by others, and there exists at least one translation for each text. However, for one reason or another, my translation happens to be almost altogether different from those done previously. For one thing, I have been trying to look at those texts from a different perspective : the previous translators have looked at them from the point of view of monistic idealism, while I have looked at them from the point of view of realistic pluralism. This, I think, is enough justification, too, for my new translation.

As for the interpretation of the texts, as I have suggested above, it is an exploration into the possibility of looking at them from a perspective different from the traditionally accepted one. It has been the belief that the Yogācārins had broken away from the early Buddhist schools by replacing the latter's realistic pluralism with a monistic idealism. In contrast to this traditional belief, my contention is that the Yogācāra position need not be interpreted as a total rejection of the realistic pluralism of the early Buddhism. My conviction is that the Yogācāra metaphysics is basically the same as that of the early Buddhism. The same old categories are retained but, classified under new terms and concepts. Such new terms and concepts under which the Yogācārins have classified the old categories are mainly: *ālaya-vijñāna* (store-consciousness), *para-tantra-svabhāva* (other-dependent nature), *parikalpita-svabhāva* (imagined nature), *pariniṣpanna-svabhāva* (absolutely accomplished nature), *anabhilāpya* (ineffable), *abhūta-parikalpa* (imagination of the unreal), and *śūnyatā* (emptiness), this latter term being one that was borrowed from the Mādhyamikas, but reinterpreted.

My thesis, however, is much more modest than it might sound. My ultimate aim is not so much to convince the reader that the Yogācāra position is definitely realistic pluralism (although I have done my best to do so), as to point out that there is a real possibility of interpreting the Yogācāra writings, at least the ones I have analysed, in terms of realistic pluralism. It is an invitation to a re-evaluation of the traditional interpretation rather than a categorical rejection of it. All the same, in building up my arguments for a realistic pluralism in the Yogācāra writings, I have generally used confident expressions and a rather assertive tone. This is because, on the one hand, for my part I am convinced of my arguments, and, on the other, because I felt that to present an argument against a widely accepted position a convincing style of language was necessary.

An important suggestion of the present thesis for an historian of religion is that Buddhism, throughout its long history of development, has ever retained the original inspiration of its founder, the Buddha. The latter believed in a multiplicity of real, individual, beings, a belief that has never been seriously questioned by any of his followers. The different stages in the history of Buddhism mark, if anything, the different ways of looking at the same teaching of the Buddha. Consequently, the different schools within Buddhism distinguish from each other not so much in their philosophy as in their practices. If, for example, there has been a movement from the non-theistic Theravāda school of Buddhism to the theistic Mahāyāna school of the same, it is a change only in the religious practices, and not a change in the philosophical convictions. Therefore, I fully endorse the words of Dr. Walpola Rahula, "The great Buddhist doctors like Nāgārjuna, Asaṅga or Vasubandhu, as has been noted earlier, were not presenting a system of their own which could be called Nāgārjuna's or Asaṅga's or Vasubandhu's philosophy, but they were only explaining and interpreting anew, putting the old teaching found in the Canonical texts into new garb."[9] One thing remarkable about the entire history of the Buddhist thought is that, at none of its stages, is any concept or term belonging to the former stages totally denied. The arrival of a new school is signalized almost always by the introduction of some new concepts and terms rather than by the denial of the old ones. The new concepts and terms are thus introduced as if they were the missing links in the original Buddhism, and, therefore, under the pretext of, or with the intention of, making explicit what was already implicit in it. The genius of each school then consists in fitting the new concepts and terms into the original scheme of thought by reinterpreting or readjusting it.

As for the procedure of my work, the first chapter is a general introduction to my line of interpretation of the texts. This is presented by way of stating my thesis and outlining the arguments for it in rather general terms. This chapter is intended to put the whole work into perspective.

Chapters II to V are translation along with my interpretation, respectively, of the four texts chosen for this study. Each of

9. Walpola Rahula, *Zen and the Taming of the Bull, Towards the Definition of Buddhist Thought*, (London : Gordon Fraser, 1978), p. 81.

these chapers includes translation of the complete text concerned and my interpretation of it. These chapters are meant to substantiate the 'thesis', and to elaborate the 'arguments', which were rather hypothetically stated in the first chapter.

The second chapter, "Discrimination Between Middle and Extremes", is the translation and the interpretation of the first chapter of *Madhyāntavibhāga-kārikā-bhāṣya* (A Commentary on the Verses on Discrimination Between Middle and Extremes). This is a commentary (*bhāṣya*), unanimously attributed to Vasubandhu, on the verses (*kārikās*) on discrimination (*vibhāga*) between middle (*madhya*) and extremes (*anta*). The authorship of these verses is, however, disputed : according to some they belong to Vasubandhu's brother Asaṅga, and according to others they belong to Maitreya, whose historicity itself is again under dispute. Vasubandhu's commentary has a sub-commentary (*tikā*) called *Āgama-anusāriṇi* by Sthiramati. All these three texts, *Kārikās*, *Bhāṣya* and *Tikā*, have now been critically edited by Professor Ramchandra Pandeya (Delhi, Varanasi, Patna : Motilal Banarsidass, 1971). But before coming to this stage of being critically edited, these texts had a long history of discovery, restoration, and translation into Chinese, Japanese and Tibetan, details of which are given by Professor Ramchandra Pandeya in the introduction to his critical edition. The whole work has been divided into five chapters, of which the first has been translated into English by Th. Stcherbatsky (Bibliotheca Buddhica XXX, 1936) and by D.L. Friedmann (Amsterdam, 1937) ;[10] and the third chapter of the *Kārikā* and *Bhāṣya* has been translated and annotated by Paul Wilfred O'Brien (Monumenta Nipponica, vols. IX and X, 1953-54). At any rate, *Madhyāntavibhāga*, including the *Kārikā*, *Bhāṣya* and *Tikā*, is a very important work for any study of the Yogācāra system. First of all, it presents the whole system in all its aspects in a very organized form, and, secondly, it represents the ideas of the three official spokesmen of the system : Asaṅga/Maitreya, Vasubandhu and Sthiramati.

My study includes, besides general references appearing in the first chapter, the translation and my interpretation of the

10. I have not seen D. L. Freidmann's translation myself.

first chapter of the *Kārikā* and *Bhāṣya*. I thought it better to limit myself to this one chapter for two reasons. First of all, as I have been concentrating on the theoretical side of the Yogācāra system, this is the only chapter that is directly concerned with my present study. Secondly, consideration of the space-limit would not allow me to add analysis of more sections. In fact, I have made a translation of the third chapter. too, which has indeed some theoretical implications. However, for want of space I decided not to include it in the present work. Instead, I contented myself by summarily referring to its central idea of 'basic truth of fact' (*mūla-tattva*) in the first chapter of this study (pp. 19-21).

My third chapter, "A Treatise on the Three Natures (*Trisvabhāva-nirdeśa*)", is the translation and analysis of a small treatise consisting of thirty-eight stanzas, called *Trisvabhāva-nirdeśa*. A critical edition, that I know of this text, is by Sujitkumar Mukhopadhyaya (Calcutta, 1939), which gives also an English translation. The text had already been translated twice into Tibetan. The original Sanskrit text as well as the first Tibetan translation mentions Vasubandhu as the author of this text. But the second Tibetan translation is said to ascribe it to Nāgārjuna, which seems to be a mistake. In any case, judged from the undisputably Yogācāra contents of the text, it cannot possibly be a work of Nāgārjuna, the founder of the Mādhyamika school. That it belongs to the Yogācāra system of Vasubandhu is beyond dispute. Its style might appear a little different from the other works of Vasubandhu. If that can be ignored, one would reasonably say that this text forms an integral part of his independent works, with *Triṃśatikā* (A Treatise in Thirty Stanzas) and *Viṃśatikā* (A Treatise in Twenty Stanzas). That is, the three main areas, namely metaphysics, psychology and epistemology, which were all briefly discussed in *Madhyānta-vibhāga-bhāṣya*, are now discussed each in detail respectively in *Trisvabhāva-nirdeśa*, *Triṃśatikā* and *Viṃśatikā*.

The translation and interpretation of "A Treatise in Thirty Stanzas" (*Triṃśatikā*), which is, as suggested above, mainly an analysis of the psyche, are the contents of my fourth chapter. Together with *Viṃśatikā* (A Treatise in Twenty Stanzas) it is often called *Vijñapti-mātratā-siddhi*. That Vasubandhu is its author, has never been questioned by anybody. This small treatise has been subsequently commented upon by as many as ten writers. The Chinese author Hsüan-tsang in his *Ch'eng Wei-shih Lun* (later translated into English by Wei Tat under the title *The Doctrine of Mere-Consciousness*, (Hong Kong, 1973) is an exposition of *Triṃśatikā* synthesizing all those ten commentaries on it. With regards to my interpretation, I have made frequent reference to Sthiramati's commentary (*bhāṣya*) on this text.

The fifth chapter, "A Treatise in Twenty Stanzas (*Viṃśatikā*)" is the translation and interpretation of *Viṃśatikā*, which is for the most part a presentation of Vasubandhu's theory of knowledge. Like its sister-treatise *Triṃśatikā*, this text, too, is unanimously ascribed to Vasubandhu. There is, further, an explanatory work, called *Vṛtti*, on it by Vasubandhu himself. Both *Viṃśatikā* and *Vṛtti* have been translated from Chinese into English by C.H. Hamilton under the title *Wei Shih Er Shih Lun Or The Treatise in Twenty Stanzas on Representation only* (New Haven : American Oriental Society, 1938). The present chapter of my work contains the full translation of *Viṃśatikā*, and interprets it following very closely Vasubandhu's own explanatory work, *Vṛtti*. The full translation of this latter work is, then, added in the appendix.

The sixth and final chapter, "Idealism or Realism ?", is a restatement and re-examination of the thesis that was proposed in the first chapter, "A General Statement of the Thesis and Arguments". This is done mainly by asking myself, 'what might have led the traditional interpreters to take Vasubandhu's system for a monistic idealism ?'. In answer to this question I have analyzed certain terms, phrases and texts which on the face of it might sound idealistic, but on deeper analysis prove otherwise : such are the cases, for example, of the terms or phrases like *vijñapti-mātra*, *vijñāna-pariṇāma*, *abhūtaparikalpa*, and the apparently idealistic tone of the text, *Viṃśatikā*. I have also discussed some points to which the traditional interpreters seem to have paid very little attention, such as Vasubandhu's clear distinction between the ineffable (*anabhilāphy*) and the imagined (*parikalpita*) nature of things, and his understanding of emptiness (*śūnyatā*). This final chapter has been so designed that it may also bring together all the central terms and concepts of Vasubandhu's Yogācāra system, such as *vijñapti-mātratā, vijñāna-pariṇāma, ālaya-vijñāna, abhūta-parikalpa, para-tantra-svabhāva, parikalpita-svabhāva, parinispanna-svabhāva, anabhilāpya, śūnyatā, grāhya-grāhaka-vikalpa* and *lokottara-jñāna*. Thus it also provides a complete picture of the theoretical framework of Vasubandhu's Yogācāra system.

I may add a word about the phrase 'realistic pluralism', which I have used to describe Vasubandhu's system of thought. I am well aware that it is too vague a phrase for this purpose. As a matter of fact Vasubandhu's understanding of reality defies all descriptions, because for him reality is ineffable (*anabhilāpya*). Therefore Vasubandhu himself would not have any label put on his view of reality. Hence my choice of the phrase 'realistic pluralism' means only that it is the nearest possible description I can find for Vasubandhu's system of thought.

Finally, this study could be further pursued by comparing Vasubandhu's system with some relevant systems in the Western tradition. For example, one could make a fruitful comparison between Kant's distinction between the 'noumenon' and the 'phenomenon' on the one hand, and Vasubandhu's distinction between the 'ineffable' and the 'saṃsāric' on the other, and between Descartes' theory of 'transcendental dream' and that of Vasubandhu. However, to make such comparisons was not within the scope of the present study, and therefore I have contented myself with occasional references to Kant's distinction between the 'noumenon' and the 'phenomenon'.

This study under the title, *Vasubandhu the Yogācārin : A New Translation and Interpretation of Some of His Basic Works*, was originally submitted in 1978 to the University of Lancaster, U.K., in fulfilment of the requirements for my degree of Doctor of Philosophy. I should like to express my sincere gratitude to all those who, at different times and in various ways, have helped me in preparing this work. My very special thanks are due to

Professor Ninian Smart, and Dr. Andrew Rawlinson, for their guidance. It has been very kind of them to spend so much time going through the manuscripts, and giving me very helpful suggestions and comments. Above all, the encouragement I received from them throughout this work has been most valuable.

ABBREVIATIONS

MV.	*Madhyānta-vibhāga* (which includes *Madhyānta-vibhāga-kārikā*, *Madhyānta-vibhāga-kārikā-bhāṣya* and *Madhyānta-vibhāga-kārikā-bhāṣya-ṭīkā*)
MVK.	*Madhyānta-vibhāga-kārikā*
MVKB.	*Madhyānta-vibhāga-kārikā-bhāṣya*
MVKBT.	*Madhyānta-vibhāga-kārikā-bhāṣya-ṭīkā*
TSN.	*Trisvabhāva-nirdeśa*
Triṃś.	*Triṃśatikā*
Viṃś.	*Viṃśatikā*
Viṃś. Vṛ.	*Viṃśatikā-vṛtti*

CHAPTER ONE

INTRODUCTION : A GENERAL STATEMENT OF THE THESIS AND ARGUMENTS

1. Realistic Pluralim, Not Monistic Idealism

My minimum contention is that the Yogācāra writings, especially those under discussion, are *open* to interpretation in terms of realistic pluralism. Here I am obviously disagreeing with those who describe the Yogācāra system as "absolute idealism",[1] as "spiritual monism",[2] as "*idealism par excellence*"[3] or as "metaphysical idealism".[4] I do not, however, mean to say that those descriptions are entirely without foundation. There are indeed passages in the Yogācāra literature, which apparently support an idealistic monism. But I maintain that the entire system, when understood in terms of realistic pluralism, makes better sense and that, therefore, even those passages which apparently support idealistic monism, have to be interpreted in accordance with realistic pluralism. By realistic pluralism I mean a theory that recognizes a plurality of beings which really exist and operate independently of each other. It positively holds that individuals are real as well as mutually independent beings. What it denies are: (i) that the absolute mode of reality is

1. For example, see C. D. Sharma, *A Critical Survey of Indian Philosophy*, (Delhi, Varanasi, Patna: Motilal Banarsidas, 1964). p. 121.

2. See Th. Stcherbatsky, trans., *Madhyānta-vibhāga*: *Discourse on Discrimination Between Middle and Extremes*, (Bibliotheca Buddhica, vol. XXX, 1936; reprint ed., (Calcutta: Indian Studies, Past and Present, 1971) p. 8.

3. See T. R. V. Murti, *The Central Philosophy of Buddhism*, (London: George Allen and Uuwin Ltd., 1955; 2nd ed., 1960), p. 316.

4. See Edward Conze, *Thirty Years of Buddhist Studies*, (Oxford: Bruno Cassirer Ltd., 1967) p. 78; see also C. H. Hamilton, *Wei Shih Er Shin Lun Or the Treatise in Twenty Stanzas on Representation-only*, (New Haven: American Oriental Society 1938) p. 6.

consciousness/mind/ideas, (ii) that the individual beings are transformations or evolutes of an absolute consciousness/mind/idea, (iii) that the individual beings are but illusory appearances of a monistic reality.

However, a realistic pluralism does not rule out the possibility of having a transcendental unity of beings which will not endanger their individual identity. By transcendental unity of beings I mean a unity which is implied by the concept of 'universal', to take just one example. A 'universal', although it conceptually unifies and embraces all the 'particulars' coming under it, is not anything existential, or concrete. It is rather an 'ideal' or an 'epistemological requirement'. It does not endanger the identity of the particulars, either. In fact, in contrast to the 'universal', the particulars are the only real, concrete and existential beings. It is worth noticing that the Buddhist logicians immediately following the Yogācārins, and themselves belonging to the Yogācāra school, classified 'universals' (*sāmānyalakṣaṇa*) as mental constructs (*vikalpa* or *kalpanā*). For them 'universal' is what the mind imposes on, or constructs over, the particulars,[1] the latter alone having own-nature (*sva-lakṣaṇa*).

By saying that a realistic pluralism does not rule out the possibility of having a transcendental unity of beings, I do not mean that the Yogācāra writings positively speak of such a transcendental unity of beings. On the contrary, in my interpretation no such possibility figures, and I believe that one can very well understand the Yogācāra writings without bringing in the idea of a transcendental unity of beings. However, if someone feels that the idea of such a unity is necessarily part of the Yogācāra system, I can easily concede his point, as it does not contradict my thesis of realistic pluralism.

2. What is Denied is Duality, Not Plurality

What made me disagree with the traditional interpretation of the Yogācāra system as monistic idealism is firstly the fact

1. *Sāmānyena lakṣaṇam sāmānyalakṣaṇam. Sādhāraṇam rūpam-iti-arthaḥ Samāropyamānam hi rūpam sakala-vahni-sādhāraṇam. Tataḥ tat-sāmānya-lakṣaṇam.* (Dharmakirti, *Nyāya-bindu*, The Chowkhamba Sanskrit Series, Banaras, 1954, I. 16).

that nowhere in the texts I have analysed, which are in any case the basic works in this system, is there an explicit statement of such a position. Moreover, the only sort of distinction the authors object to is that between graspable and grasper (*grāhya-grāhaka-vikalpa*). For example, the whole of *Madhyānta-vibhāga* in general, and particularly its first chapter, is devoted to show that the distinction between graspable and grasper is unreal or rather non-existent (*abhūta*). That the dualism between graspable and grasper is merely mental construction (*parikalpa*) and that it is, therefore, non-existent (*nāsti* or *na vidyate* or *na bhavati*) is repeated time and again, while not even once is there a positive denial of a plurality of beings. That means, what the Yogācārins are concerned about is the problem of duality, not of plurality. That there is a plurality of beings is taken for granted, while the dualistic view of reality is emphatically denied.

It should be emphasized that for the Yogācārins dualism means basically the dualism between *grāhya* (graspable) and *grāhaka* (grasper),[1] which being merely mental construction,[2] is nothing existent.[3] To say that duality is denied while accepting plurality, might sound a contradiction in terms. However, it should be by now clear that the 'plurality' and 'duality' under discussion refer to two different universes of discourse: the former refers to the ontological universe of discourse and stands for plurality of beings, while the latter refers to the epistemological/experiential universe of discourse and stands for duality of understanding. Therefore, there is no contradiction in accepting plurality of beings while denying duality of understanding. For the Yogācārins, there can be and there is, a plurality of beings, although they do not tolerate the distinction of those beings into graspable and grasper, enjoyable and enjoyer, experience-able and experiencer, knowable and knower, or object and subject. Each of those many beings has to be understood as characterized neither by subjectivity nor by objectivity; it is empty of both subjectivity and objectivity as well. This

1. *Dvayam grāhyam grāhakam ca.* MVKB. I. 2
2. *Tatra-abhūta-parikalpo grāhya-grāhaka-vikalpaḥ.* Ibid.
3. *Dvayam tatra na vidyate.* MVK. I. 2.

indeed is the meaning of "emptiness" (*śūnyatā*) for the Yogācārins, namely the emptiness of subject-object characterization[1] with reference to each individual being.

3. What is Imagined is the Graspable-Grasper Duality, Not the Thing-in-Itself

Another strong case for my refusal to recognize monistic idealism in the Yogācāra writings is the fact that what the authors attribute to the operation of imagination (*parikalpa*) is only the distinction between graspable and grasper, not the entire external world, as a monistic idealism would have one believe. Right in the beginning of his *Madhyānta-vibhāga-kārikā-bhāṣya* Vasubandhu makes it unquestionably clear that "the imagination of the unreal [*abhūta-parikalpa*] means the discrimination between graspable and grasper [*grāhya-grāhaka-vikalpaḥ*].[2] Then the text goes on to say how the whole world of experience, including the experiences of inanimate and animate beings, self and ideas, is mere imagination of the unreal,[3] and how it rests on the unreal distinction between graspable and grasper.[4] Thus the basic experience of *saṃsāra* is the illusory consciousness of *grāhya-grāhaka* distinction, the cessation of which will automatically result in one's liberation (*mukti*).[5] Thus, graspable-grasper distinction is the only factor the Yogācārins attribute to the operation of imagination. Is it reason enough to call their system idealism ? All that they characterize as illusory (*bhrānti*) is the experience of graspable-grasper distinction.[6] Is it, again, reason enough to call their system monism ? The answer to these questions being definitively negative, the Yogācāra system is neither monism nor idealism.

1. *Śūnyatā tasya-abhūta-parikalpasya grāhya-grāhaka-bhāvena virahitatā*. MVKB. I. 2; for more explanation of this statement see below pp. 30 ff.
2. *Tatra-abhūta-parikalpo grāhya-grāhaka-vikalpaḥ*. MVK. I. 2.
3. See MVK. I. 4-5, and my analysis of these stanzas below pp. 56 ff.
4. For more details see my analysis of MVK. I. 4-5 below pp. 45 ff.
5. *Tat-kṣayān-mukti-riṣyate*. MVK. I. 5.
6. *Yathā grāhya-grāhakatvena bhrānti-rudbhāvitā-api*... MVKBT. I. 5.

It is true that the Yogācārins themselves have described their system as *vijñapti-mātratā-vāda*, a theory which says that all is mere representation of consciousness. However, the application of this description is much more restricted than traditionally believed. From the above paragraph it follows that the factors which the mind contributes to the picture of the universe are basically 'graspability', 'grasperhood', and the distinction between them. Hence, those factors are rightly described as the externalization of ideas or as mere representations of consciousness. That is, but for the constructive imagination (*parikalpa*), characterizations of individual streams of existence as 'graspable' or 'grasper' would make no sense. Thus the graspable-grasper characterizations are entirely imagined (*parikalpita*), and are, therefore, mere represen:ations of consciousness (*vijñapti-mātra*). This indeed is what the Yogācārins mean when they describe their system as *vijñapti-mātratā-vāda*, a theory which says that all is mere representation of consciousness.

However, the fact is that the effect of the superimposed distinction between graspable and grasper is so far-reaching that it makes the whole universe appear (*ābhāsa*) in a way much different from what it really is. Consequently the entire cosmos as it appears is rightly called a mental construction (*parikalpita*), and is, therefore, described as mere representation of consciousness (*vijñapti-mātra*). Hence in the final analysis the phrase *vijñaptimātratā-vāda* means a theory which says that the world *as it appears* to the unenlightened ones is mere representation of consciousness. Therefore, any attempt to interpret *vijñapti-mātratā-vāda* as idealism would be a gross misunderstanding of it.

4. A Theory of Experience, Not a System of Ontology

It should then be noticed that the theory of *vijñapti-mātratā* in the Yogācāra writings is meant to be an explanation of experience, rather than a system of ontology. Contrasting the *citta-mātratā* theory of the *Laṅkāvatāra* and the *vijñapti-mātratā* theory of the Yagācārins D. T. Suzuki has pointed out that "The philosophy, if there is any such thing in the *Laṅkāvatāra*, is ontology and not epistemology. Whereas the doctrine of Vijñapti-mātratā is epistemological".[1] The point is that the *Laṅkāvatāra* has explicitly identified the absolute state of reality with *citta*,[2] and has positively said that in the final analysis "there is nothing but *citta*."[3] But not even once in the four Yogācāra works I am studying has the term *vijñapti* been used to describe the absolute state of reality, nor is there any indication that the final state of existence has to be defined in terms of *vijñāna*. Instead, as already observed, the absolute state of reality is defined simply as emptiness, namely the emptiness of subject-object distinction. Once thus defined as emptiness (*śūnyatā*), it receives a number of synonyms,[4] none of which betrays idealism. The synonyms enumerated in *Madhyānta-vibhāga* are *tathatā* (suchness), *bhūta-koṭi* (limit of existence), *animittam* (uncaused), *paramārthatā* (absoluteness) and *dharma-dhātu* (source-reality[5]).[6] It is obvious from this list of synonyms for emptiness—emptiness which is the same as the thing-in-itself (*Yathābhūta-vastu*)—that to conceive the latter in idealistic terms does not occur to the Yogācārins. I have of course come across a few instances which a casual reader might take to mean idealism. For example, Vasubandhu in his *Madhyānta-vibhāga-kārikā-bhāṣya* says that *śūnyatā* is the subject-object distinctionless state of the imagination of

1. D. T. Suzuki, *Studies in the Lankavatara Sutra*, (London and Boston: Routledge and Kegan Paul Ltd., 1972) p. 280.

I cannot, however, agree with Suzuki if he is arguing on the basis of terminology, for the phrases *citta-mātra* and *vijñapti-mātra* have been synonymously used both by *Laṅkāvatāra* and the Yogācārins. Suzuki himself has quoted three instances of *vijñapti-mātra* and four instances of *prajñapti-mātra* from *Laṅkāvatāra* used in the same sense as *citta*. (See p. 181). And right in the very beginning of his *Viṃśatikā-vṛtti* Vasubandhu declares that for him *vijñapti* is synonymous with *citta*. See also his *TSN*. 36.

2. "Suchness, emptiness, the limit, Nirvāṇa, Dharmadhātu, variety of will-bodies—they are nothing but Mind (*citta*) "*Laṅkāvatāra*, 31, quoted and translated by Suzuki, Ibid.. p. 242.

3. *Laṅkāvatāra* 29-33.

4. *paryāyaḥ*.

5. My translation of *dharma-dhātu* as source-reality is based on the following commentary of Vasubandhu: *Ārya-dharma-hetutvāt dharmadhātu, ārya-dharmāṇām tad-ālambana-prabhavatvāt. Hetu-artho hi-atra dhātu-arthaḥ*. MVKB. I. 16.

6. MVK. I. 15.

the unreal (*abhūta-parikalpa*).[1] It could be taken to suggest idealism, if the imagination of the unreal in its subject-object distinctionless state could still be called 'imagination', or 'mind', or 'conciousness', or some other idealistic name. But the fact is that reality is called, in the Yogācāra writings, '[creative] imagination', or 'mind', or 'imagination', only in its creative aspect, when it is capable of discriminating between subject and object. Once it is freed of the subject-object prejudice, it is just suchness, or emptiness, or the thing-in-itself.

Another instance of apparent idealism is found in Sthiramati's commentary on the *Triṃśatikā*. Speaking of the purpose of the treatise *Triṃśatikā*, he says : "The present treatise has been composed to repudiate two exclusive claims : one, that *vijñeya* [the knowable or the object] is as much a reality[*dravyataḥ*] as *vijñāna* [knowledge or consciousness] itself; two, that *vijñāna* [knowledge or consciousness is as much a convention [*saṃvṛtitaḥ*] as *vijñeya* [the knowledge or the object] itself."[2] This statement does apparently imply that what is real is *vijñāna* and that *vijñeya* is only conventional. My reaction, however, is that Sthiramati is either misinterpreting Vasubandhu, or means only that *vijñāna* is more real than *vijñeya*, without implying that the former is the only real. That the subjective element (i.e. *vijñānam* or *vijñapti* or *abhūta-parikalpa*) is more real than the objective one (i.e. *vijñeya* or *viṣaya* or *artha* or *parikalpita*) and, therefore, more difficult to get rid of is certainly the general thesis of the Yogācārins.[3] In any case I cannot accept Sthiramati if he means that for the previous Yogācārins *vijñāna* marks the ultimate state of reality or existence. For, MV I.4 clearly says that *vijñāna* is the name of reality when the latter *is born* in the form of inanimate and animate beings, self and representations of consciousness.[4] That means, *vijñāna* is not the ultimate state of reality, but only one of its "born" states. One might argue

1. *Śūnyatā tasya-abhūta-parikalpasya grāhya-grāhaka-bhāvena virahitatā*. MVB. I. 2.

2. ... *vijñāna-vad-vijñeyam-api drdvyata eva iti kecin-manyata vijñeya-vad vijñānam-api saṃvṛtita eva na paramārthata iti-asya dviprakārasya-api-ekāntavādasya pratiṣedhārtaḥ prakaraṇārambhaḥ*. (*Triṃśatikā-bhāṣyam*, Introduction).

3. This is clear from passages like *MVK* I. 7; *TSN*. 36 etc.

4. *Artha-sattva-ātma-vijñapti-pratibhāsam prajāyate vijñānam*. MVK. I. 4.

that the verse under reference could be differently translated to mean that "*vijñāna*, [the ultimate realty], is born [i.e. manifests itself] in the forms of animate and inanimate beings, self and representations of consciousness". This translation, although grammatically correct, does not fit in with the context, for the latter part of the verse is an unambiguous denial of any ultimate reality to *vijñāna*. It says that the knowable objects being non-existent, the knowing *vijñāna*, too, is non-existent.[1] This statement implies that the term *vijñāna*, which means nothing ultimate, would make sense only as long as one is under the illusion of subject-object distinction.

I have been saying that the *vijñapti-mātratā* theory of the Yogācārins is more an explanation of experience that a system of ontology. To pursue this point further, I must point out that the terms *vijñapti* as well as *vijñāna* have been employed not to describe any ontological state of reality, but to denote the subjective part of an experience (*grāhaka*), and are always contrasted with its objective part (*grāhya*) which is denoted by terms like *artha* and *vijñeya*. I may refer to one or two typical passages to this effect. First of all there is MVK I.7:

> Depending upon perception
> There arises non-perception,
> And depending upon non-perception
> There arises non-perception.[2]

And its commentary by Vasubandhu, which may be paraphrased as follows:

> That is, from the perception that there is only *vijñapti*, arises the perception that there is no *artha* [object]; and then from this non-perception of *artha* arises the perception that there is not even mere *vijñapti*.[3]

1. . . . *nāsti ca-asya vijñānasya arthas-tad-abhāvāt tad-api asat.* Ibid.
2. *Upalabdhim samāśritya nopalabdhiḥ prajāyate,*
Nopalabdhim samāśritya nopalbdhiḥ prajāyate. MVK. I.7
3. *Vijñapti-mātropalabdhim niśritya-artha-anupalabdhir-jāyate. Arthānūpalabdhim niśritya-vijñapti-mātra-anupalabdhir-jāyate.* MVKB. I. 7. For literal translation and explanation of this text see below p. 61.

These passages clearly show that the terms *vijñapti* and *artha* do not stand for any ontological states of reality, but merely denote two polar concepts, namely those of subjectivity and objectivity respectively. I call them 'polar concepts' in the sense that "each of them is essentially contrasted with the other; indeed, it gets its sense by way of this contrast".[1] In other words, they do not make sense without referring to each other. If, therefore, any one of them could be proved to be non-sensical, the other one, too, is at once proved to be non-sensical. This is exactly what the above quoted passages get across: *vijñapti* and *artha* are contrasted to each other as standing for the polar concepts of subjectivity and objectivity; then the non-sensical character of the concept of *artha* is established from the fact that there is only *vijñapti*; then, finally, from the non-sensical character of the concept of *artha*, is established the non-sensical character of the concept of *vijñapti* itself.[2] Thus the concepts of both *vijñapti* and *artha* turn out to be non-sensical and, therefore, irrelevant, too. Incidentally, it must be noted that this is the whole point and central argument of the Yogācāra philosophy: the entire lot of *saṃsāra* experience hinges on the polar concepts of subjectivity and objectivity (*grāhakatva* and *grāhyatva*) namely that one is the subject of experience (*bhoktṛ*), while all else are object of one's experience (*bhojya*); then the concept of objectivity is proved to be mere imagination, which will in turn prove the concept of subjectivity as well to be mere imagination;[3] thus the concepts of subjectivity and objectivity collapsing, the whole *saṃsāra* experience, too, collapses, and there automatically results release (*mokṣa* or *mukti* or *nirvāṇa*). I shall return to this point a little later. What interests me at the moment are the following facts: (i) the terms *vijñapti* and *artha* under discussion do not refer to anything onto-

1. This is how a pair of polar concepts is described by D. W. Hamlyn, *The Theory of Knowledge*, (London and Basingstoke: The Macmillan Press Ltd., 1970; reprint ed., 1974), p. 16.

2. From the logical point of view, this argument implies a vicious circle, and is, therefore, fallacious. The fact, however, is that it is meant to be a process of realization rather than a logical argument: one first realizes that the concept of *artha* is non-sensical, which will lead one to the realization that the concept of *vijñapti* itself is non-sensical. For more explanation see below. p. 61.

3. *Grāhya-grāhakayoḥ paraspar-nirapekṣatvāt.* MVKBT. I. 7.

logical (*vastu*), but only to the epistemological concepts of subjectivity and objectivity; (ii) therefore the denial of existence (*sattā* or *bhāvatva*) to *vijñapti* and *artha* does not amount to the denial of the concepts of subjectivity and objectivity as something more than mere imagination; (iii) hence the main concern of the Yogācārins, in contexts such as that referred to above, is not about the multiplicity of beings, but about unwarrantedly categorizing them as subjects and objects.

A similar analysis could be carried out with *Trisvabhāva-nirdeśa*, 36, where the polar concepts of *citta* and *jñeyārtha* are contrasted with each other, and then the meaningfulness of each of them is denied using the same argument as that used in the case of *vijñapti* and *artha*.[1] Again, in MV. I.4 the concept of *vijñāna* is contrasted with that of *artha*, (which in this instance includes the concepts of inanimate and animate beings, self and representations of consciousness), and subsequently the validity of both of them is denied.[2] In fact there are many more instances of this kind.

Thus speaking in an epistemological context the Yogācārins are seeking to find out what are the contents of one's experience, rather than what are things-in-themselves. The question before them is what things are got at through experience, rather than what things are there in fact. That there are many things or many individual streams of existence is taken for granted. But does one's epistemological experience reach them ? The answer is negative. All that one reaches through experience are one's own mental constructions (*kalpanā* or *parikalpa*), or rather appearances (*pratibhāsa*) of one's own consciousness, which have nothing to do with things-in-themselves (*parinispanna-svabhāva* or *tathatā*). This is to my mind the message of, for example, MV. I.4, which on the one hand says that the categories of inanimate and animate things, self and representations of consciousness as

1. *Citta-mātra-upalambhena jñeya-artha-anupalambhatā, jñeya-artha-anupalambhena syāc-citta-anupalambhatā.* TIN. 36.

2. *Artha-sattva-ātma-vijñapti-pratibhāsam prajāyate, vijñānam nāsti ca-asya-arthas-tad-abhāvāt tadapi-asat.* MVK. I. 4; see also the subsequent commentaries of Vasubandhu and Sthiramati.

experienced are nothing but different appearances (*pratibhāsa*) of consciousness itself, and, on the other hand, that they are either deprived of objectivity (*ākāratva* or *prakāratva*) or are different from what they appear to be. After making a detailed analysis of this stanza elsewhere,[1] I came to the following conclusion. The categories of consciousness, self, representations of consciousness, living beings and inanimate beings, in so far as they fall within the range of experience, are nothing but subjective constructions, and for that reason non-beings, too. Neither of these categories ever reaches the thing-in-itself. The thing-in-itself is thus beyond the range of experience. Those categories, subjective forms as they are, are experienced either as subjects or objects. The categories of inanimate and living beings, in so far as they are objects of experience, are non-beings, because they do not represent any objective form, but only subjective forms. The categories of self and representations of consciousness, in so far as they are objects of experience, are only mentally constructed forms, and are, therefore, non-beings, having nothing to do with things-in-themselves. Self and representations of consciousness, in so far as they are subjects of experience, are likewise mentally constructed forms and non-beings, and as such are false appearances of consciousness. Consciousness itself, in so far as it is subject of experience, is non-being. Thus, in short, whatever is referred to as subject or object is mere subjective construction and therefore non-being; the thing-in-itself is neither subject nor object. Above all, what is described as 'subjective construction and therefore non-being' is only the concept of subjectivity and objectivity, not in any case the thing-in-itself.

5. The Motive is Practical Rather Than Theoretical

The next point I want to emphasize is the fact that the ultimate motive of the Yogācārins in building up their system is religious rather than merely philosophical. Their primary interest is to explain the *saṃsāra* experience and to suggest a way out of it. As Sthiramati puts it, they are concerned about the

1. See below pp. 54-55.

ways and means of "producing the totally intuitive knowledge proper to the Buddhas".[1] Or, in the words of MV, they are trying to find out what must be extinguished to result in one's *mukti* (release or liberation).[2] Hence, the whole system has to be viewed as converging on the main themes of *saṃsāra* and *mukti*.

What then is the characteristic mark of *saṃsāra* ? Early Buddhism characterized it as *duḥkha* arising from *tṛṣṇā* (desire) or *upādāna* (clinging = passionate attachment). The Yogācārins now go further and trace *tṛṣṇā* or *upādāna* itself to the arch-idiosyncrasy for discrimination between graspable and grasper. Sthiramati says, '*upādāna* which is the same as craving for *pudgala* and *dharma*, *is based on graspable-grasper duality*, and is, therefore, of imagined nature'.[3] It is quite understandable why desire (*tṛṣṇā* or *upādāna* or *abhiniveśa*) and other allied passions should be attributed to the graspable-grasper distinction, for desire obviously presupposes a subject who desires and an object which is desirable. Without making a distinction between subject and object one cannot speak of either desire or clinging or attachment or enjoyment, which are all, for the Buddhists, basic experiences of *saṃsāric* existence. Therefore, as I have already suggested, discrimination between graspable and grasper (*grāhya-grāhaka-vikalpa*) is the arch-idiosyncrasy to which one in the state of *saṃsāra* is subject, and to which all other perverted distinctions and the consequent distorted picture of the universe are all to be traced. The experience of *saṃsāra* consists basically in one's being forced to view oneself as the grasper (*grāhaka*), the enjoyer (*bhoktṛ*), the knower (*jñātṛ*) of all other beings, which then are viewed as the graspable (*grāhya*), the enjoyable (*bhojya*), the knowable (*jñeya*). There one cannot help mentally constructing the distinction between the subject and the object, the grasper and the graspable, the enjoyer and the enjoyable. There one

1. *Kimartham-idam śāstram praṇītam, Buddhānām bhagavatām samyag-nirvikalpajñāna-utpādanārtham.* MVKBT. I. 1.

2. ... *tad-kṣayān-muktir-iṣyate* MVK. I. 5; *yat-kṣayān-muktir-iṣyate.* MVK. II. 27.

3. *Sa ca* (*pudgala-dharma-abhiniveśaḥ = upādānam*) *dvayapatitatvāt parikalpitaḥ svabhāvaḥ.* MVKBT. III. 6. Here *dvayam* means *grāhya* and *grāhaka.*

is led to believe that one is the subject knowing and enjoying all other streams of existence around one, which then inevitably appear as the objects of one's knowledge and enjoyment.

Now, therefore, all that an aspirant to buddhahood should be warned against is the idiosyncrasy for the graspable-grasper distinction. And this indeed is the central message of the Yogācārins. That the graspable-grasper distinction is mere imagination,[1] and that, therefore, it is non-existent[2] and illusory,[3] is repeated time and again. MV. I. 7 is particularly worth noticing in this respect.[4] It shows the illusory nature of every experience that involves a distinction between graspable and grasper. Introducing this stanza Vasubandhu says that it suggests a means (*upāya*) of understanding the nagative definition (*asal-lakṣaṇa*) of the imagination of the unreal (*abhūta-parikalpa*).[5] Sthiramati further makes it clear that by the negative definition of the imagination of the unreal Vasubandhu means the non-existence of graspable and grasper.[6] An individual in the state of *saṃsāra*, when he is endowed with, and almost identified with,[7] the power of the imagination of the unreal, is bound to think of himself as the subject knowing and enjoying other things which he takes for objects. So he must be warned against the non-existence (*asattvam*) of the objectivity (graspability) and subjectivity (grasperhood). He must be told that the objectivity and subjectivity are merely his own imagination, and that, therefore, he should not cling to such deceptive fancies. If he is not so warned, "The imagination of the unreal [*abhūta-parikalpa*], unaware of the negative definition, works in favour of the defilements of *kleśa*, *karma* and *janma*".[8] Thus the

1. *Tatra-abhūta-parikalpo grāhya-grāhaka-vikalpaḥ.* MVB. I. 2.
2. *Dvayam* (*=grāhyam grāhakam ca*) *tatra na vidyate.* MVK. I. 2.
3. *grāhya-grāhakatvena bhrāntir-udbhāsitā.* MVKBT. I. 5.
4. For a detailed analysis of this text see below pp. 61 ff.
5. *Idānīm tasmin-neva-abhūta-parikalpe-asal-lakaṣaṇam pradīpayati.* MVKB. I. 7.
6. *grāhya-grāhakayor-asattvam-eva asal-lakṣaṇam.* MVKBT, I. 7.
7. Such an identification is suggested, for example, by the passage quoted below under note 8.
8. *Aparijñāta-asal-lakṣaṇo hi-abhūta-parikalpaḥ kleśa-karma-janma-saṅkleśāya sampravartate.* MVKBT. I. 7.

ultimate motive of the authors is moral or religious, namely to dissuade the disciples from indulging in the enjoyments of *saṃsāra*. Therefore, what they are attacking is the graspable-grasper dualism, not the ontological pluralism.

6. The Things-in-Themselves Are Covered Up by Mental Constructs

As already explained, according to the Yogācārins one in the state of *saṃsāra* does not experience the things-in-themselves, but only the subjective forms of one's own consciousness. Such forms are basically those of subjectivity and objectivity. Constructed and projected by the consciousness they cover up the things-in-themselves in such a way that the latter are prevented from being perceived or experienced. This leads to the Yogācārins' concept of "coverings" (*āvaraṇas*) discussed at great length in *Madhyānta-vibhāga*, chapter II. *Āvaraṇas* include all the limitations to which one in the state of *saṃsāra* is subject, and "from the cessation of which issues liberation".[1] To describe the state of *saṃsāra* in terms of *āvaraṇa*, meaning 'covering' or 'veiling', is typical of the Yogācāra tradition. Usually the Indian systems, including the early Buddhist systems, look at *saṃsāra* as a state of *avidyā* (ignorance). But, for the Yogācārins even this *avidyā* is basically a 'covering'. For example, in MV. I. 11 the first link of the dependent origination (*pratītya-samutpāda*), which was traditionally called *avidyā*, has been interpreted as *ācchādana*, literally meaning "covering". Then Vasubandhu comments, "here *ācchādana* means *avidyā*, which prevents the vision of reality as such [*yathā-bhūta-darśana*]".[2] Sthiramati then adds, "*avidyā* by nature is non-vision [=non-seeing]. Therefore by it is covered [=concealed] the object of *bhūta-darśana*. *Bhūta-darśana* is mainly supra-mundane wisdom ... *avidyā*, impeding the *bhūta-darśana* becomes the source [=condition] of *saṃskāras*, and thus by it is the *jagat* tormented."[3] The theory of *āvaraṇas*,

1. *Yat-kṣayān-muktir-iṣyate* MVK. II. 17.
2. *Tatra ācchādanād-avidyayā yathā-bhūta-darśana-avabandhanāt.* MVKB. I .11.
3. *Avidyā hi-adarśana-ātmakatvād bhūtadarśana-viṣaye pracchādite bhūta-darśanam notpadyate' to bhūta-darśana-utpatti-vibandhanād-avidyā bhūta-darśana-vibandhaḥ.* MVKBT. I. 11.

then, should be considered as an extension of the view of *avidyā* as 'covering', and accordingly there are its descriptions such as "that which prevents knowledge from coming into being",[1] "covering which obstructs the vision of truth",[2] "covering of non-illusory vision",[3] and so on. In short, *āvaraṇa* is that which makes the experience of things-in-themselves impossible, which for the Yogācārins is none other than one's bias towards subject-object distinction. Such a bias towards subject-object distinction not only prevents one from seeing things as they really are, but also arouses one's selfish interests and passions, and makes one cling to the so-called objects of enjoyments. So what have been traditionally called as *kleśas*, *upakleśas*, *tṛṣṇā*, *saṃyojanāni*, *utpāda-satya* etc. etc. are all subsumed under the heading *kleśa-āvaraṇa*. They are *āvaraṇas* 'consisting of *kleśas* themselves, including *upakleśas* as well'.[4] It should be noticed that under the heading *kleśa-āvaraṇas* the Yogācārins are not introducing any new topic, but are only interpreting the old list of *kleśas* and *upakleśas* as *āvaraṇas*. But they ingeniously speak of a second group of *āvaraṇas*, namely *jñeya-āvaraṇas*, which can hardly find a place in early Buddhism. "*Jñeya-āvaraṇas* consist of knowables [*jñeyas*] themselves."[5] The whole idea is that for the Yogācārins belief in *jñeyas*, namely that there are knowable objects, is a serious impediment in understanding things-in-themselves. Sthiramati says: "*Jñeya-āvaraṇas* are so called because *jñeyas* themselves are *āvaraṇas*. It means that the really knowables being covered by it [i.e. by *jñeya-āvaraṇa*], there is no object of real knowledge".[6] In this passage the term *jñeya* is used in two different meanings.[7]

1. *jñanotpatti-pratibandhaka* MVKBT. II. 1.
2. *tattva-darśanasya āvaraṇam* MVKBT. II. 3.
3. *abhrānti-darśanasya āvaraṇam* MVKBT. II. 3.
4. *Kleśa eva-āvaraṇam-iti-āvaraṇasya kleśa-dharmatvena sārūpyād-iha-upakleśo'-pi kleśa-śabdena gṛhyate.* MVKBT. II. 1.
5. *Jñeya eva-āvaraṇam-iti jñeyāvaraṇam.* MVKBT. II. 1.
6. *Tena jñeya-prāvṛtatvāt jñānasya viṣaya eva nāsti.* MVBT. II. 1.
7. The reason why I suggest two meanings for the term *jñeya* is simply that otherwise the passage under reference would make no sense. Besides, to use a term in different meanings, and that, too, without any warnings, is not unusual in MV. and its commentaries. A typical example is the term *artha*, used very often to mean 'object' in general, or 'meaning' of a term, and in few cases also to mean 'inanimate beings' (e.g. see MV. I. 4).

This term means, on the one hand the mentally constructed forms of knowables (*parikalpita-jñeya*), and, on the other, the really knowables (*pariniṣpanna-jñeya*). In the phrase *jñeyāvarāṇa* the term *jñeya* is used in the former meaning, and in the phrase *jñeya-prāvṛtatvāt* it is used in the latter meaning. As the mentally-constructed-knowables cover the real-knowables, vision of reality as it is, (*yathā-bhūta-darśana*), is made impossible. *Jñeya* as mentally-constructed-forms are false objects and as such lead to illusion (*bhrānti*), while *jñeya* as really-knowables are things-in-themselves (*tathatā* or *tathā-bhūta-vastu*), and as such are objects of realization (*sākṣāt-kāra*) or *yathā-bhūta-darśana*.

What I make of the above discussion on the *āvaraṇas* is that they are all different expressions of the idiosyncrasy for subject-object distinction. Consequently, freedom from this idiosyncrasy is the essential mark of the state of *nirvāṇa*. There one sees individual beings not as subjects and objects, nor as enjoyers and enjoyed, but as mutually independent streams of existence. They are related to each other neither as knower and known, nor as cause and effect, nor as enjoyer and enjoyed. To the unenlightened the streams of existence would never appear in their suchness (*tathatā*), but as essentially related to each other in one way or another, criss-crossing each other, and thus blurring the identity of each other. But seen through the yogic eyes of the enlightened, they will appear in their suchness, mutually unrelated and independent, never liable to the categories of subject and object. *Madhyānta-vibhāga*, chapter III and its commentaries by Vasubandhu and Sthiramati examine the categories of *skandha*, *dhātu*, *āyatana*, *pratītya-samutpāda*, *sthāna-asthāna*, *indriya*, *adhvā*, *satya*, *yama* and *saṃskṛta-asaṃskṛta*, and show how seen through yogic intuition they bring out the non-sensical and irrelevant character of the language of relations. The *skandhas* are, thus, mere collections of discrete, momentary, elements which are neither objects nor subjects of any experience; the eighteen *dhātus* are reduced to independently evolving seeds (*bījas*); the *āyatanas* are explained in such a way that the myth of an experiencing subject is exploded; the principle of *pratītya-samutpāda* is understood as meant to dispense with the belief in causality; the rule of *sthāna* and *asthāna* is explained as implying moral retribution without recourse to a retributor, or creator; *indriyas* are explained in such a way that the individual beings are objects of no other power than themselves : everyone determines and controls himself.[1]

7. The Same Old Realistic Pluralism

Let me once again make my position clear : I hold that the Yogācārins retain the Buddha's pluralistic and realistic conception of reality. The Buddha and his immediate disciples analysed existence into an interplay of a plurality of subtle, ultimate, not further analysable elements (*dharma*) of matter (*rūpa*), mind (*nāma* = *citta*) and force (*saṃskāra*). For the Yogācārins, too, existence is composed of so many discrete, mutually independent, further unanalysable elements. As already mentioned, nowhere in the Yogācāra writings does one come across a conclusively monistic conception of the world. Instead, there are many passages which are unintelligible without presupposing a pluralistic view of reality. For example, a repeatedly raised question is how the same objects are experienced differently by different individuals : objects appearing in dreams are seen only by the dreamer, not by others;[2] extraordinary objects are seen by people having bad eyes, not by others;[3] rivers in hell appear to ghosts as filled with putrid stuffs, excrements and urine, whereas the same rivers appear to ordinary human beings as filled with clear, cool, water with nothing unpleasant about it.[4] In all these instances the basic presupposition is that there are different individuals having different experiences. Then the question is how, the circumstances and objective conditions being the same, they come to have different experiences. Unless one supposes that there are different experiencing individuals, this question would be redundant. On the other hand, supposing that there are different individuals, the Yogācārins have very cleverly answered it saying that experience differs from one individual to another according to his psychological disposition and historical past. Sthiramati says : "Each individual stream of mind

1. Cf. MV. III, 17-20.
2. See Viṃś. 4.
3. Ibid.
4. MVKBT. I. 4.

from its own seeds produces consciousness appearing in different forms of objects, which are consequently perceived by the same individual. This explains how one and the same thing can be experienced by different individuals in different ways''.[1] So are to be explained the extraordinary experiences of the yogins who perceive objects which are not perceived by ordinary people.[2]

Again, frequent reference to different streams of existence is clear indication that the Yogācārins do believe in the mutually independent and irreducible individuals. For example, Sthiramati in the above quoted passage refers to 'different individual streams of mind each of which produces its own subjective forms of consciousness',[3] and Vasubandhu while interpreting the term *sattva* makes a distinction between one's own and other people's streams of existence.[4] Again in Vasubandhu's *Viṃśatikā-vṛtti* there is an explicit admission of a plurality of beings (*sattvas*), which are each a separate, real, stream (*santāna*), influencing each other through their respective representations of consciousness (*anyonya-vijñapti-ādhipatyena*).[5] One might object that the 'mutual influencing of individuals' referred to in the latter instance applies only at the conventional (*saṃvṛti*) level. Of course, it is true that the Yogācārins do not mean that the individuals interact at the noumenal level. Even so, my thesis stands, namely that the Yogācārins admit the existence of different individuals, although the 'representations of consciousness' proceeding from these individuals have only conventional (*saṃvṛti*) or practical (*vyāvahārika*) value.

1. ... *bhinnārtha-svarūpam-asannapi citta-santāna-pratiniyamena svabījāt pratyeka-ātma-gṛhītam bhinna-artha-ādi pratibhāsam vijñānam prasūyate*. MVKBT. I. 4.

2. Cf. MVKBT. I. 4.

3. See above note 1.

4. *Sattva-pratibhāsam yat pañca-indriyatvena sva-para-santānayoḥ*. MVKB. I. 4.

5. *Anynya-adhipatitvena vijñapti-niyama mithaḥ* (Viṃś. 18). Commenting on these words of his own, Vasubandhu says: *Sarvam hi sattvānām anyonya-vijñapti-ādhipatyena mitho-vijñapter-niyamo bhavati yathāyogam ... ataḥ santāna-antara-vijñapti-viśeṣāt santāna-antare vijñapti-viśeṣa utpadyate ...* (Viṃś. Vṛ, 18.)

Considering all that, I have been saying so far, I hold that whatever the Yogācārins say about reality applies to, and only to, each individual stream of existence. They are looking into the meaning of individual streams of existence making up a pluralistic cosmos. Each of those individuals, for them, has a beginningless past, an empirical present and is a potential Buddha. It is each of those individuals that is said to take on the three natures (*svabhāva*), namely *para-tantra*, *parikalpita* and *pariniṣpanna*. Similarly, all other concepts discussed in the Yogācāra writings can rightly be understood as referring to individuals taken separately, rather than to reality conceived in monistic terms. To suggest one more example, far from being a "cosmic unconscious", the *ālaya-vijñāna*[1] in the Yogācāra writings is a "personal unconscious", a storage of the idiosyncratic ideas of the respective individual.

Perhaps the concept of *mūla-tattva*, appearing in MV. III requires a special comment. Translating that term as "basic reality" a random reader can be very easily led to take it as betraying a monistic view of reality. The fact, however, is that *mūla-tattva* in this context is just another name for the three natures, namely *para-tantra*, *parikalpita* and *pariniṣpanna*, all of them referring, as I have already suggested, to different phases of an individual's life, not to any monistic reality. Commenting on MVK. III. 1, Vasubandhu says: "There *mūla-tattva* is 'the threefold nature' [MVK. III. 3], namely *parikalpita*, *paratantra* and *pariniṣpanna*, for on it [i.e. the threefold nature] are established the other *tattvas*".[2] Moreover, it should be particularly noticed that here the term *tattva* does not at all mean any 'ontological reality', but 'an abstract truth' or 'a fact'. Sthiramati has consistently defined *tattva* as "unchanging". In MVKBT. I, he says, "*tattvam aviparyāsaḥ* [= *tattva* is that which does not change] ".[3] Then again commenting on MVK. III.3 he says, "*aviparito hi tattvārthaḥ* [= the term *tattva* is used in the

1. References to *ālaya-vijñāna* are found, for example, in MV. I. 10; III. 22; Triṃś. 2.

2. *Tatra mūla-tattvam svabhāvas-trividhaḥ : parikalpitaḥ, para-tantraḥ, pariniṣpannaś-ca. Tatra-anya-tattva-vyavasthāpanāt.* MVKB. I. 3.

3. MVKBT. I. 1

sense of 'unchanging'] ."[1] Therefore the question in MV III, which is entitled 'A Chapter on *Tattva*', is what is 'unchanging'. Again, that it is a question concerning 'the truth about reality' (which, incidentally, is pluralistic), rather than about reality itself, becomes clear when one considers the issue, "what indeed is the *tattva* in those three natures [i.e. *paratantra*, *parikalpa* and *pariniṣpanna*] ?"[2] This latter issue has been raised by the authors immediately after the above quoted statement that "There *mūla-tattva* is 'the threefold nature' [MVK. III.3], namely *parikalpita*, *paratantra* and *pariniṣpanna*. . ."[3] In other words, after having established the three natures as the basic *tattva*, the authors are then asking about the *tattva* of those three natures themselves. The term *tattva* in this latter instance cannot mean anything other than 'truth'. Otherwise the question, "what indeed is the *tattva* in those three natures ?" would make no sense. On the contary, translating *tattva* as 'truth' the question could be meaningfully recast as "What is the truth about each of those three natures ?", or as "What are the unchanging factors in them ?". That this is exactly the question at issue is further confirmed by the subsequent answer.[4] An observation of P. W. O'Brien is worth quoting : "The meaning of *tattva* must swing from reality to truth, errorlessness . . . But the difficulty is still not cleared up. What is true? One of the natures ? Rather, some statement about the natures, . . . The imaginary nature is not true, but the statement 'the nature is non-existence' is true. The relative nature is not true, but the statement 'the relative nature exists yet not absolutely' is true. In the same way we might say 'headless horses are true or real' meaning that the statement 'headless horses have no heads' is true. There is question, then, not of the reality of the three natures, but of the truth of three aspects of one reality."[5] In short, MV. III, "A Chapter on *Tattva*", is

1. MVKBT. III. 3.
2. *Kim-atra svabhāva-traye tattvam-iṣyate*? MVKB. III. 3.
3. See above note 2, p. 19.
4. This answer may be paraphrased as follows: The truth (*tattva*) about the three natures, namely *parikalpita-svabhāva*, *paratantra-svabhāva*, and *pariniṣpanna-svabhāva*, is that they are, respectively, permanently non-existent (*asat-nityam*), existent but not really (*sad-apiatattvataḥ*) and existent as well as non-existent (*sad-asat*). (MV. III. 3).
5. P. W. O'Brien, "A Chapter on Reality from the Madhyāntavibhāgaśāstra", *Monumenta Nipponica*, Vol. IX (1953), p. 289.

dealing with various 'truths' or 'factors' about reality, which is basically the individual rather than a monistic whole. And, the basic truth or fact (*mūla-tattva*) about this reality is that is takes on three natures.[1] Having said that, the authors then proceed to discuss the various 'truths' or 'facts' about those three natures themselves looked at from different angles. That is all "A Chapter on *Tattva*" is about. Therefore, it is unwarranted to say that this chapter in general, or the concept of *mūla-tattva* therein, advocates a monistic view of world.

8. More Arguments from Viṃśatikā

It may be noticed that I have been so far referring mainly to the *Madhyānta-vihhāga*. However, I can ensure that my thesis of realistic pluralism applies equally to the other texts under discussion, as well, Of them *Triṃśatikā* which presents a detailed analysis of the psyche, is at the same time an abridged version of *Madhyānta-vibhāga*, while *Trisvabhāva-nirdeśa* is an elaboration on the theme of 'three natures'. Vasubandhu's *Viṃśatikā* can, however, be a little confusing to a casual reader. A strong polemic against belief in *objects* (*artha*), it is very easily mistaken for a polemic against belief in things as such,[2] The central thesis of the text is that the objects experienced by an unenlightened man are like those experienced by one in a dream or one with bad eyes : just as the objects experienced by one in a dream or one with bad eyes, are merely one's own mental constructions, so are those experienced by an unenlightened one in the state of *saṃsāra*.[3] The ultimate conclusion of the text, therefore, is that in the state of *saṃsāra* every individual is in a transcendental dream.[4] It does not imply that there is only *one* dreaming

1. *Tatra mūla-tattvam 'svabhāvas-trividhaḥ': parikalpitaḥ, para-tantraḥ pariniṣpannaś-ca. Tatra anya-tattva-vyavasthāpanāt.* MVKB. III. 3.

2. In phrases like '*asad-artha-avabhāsanāt*', (Viṃś. 1), *na so'rtho dṛśyate*, (Ibid. 16) etc. the term *artha* stands for object of experience, not for thing-in-itself. Moreover, *artha* is never found used to mean things in general.

3. *Vijñapti-mātra-eva-etad-asadartha-avabhāsanāt; Yathā taimirikasya-asat-keśa-candrādi-darśanam.* Viṃś. 1. *Svapna-upaghātavat-kṛtya-kriyā.* Viṃś. 4.

4. *Svapne dṛgviṣaya-abhāvam na-aprabudho'avgacchati.* Viṃś. 17 Vasubandhu then comments on this line : *Evam vitatha-vikalpa-abhyāsa-vāsanā-nidrayā prasuptalokaḥ svapna iva-abhūtam-artham paśyan-na prabudhas-tad-abhāvam*

individual. On the contrary, there are clear indications that there is a plurality of individuals undergoing the transcendental dream of *saṃsāra* : for example, there are references to individuals, who by virtue of their mental representations,[1] influence each other,[2] and injure each other.[3] In fact, a major part of the text,[4] taking for granted the plurality of individuals who in their inexpressible nature[5] do not fall within the range of mutual experience, is trying to justify the commonsense language of action and reaction involving different sorts of relations. To a great extent, therefore, this treatise is an attempt to establish a practical (*vyāvahārika*) bridge between the noumenal (*paramārtha*) and phenomenal (*saṃvṛti*) worlds.

Speaking about 'knowledge of other minds' Vasubandhu makes it clear that every individual has an ineffable nature perceived only by the enlightened ones.[6] and that, therefore, nobody in the state of *saṃsāra* knows anybody's mind, not even one's own.[7] To explain it further, he says that the reason why one in the state of *saṃsāra* does not know individuals, whether oneself or others, in their ineffable nature, is that one is still subject to the idiosyncrasy of graspable-grasper distinction,[8] which is responsible for the appearance of false forms.[9] Here, again, it should be noted that the basic 'evil' of *saṃsāra* experience is one's idiosyncrasy for graspable-grasper

yathāvan-nāvagacchati. Yadā tu tat-pratipakṣa-lokottara-nirvikalpa-jñāna-lābhāt-prabudho bhavati tadā tat-praṣṭha-labdha-aśudha-laukika-jñāna-sammu-khībhāvād-viṣayābhāvam yathā-vad-avagacchati-iti-samānam-etat. (Viṃś. Vṛ. 17).

1. *Sarveṣām hi sattvānām anyonya-vijñapti-ādhipatyena mitho vijñapter-niyamo bhavati.* Viṃś. Vṛ. 17.
2. See Ibid.
3. See Viṃś. 18-20.
4. See, for example, Viṃś. 18-21.
5. *anabhilāpyena-ātmanā.* Viṃś. Vṛ. 10.
   nirabhilāpyena-ātmanā. Viṃś. Vṛ. 10.
6. . . . *anabhilāpyena-ātmanā yo buddhānām viṣayaḥ iti.* Vimś. Vṛ. 10. *nirabhilāpyena-ātmanā buddhānām gocaraḥ.* Vimś. Vṛ. 21.
7. *Para-cittavidām jñānam-ayathārtham katham yathā sva-citta-jñānam.* Viṃś.21.
8. . . . *tad-ubhayam [para-citta-jñānañ-ca sva-citta-jñānañca] na yathārtham vitatha-pratibhāsatayā grāhya-grāhaka-vikalpasya-aprahīṇatvāt.* Vimś. Vṛ. 21.
9. See *vitatha-pratibhāsatayā* in note 8.

distinction, which constructs false appearances[1] of objects and subjects.[2]

Again, more than once does Vasubandhu refer to a mutiplicity of enlightened ones (*buddhas*)[3], implying that the individuals, once emancipated from the spell of transcendental dream, retain their individuality in the *nirvāṇa* state as well. There they remain, and recognize each other in their 'ineffable nature'.[4]

Another illuminating point brought out by *Viṃśatikā* is that the theory of *vijñapti-mātratā* is just another way of putting the old theories of *pudgala-nairātmya* and *dharma-nairātmya*; or rather that it explains the real meaning of the latter theories :

> "The theory of *dharma-nairātmya* does not mean that *dharma* is non-existent in all respects, but only in its 'imagined nature' (*kalpita-ātmanā, Viṃś.* 10). The ignorant imagine the *dharmas* to be in the nature of *grāhya, grāhaka* etc. Those *dharmas* are non-substantial (*nairātmya*) with reference to that imagined nature (*tena parikalpitena ātmanā*), not with reference to their ineffable nature (*natu anabhilāpyena-ātmanā*), which is object of the knowledge of the enlightened ones alone. Similarly the non-substantiality (*nairātmya*) of *vijñapti* (=*pudgala*), too, is to be understood with referenc to the self imagined (and super-imposed) by other *vijñaptis* (=by other *pudgalas*). Thus through the theory of *vijñapti-mātra* the non-substantiality of all *dharmas* is taught, not the denial of their existence."[5]

1. *asad-artha-avabhāsana.* Viṃś. 1.
2. (same as preceding three notes).
3. Some examples are : *anabhilāpyena-ātmanā yo buddhānām viṣayaḥ iti.* (Vimś. Vṛ. 10); *nirabhilāpyena-ātmanā buddhānām gocaraḥ* (Ibid. 21). I am, however, aware that the plural form *buddhāḥ* need not necessarily refer to a plurality of beings, but that it may well be just a reverential way of addressing the enlightened one. So a plural form like *buddhāḥ* cannot be by itself a conclusive argument for a plurality of beings. It can, however, serve as a persuasive argument.
4. *anabhilāpya-ātman* (Vims. Vṛ. 10); *nirabhilāpya-ātman* (Ibid. 21).
5. *Na khalu sarvathā dharmo nāsti-iti-evam dharma-nairātmya-praveśo bhavati. Api-tu, 'kalpita-ātmanā'* (Vimś. 10). *Yo bālair-dharmāṇām svabhāvo grāhya-grāhakādiḥ parikalpitas-tena kalpitena-ātmanā teṣām nairātmyam na tu-anabhilāpyena-ātmanā yo buddhānām viṣaya iti. Evam vijñapti-mātrasya-api vijñapti-antara-*

I feel that this passage alone is sufficient to substantiate my thesis of realistic pluralism : it admits a plurality of *dharmas*, *pudgalas*, and *buddhas* : it distinguishes between the ineffable and imagined natures of things; of them the ineffable nature is totally beyond the realm of the experience of an ordinary individual, it is perceived by the enlightened ones alone; on the contrary, the imagined nature is what is experienced by an individual on the *saṃsāra* level, it is characterized by the subject-object distinction, the old theory of *nairātmya* is thus explained as meaning the non-substantiality of the imagined nature, not of the ineffable nature; finally, and most important of all, the identification of the theory of *nairātmya* with that of *vijñapti-mātratā* clearly indicates that the Yogācārins do not want to conradict the realistic pluralism of original Buddhism.

It is in the light of his distinction between the "ineffable" and "imagined" natures that Vasubandhu's 'refutation of realism' occurring in *Viṃśatikā* 11-15 should be understood. His objection is directed mainly to the atomic realism of the Vaiśeṣikas, who without making a distinction between the 'ineffable' and the 'imagined', claim abolute reality to all objects (*viṣaya*) of experience. And then by implication his arguments apply to any system which holds that the object (*viṣaya*) of experience should be accepted as real at its face value. Thus Vasubandhu's objection is only to those who refusing to distinguish between the 'ineffable' and the 'imagined', claim reality even to the phenomenal object. It is clear from the fact that his 'refutation of realism' appears immediately after his clear statement that the non-substantiality (*nairātmya*) applies only to the imagined nature, not to the ineffable one.[1] It should again be noted that his 'refutation of realism' is given in reply to the opponent's insistence that 'whatever *rūpa* etc. happen to be the objects of one's *vijñapti*, each should be considered as really existent being'.[2] And, finally, right from the beginning of the refutation what Vasubandhu calls

parikalpitena-atmanā nairātmya-praveśāt vijñapti-mātra-vyavasthāpanayā sarva-dharmāṇām nairātmya-praveśo bhavati na tu tad-astitva-apavādāt. Vimś. Vṛ. 10.

1. Cf. Vimś. and Vimś. Vṛ. 10.

2. *Katham . . . na punaḥ santi-eva tāni yāni rūpādi-vijñaptīnām pratyekam viṣayī-bhavanti-iti. Yasmāt . . .* Vimś. Vṛ. 10.

into question is the reality of objects (*viṣaya*) of *vijñapti*, not of things in general.[1] From all these I conclude that what Vasubandhu is fighting against, is the 'indiscriminate realism, which does not take the trouble to distinguish between the phenomenal and the noumenal, the imagined and the real, the *parikalpita* and the *pariniṣpanna*.

9. In the Light of the Later School of Logic

A final, but very convincing, argument for my position refers to the Yogācāra school of logic founded by Diṅnāga and developed by his disciple Dharmakīrti.[2] Diṅnāga was himself a student of Vasubandhu. Now one must naturally expect that Diṅnāga and Dharmakīrti, as the immediate followers and disciples of Vasubandu, subscribed to the latter's teaching. In fact some authors do agree with me on this point. A.K. Chatterjee for one in his *The Yogācāra Idealism* says, "Their essential teaching was that of the Yogācāra as is evident from Diṅnāga's *Ālambanaparīkṣā* and Dharmakīrti's section on the *Vijñaptimātratā-cintā* in his *Pramāṇavārttika*".[3] Then, if two systems claim to have the same teaching, it is only reasonable to interpret the less clear one of them in the light of the other. And, of the two systems under reference, that of Diṅnāga is obviously clearer than that of Vasubandhu. Therefore, I propose to interpret the latter in the light of, and in accordance with, the former. What then is the teaching of the school of Diṅnāga on reality? To start with, Diṅnāga and Dharmakīrti were staunch defenders of the old theory of momentariness (*kṣaṇika-vāda*). Then they based the entire edifice of their epistemology on a clear-cut distinction between the realms of things-in-themselves and commonsense-experience, which they named respectively as *svalakṣaṇa* and *sāmānya-lakṣaṇa*. The former is the sphere of first order reality (*paramārtha-sat*), whereas the latter is the sphere of empirical reality (*saṃvṛti-sat*). The most

1. *Na tad-ekam na ca-anekam viṣayaḥ paramāṇuśaḥ* . . . Viṃś. 11 Note that Vasubandhu is here using the term *viṣayaḥ*.

2. Dharmakirti's teacher was Īśvarasena, a student of Diṅnāga.

3. A. K. Chatterjee, *The Yogācāra Idealism*, 2nd rev. ed., (Delhi, Varanasi, Patna: Motilal Banarsidass, 1975), p. 41.

important point about the distinction between *sva-lakṣaṇa* and *sāmānya-lakṣaṇa* is that they are contrasted respectively as the non-constructed, and the constructed[1], the non-artificial and the artificial,[2] the non-imagined and the imagined,[3] the unutterable and the utterable,[4] etc. In short, whatever comes within the range of empirical experience is characterized as mentally constructed, artificial, imagined, linguistically expressible and, finally, unreal (*avastu*) ; whereas the things-in-themselves (*sva-lakṣaṇāni*) are characterized as untouched by mental construction, artificiality, imagination, as beyond the realm of language, and, finally, as real (*vastu*).[5] What I am suggesting, therefore, is that the distinction between *sāmānya-lakṣaṇa* and *sva-lakṣaṇa*, and the entire philosophy behind it, were already implied and meant by Asaṅga and Vasubandhu when they distinguished between *parikalpita* and *pariniṣpanna*, or *parikalpita-ātma* and *anabhilāya-ātma*. In other words, the central insight of the school of Diṅnāga was inspired by the school of Asaṅga and Vasubandhu: the central theme of the former school has kept clear continuity with that of the latter school. This implies a continuity of essential details of the same theme too. Now, Diṅnāga and his followers thought that a realistic pluralism was essential to their central theme, namely the distinction between *sāmānya-lakṣana* and *sva-lakṣaṇa*. Similarly Asaṅga and Vasubandhu, too, must have felt it necessary to maintain a realistic pluralism; indeed it should be from them that the school of Diṅnāga borrowed its realistic pluralism.

1. *nirvikalpaka* and *kalpita*.
2. *akṛtrima* and *kṛtrima*.
3. *anāropita* (= *akalptta*) and *āropita* (=*kalpita*). *āropita* and *anāropita* could be better translated as 'superimposed' and 'not superimposed'.
4. *anabhilāpya* and *abhilāpya*.
5. Some relevant passages are : *Tad-sva-lakṣaṇam. Tad-eva paramārtha-sat* (Dharmakīrti's *Nyāyabindu*, 13-14). *Paramārtho'kṛtrimam anā-ropitam rūpam. Tena-asti-iti paramārtha-sat . . . tad-eva sva-lakṣaṇam* (Dharmottara's *Ṭīka* on the above passage) . . . *atas-tad-eva sva-lakṣaṇam na vikalpa-viṣayam* (Dharmottara on *Nyāyabindu*, 15) *Anyat-sāmānyalakṣaṇam* . . . (*Nyāyabindu*, 16). For more details see my *A Study of the Buddhist Epistemology According to Dharmakīrti's Nyāyabindu* (M. A. Dissertation, of Poona, 1974), especially pp. 9ff.

CHAPTER TWO

DISCRIMINATION BETWEEN MIDDLE AND EXTREMES (*MADHYĀNTA-VIBHĀGA*)

1. Introduction

Having paid homage to the founder of this science,
Son of the well-gone,
And also to its expositor for people like me,
May I now endeavour to analyse its meaning.[1]

This is how Vasubandhu opens his commentary (*bhāṣya*) on *Madhyānta-vibhāga-kārikā*. To begin a literary work with a prayer, or paying homage to one's teachers, or, at least, with a noble thought, is traditional in India. Accordingly, Vasubandhu right in the beginning of his commentary devotes this stanza to the honour of the founder (*praṇetṛ*) and the expositor (*vaktṛ*) of this science (*śāstra*). By the term *praṇetṛ* Vasubandu means Maitreya,[2] who is generally accepted as the founder of the Yogācāra system. The same Maitreya is then qualified as "son of the well-gone" (*sugata-ātmaja*), an epithet of any Bodhisattva. "The well-gone" (*sugata*) refers to the Buddha himself, and therefore *suguta-ātmaja* means the son of the Buddha. According to Sthiramati, Maitreya is called "son of the Buddha" either because he shares the intuitive knowledge (*nirvikalpaka-jñāna*) of the Buddha, or because he is born in the latter's lineage.[3]

1. *Śāstrasya-asya praṇetāram-abhyarhya sugata-ātmajam*
Vaktāram ca-asmad-ādibhyo yatiṣye'rtha-vivecane. MVKB. (Introduction)
2. *Kārikā-śāstrasya-ārya-maitreyaḥ praṇetā.* MVKBT. (Introduction)
3. . . . *nirvikalpaka-jñāna viśeṣa-ātmakaḥ sugataḥ, taj-janitatvānnirvikalpasya jñānasya. Tasmāt-tasmin vā jātaḥ sugata-ātmajaḥ. Athavā sugata-ātmanā jātaḥ iti sugata-ātmajaḥ. Yathā-uktam sūtra-antare jāto bhavati tathā-gata vaṃśe tad-ātmaka-vastu pratilābhād-iti.* MVKBT (Introduction).

By the expositor (*vaktṛ*) of this science is meant Vasubandhu's own brother Asaṅga. As legend has it, the Yogācāra system was revealed to Asaṅga by Maitreya, and the former then wrote it down in the form of verses.[1] Thus he is aptly called the *vaktṛ* (expositor or spokesman) of this science (*śāstra*), contained in the *Madhyānta-vibhāga-kārikā*. The central thesis of this text claims to be a middle position between the two extreme views, namely, the extreme realism of the *Sarvāstivādins* and the extreme relativism of the Mādhyamikas. Hence the title *Madhyānta-vibhāga-kārikā*, which means "The Verses on Discrimination between Middle and Extremes".

The various topics discussed in this book are stated in MVK I. 1:

[MVK I. 1] The definition,
The coverings,
The truth,
Meditation of the opposite,
Its stages,
Attainment of result,
And the pre-eminence of the path.[2]

Commenting on this stanza Vasubandhu says:

These are the seven topics discussed in this science. They are namely the definition, the coverings, the truth, meditation of the opposite, stages of that meditation, attainment of result, and, seventhly, the pre-eminence of the path.[3]

Of these seven topics the first one makes the subject-matter of the first chapter of *Madhyānta-vibhāga-kārikā*, entitled "A Chapter on Definitions".[4] which, along with its commentary

1. *Vaktāram-iti . . . sa punar-ārya-asaṅgaḥ. Tasya hi-idam śāstram abhivyaktam, ākhyātam ca-ārya-maitreya-adhiṣṭhānāt-dharma-santānena.* Ibid.

2. *Lakṣaṇam hi-āvṛtis-tattvam pratipakṣasya bhāvanā*
Tatra-avasthā phala-praptir-yāna-ānuttaryam-eva ca. MVK 1.1.

3. *Iti-ete sapta-arthā hi asmin śāstra upadiśyante. Yad-uta—lakṣaṇam, āvaraṇam, tattvam, pratipakṣasya bhāvanā, tasyām-eva ca pratipakṣa-bhāvanāyām-avasthā, phalaprāptiḥ, yāna-ānuttaryam ca saptamo'rthaḥ.* MVKB 1.1

4. *lakṣaṇa-pariccheda.* The term *lakṣaṇa*, literally meaning a "sign", "mark" or "characteristic", is technically used to mean a "definition" or a "scientific description".

by Vasubandhu, I propose to analyse in the following pages. This chapter tries to define, or rather describe, reality in its phenomenal as well as absolute aspects. Consequently this chapter may be subdivided into two main sections:

(i) *Verses* 2-11, dealing with reality in its phenomenal aspects. This section may be entitled 'the imagination of the unreal' (*abhūta-parikalpa*). The central theme of this section is that reality as it is experienced by one in the state of *saṃsāra* is there owing to 'the imagination of the unreal' (*abhūta-parikalpa*). In other words, it establishes that the form of subjectivity and objectivity, under which alone things are experienced, are 'imagination of the unreal'.

(ii) *Verses* 12-23, dealing with reality in its absolute aspects. This section may be entitled 'the emptiness' (*śūnyatā*). The central theme of this section is that reality in its absolute state is empty (*śūnya*) of subject-object distinction, or rather that it is beyond subject-object characterization.

2. The Imagination of the Unreal

Terms explained

Verse 2, which opens the main discussion, makes a few crucial statements, which along with Vasubandhu's commentary on them, should be considered the key-stones of the whole system. "There, beginning with the definitions, [the text] says":

[MVK I. 2] There exists the imagination of the unreal,
There is no pair,
But there is emptiness,
Even in this there is that.[1]

This stanza contains four clear statements which I consider to be the key-stones of the entire system. Those statements are:

1. *Abhūta-parikalpo'sti dvayam tatra na vidyate*
Śūnyatā vidyate tu-atra tasyām-api sa vidyate. MVK I.2

(i) an assertion of the imagination of the unreal: *abhūta-parikalpo'sti,*

(ii) a negation of duality: *dvayam tatra na vidyate,*

(iii) an assertion of emptiness: *śūnyatā vidyate tu-atra,*

(iv) an assertion of the co-existence of the imagination of the unreal (*abhūta-parikalpa*) and the emptiness (*śūnyat*.): *tasyām-api sa vidyate.*

These four statements involve three key-terms, namely:

(i) the imagination of the unreal (*abhūta-parikalpa*),

(ii) pair (*dvayam*), and

(iii) emptiness (*śūnyatā*).

A correct understanding of these three key-terms leading up to a correct understanding of the above four key-statements will provide all necessary clues to the understanding of the entire system of Vasubandhu. Now Vasubandhu himself has explained those terms and statements in his subsequent commentary as follows:

> There, the imagination of the unreal means the discrimination between the graspable and the grasper. The pair is the graspable and the grasper. Emptiness means that state of the imagination of the unreal which is lacking in the form of being graspable or grasper. Even in this [emptiness] there is that, namely, the imagination of the unreal. Thus, when something is absent in a receptacle, then one, [seeing] that receptacle as devoid of that thing, perceives that receptacle as it is, and recognizes that receptacle, which is left over, as it is, namely as something truly existing here. Thus, the definition of emptiness is shown to imply no contradiction.[1]

I may now reconstruct verse 2 along with Vasubandhu's

1. *Tatra-abhūta-parikalpo grāhya-grāhaka-vikalpaḥ. Dvayam grāhyam grāhakam ca. Śūnyatā tasya-abhūta parikalpasya grāhya-grāhaka-bhāvena virahitatā. Tasyām-api savidyata iti-abhūta-parikalpaḥ. Evam yad yatra nāsti tat tena śūnyam-iti yathā-bhūtam samanupaśyati, yat punar-atra-avaśiṣṭam bhavati tat sad-iha-asti-iti yathā-bhūtam prajānāti-iti-aviparītam śūnyatā-lakṣaṇam-udbhāvitam bhavati.* MVKB. I.2.

commentary on it as follows:

> There exists the imagination of the unreal,[1]
> namely, the discrimination
> between the graspable and the grasper.[2]
> However, there is no pair,[3]
> such as the graspable and the grasper.[4]
> There is instead emptiness,[5]
> which means that state of the imagination of the unreal,
> which is lacking in the form of being graspable or grasper.[6]
> Even in such emptiness
> there exists the imagination of the unreal.[7]
> Thus, when something is absent in a container,
> the latter is then perceived as such;
> also, what is left over there, namely the container,
> is then recognized as such,
> namely, as uncontradictably existing there:
> this indeed is the defining characteristic of emptiness.[8]

The meaning of the three terms, *abhūtaparikalpa*, *dvayam* and *śūnyatā*, is now unambiguously clear:

Abhūta-parikalpa, the imagination of the unreal, means the discrimination (*vikalpa*) between the graspable (*grāhya*) and the grasper (*grāhaka*). This implies that whatever Vasubandhu traces to imagination (*parikalpa*) is the discrimination (*vikalpa*) between the graspable and the grasper, and whatever he describes as mental construction (*kalpita*) and therefore unreal (*abhūta*), is primarily such discrimination, and the consequent

1. *Abhūta-parikalpo'sti.* MVK I.2.
2. *Tatra-abhūta-parikalpo grāhya-grāhaka-vikalpaḥ.* MVKB I. 2.
3. *Dvayam tatra na vidyate.* MVK I. 2.
4. *Dvayam grāhyam grāhakam ca.* MVKB I.2.
5. *Śūnyatā vidyate tu-atra.* MVK I.2.
6. *Śūnyatā tasya abhūta-parikalpasya grāhya-grāhaka-bhāvena virahitatā.* MVKB I.2.
7. *Tasyām-api sa vidyate. MVK I.* 2; *tasyām-api sa vidyata iti-abhūta-parikalpaḥ.* MVKB I.2.
8. *Evam yad yatra nāsti tat tena śūnyam-iti yathā-bhūtam samanupaśyati, yat punar atra-avaśiṣtam bhavati tat sad iha-asti-iti yathā-bhūtam prajānanti-iti-aviparītam śūnyatā-lakśaṇam-udbhāvitam bhavati.* MVKB I. 2.

forms of graspability (*grāhyatva*) and grasperhood (*grāhakatva*). In other words, the distinction between graspable and grasper, and the forms of graspability and grasperhood, under which things are experienced, are all mere imagination, and therefore unreal (*abhūta*), too. Then, ultimately what Vasubandhu will describe as "mere representation of consciousness" (*vijñapti-mātra*) turn out to be the graspable-grasper forms and the distinction between them.

Dvaya, the pair, means the graspable and the grasper. Hence, wherever Vasubandhu uses the term *dvaya*, it must be taken to mean the duality between graspable and grasper. There are many instances in which Vasubandhu has used the term *dvayam* without giving any explanation.[1] In all such cases *dvayam* means the duality between grasper and graspable. Consequently, denial of duality (*dvayam* or *dvitva*) in Vasubandhu's system does not all mean denial of the multiplicity of beings, as is the case in Śaṅkara's *advaita*-system. In this latter system, for example, the statement *ekam-eva advitīyam* (one only without a second), means that there is only one being having no other being than itself. Here, therefore, the denial of duality, expressed by the term *a-dvitīya* amounts to the denial of the multiplicity (*bahutva*) of beings. But in Vasubandhu's system the denial of duality (expressed by terms like *dvayam tatra na vidyate* MVK I. 2, *advayatvena yac-ca asti* TSN 13, *dvaya-abhāva-svabhāva* TSN 16, *asaddvaya-svabhāva* TSN 18, etc.) means only that a thing in its absolute state of existence is devoid (*śūnya*) of subject-object duality, or that it is lacking in the forms of subjectivity and objectivity (*grāhya-grāhaka-bhāvena virahitatā*). Śaṅkara is speaking about the absence of a second being (*advitīya-vastu*), while Vasubandhu is speaking about the absence of a dual nature (*asad-dvaya- svabhāva*) referring to each individual being. Incidentally, it might have been the tendency to read Śaṅkara's meaning of *advitīya* into Vasubandhu's use of *asad-dvaya-svabhāva* that led many later interpreters to understand Vasubandhu's system as monistic idealism.

Śūnytā, the emptiness, means basically the state of existence, which is empty of grasper-graspable characterizations. *Śūnyatā*,

1. For example, TSN 4, 10, 13. etc.

therefore, refers to the thing as it is (*yathā-bhūta*), and is otherwise called 'suchness' (*tathatā*). Thus, *śūnyatā*, meaning the thing unqualified by subjectivity and objectivity, is far from suggesting any kind of nihilism. Again, what is denied of reality in its absolute state of existence, is not plurality of beings, but only the duality between subjects and objects, or rather the dualistic mode of apprehension that is based on graspable-grasper characterization. Also, what is attributed to mental construction is this duality between subjects and objects, not the plurality of beings. Vasubandhu in his commentary has interpreted *śūnyatā* with reference to *abhūta-parikalpa*: "Emptiness means that state of the imagination of the unreal which is lacking in the form of being graspable or grasper."[1] But 'the imagination of the unreal' itself has been defined as "the discrimination between the graspable and the grasper."[2] Therefore, the state in which 'the imagination of the unreal' is lacking in the forms of the graspable and the grasper, would mean the cessation of the 'imagination of the unreal' itself. Thus *śūnyatā* ultimately means that state of existence which is empty of 'the imagination of the unreal' and of the consequent subject-object distinction. Therefore to realize the absolute state of existence, namely, *śūnyatā*, one has only to stop imagining (i.e. mentally constructing) the unreal forms of subjectivity and objectivity.

Let me now explain the meaning of the four statements mentioned above :

Firstly, there is an assertion of the imagination of the unreal: *abhūta-parikalpo'sti*. This in effect is a strong declaration of the fact that the imagination of the unreal is an undeniably real experience for one in the state of *saṃsāra*, namely that one in the state of *saṃsāra* is bound to construct mentally the unreal forms of subjectivity and objectivity, and then to see everything as endowed with those forms.

Secondly, there is an emphatic negation of duality: *dvayam tatra na vidyate*. This implies that the imagination of the unreal, which means the discrimination between the graspable and the

1. See note 6 on p. 31.
2. See note 2 on p. 31.

grasper,[1] has only phenomenal value, and therefore is real only on the level of *saṃsāra*. As long as one is in the state of *saṃsāra* one goes on discriminating between graspable and grasper, and treats things as if they are endowed with the forms of graspability and grasperhood. But in fact graspability and grasperhood are only subjective forms of experience, and therefore do not belong to things as such (*yathā-bhūta*), and for that matter there is no duality between graspable and grasper.

Thirdly, there is an assertion of emptiness: *śūnyatā vidyate tu-atra*. This refers, as already explained, to the suchness (*tathatā*) of things, which is empty of subject-object characterizations. While the imagination of the unreal, and the consequent subject-object duality are inevitable parts of saṃsāric experience, in the state of *nirvāṇa* one no more imagines the unreal forms of subjectivity and objectivity, and no more perceives things as grouped into subjects and objects. Thus in the absolute state of existence there is emptiness of subjectivity and objectivity.

Fourthly, there is an assertion of the co-existence of the imagination of the unreal and the emptiness: *tasyām-api sa vidyate*. A literal translation of this statement would be, "Even in this [emptiness] there is that [imagination of the unreal subjectivity and objectivity]". This is, as Sthiramati says,[2] an explanation of the "mystery" of *saṃsāra* as follows: that things in their pure nature are neither subjects nor objects is a fact; but in the state of *saṃsāra* the pure nature of things is obscured by the imagination of the unreal; therefore, even in this emptiness, i.e. inspite of the fact that things are empty of subject-object characterizations, there is that imagination of the unreal, which obscuring the real nature of things accounts for saṃsāric experience, namely the experience of things as discriminated into subjects and objects.

According to Sthiramati there are four ways of understanding the present stanza:

First of all, it is a refutation of the blanket-denial of everything (*sarva-apavāda-pratiṣedhārtham*). The propounders of this

1. *Tatra abhūta-parikalpo grāhya-grāhaka-vikalpaḥ*. MVKB I.2
2. See below from the next paragraph onwards.

latter theory, whom Stcherbatsky identifies as the Mādhyamikas,[1] held that all elements are devoid of own-nature in all respects (*sarva-dharmāḥ sarvathā niḥsvabhāvāḥ*), just as the horn of a hare is devoid of own-nature.[2] Against this view the present stanza asserts the reality of 'the imagination of the unreal' and of 'the emptiness', both having own-nature in one way or another. The imagination of the unreal has own-nature,[3] which will be later identified as *para-tantra svabhāva*;[4] and the emptiness has own-nature in the absolute sense of the term,[5] which will be later identified as *pariniṣpanna-svabhāva.*[6] The emptiness though always present is obscured by the imagination of the unreal. Therefore one in the state of *saṃsāra* does not realize it, and this inability to realize it explains the bondage in which one is.[7]

Secondly, it is directed against those who held that colour etc. are substances (*dravyatvena santi*) existing independently of mind and mental factors (*citta-caittāḥ*).[8] According to Stcherbatsky the reference here is to the Sarvāstivādins.[9] Against them the first line of the stanza should be interpreted to mean that what substantially exists is the imagination of the unreal, not colour etc. Why ? Because there is no pair of subjects and objects.[10] Here Sthiramati is making a very

1. Th. Stcherbatsky, trans., *Madhyānta-vibhāga : Discourse on Discrimination between Middle and Extremes*, (Bibliotheca Buddhica XXX, 1936; reprint, Calcutta : Indian Studies, Past and Present, 1971), p. 41

2. *Kecit-virudhanti sarva-dharmāḥ sarvathā niḥsvabhāvāḥ śaśaviṣāṇa-vad-ityataḥ sarva-apavāda-pratiṣedhārthamāha abhūta-parikalpo'sti-iti.* MVKBT I.2

3. *Abhūta-parikalpo'sti-iti. Svabhāvataḥ iti vākyaśeṣaḥ.* Ibid

4. *Abhūta-parikalpaḥ para-tantra-svabhāvaḥ.* MVKB I.6

5. *Paramārthataḥ svabhāvaḥ.* MVKBT I.2

6. *Grāhya-grāhaka-abhāvaḥ [=śūnyatā] pariniṣpannaḥ svabhāvaḥ.* Ibid

7. . . . *yasmāc-chūnyatāyām-api-abhūtaparikalpo vidyate tasmād bhavanto na muktaḥ.* MVKBT I.2

8. *Citta-caittebhyo'nyatra rūpādayo dravyatvena santi iti yad darśanam tad-pratiṣedhārtham-āha* . . . Ibid

9. Th. Stcherbatsky, trans., *Madhyānta-vibhāga : Discourse on Discrimination between Middle and Extremes*, (Bibliotheca Buddhica XXX, 1936; reprint, Calcutta: Indian Studies, Past and Present, 1971), pp. 42-43

10. . . .*nāsti rūpam tad-abhūtaparikalpa-vyatiriktam dravyata iti. Kim kāraṇāt ? yasmāt "dvayam tatra na vidyate".* Ibid

important point : the forms of subjectivity and objectivity in which things are experienced, are mental constructions, and therefore are not substances existing independent of mind and mental factors. Colours etc., which are experienced as objects, are only different modes of objectivity under which things are experienced, and for that matter have no reality independent of mind and mental factors. Here what is to be particularly noted is that when Sthiramati says that colour etc. are not substances (*dravya*) other than mind and mental factors (*citta-caittebhyo 'nyatra*), by colour' etc. he means the different modes of objectivity under which things are experienced, and not those things themselves. That this is his meaning is clear from the fact that the reason he gives for saying that colour etc. are not substances existing independent of mind and mental factors, is that "there is no pair" of subjectivity and objectivity.[1] In other words, what he says is that colour etc., since they belong to the categories of subjectivity and objectivity, do not have any reality independent of mind and mental factors. To make the point clear I may formulate his argument as follows:

> All forms of subjectivity and objectivity are but mental forms, and therefore have no reality independent of mind and mental factors.
> Colour etc. are forms of objectivity under which things are experienced.
> Therefore, they, too, do not have any reality independent of mind and mental factors.

In short, whenever reality is denied to something, it invariably refers to some of subjectivity or objectivity. So Sthiramati continues his explanation in the following manner. The imagination of the unreal is itself neither grasper of anything nor is grasped by anybody. On the contrary, objectivity and subjectivity are but abstract concepts. For colour etc. are not grasped outside consciousness. Just as a dream, consciousness produces the appearance of colour etc. . . . The graspable being absent there cannot be the grasper either, for in the absence of the

1. See note 10 on p. 35

graspable there is also the absence of the grasper. Therefore, colour as an object of experience does not exist apart from the imagination of the unreal. This does not mean that there is nothing apart from the imagination of the unreal. For there is indeed the emptiness which is the basis of purity. However, it is obscured by the imagination of the unreal forms of subjectivity and objectivity. Hence the state of bondage.[1]

Thirdly, the stanza endeavours to portray the middle position between the above-mentioned extremes. On the one hand it is not an outright denial of everything (*sarva-apavāda*), for there is the assertion of the imagination of the unreal; on the other hand it is not an indiscriminate assertion of everything, for the pair of subjectivity and objectivity, which includes the sense-objects such as colour etc. has been denied. Further, the assertion of emptiness, which means the unreality of subject-object distinction, explains the meaning of non-substantiality (*nairātmya*). This latter theory does not mean "the absence of a person who acts from within" (*antar-vyāpāra-puruṣa-rahitatā*), but only the absence of subject-object characterization.[2] However, the state of emptiness is obscured by the imagination of the unreal, and therefore the state of bondage.[3]

Fourthly, the stanza brings home the distinction between the two realms of existence, namely the realms of defilement (*saṅkleśa*) and of purity (*vyavadāna*).[4] The imagination of the unreal belongs to the realm of defilement, for it is characterized by illusion (*bhrānti*).[5] That is, the imagination of the unreal is

1. *Na hi abhūta-parikalpaḥ kasyacid grāhako na-api kenacit gṛhyate. Kim tarhi grāhya-grāhakatvam bhāva-mātram-eva. Yato vijñānāt bahi rūpādayo na gṛhyante. Svapna-ādivad vijñānam rupādyābhāsam-utpadyate. . . .Grāhya-abhāve grāhakasya-abhāvād grāhye'sati grāhako bhavitum na yujyate. Tasmān-narūpam-abhūta-parikalpāt-pṛthag-asti. . . . Śūnyatā vidyate tu-atra. . .śūnyatā hi viśuddhi-ālambanā. Sā ca grāhya-grāhaka-rahitatā. . .abhūtaparikalpa-āvṛtatvān-na gṛhyate.* MVKBT I.2

2. *Anyair-antar-vyāpāra-puruṣa-rahitatā dharmāṇām śūnyatā-iti-ucyate. Ataḥ śūnyatā-apavāda-pratiṣedhārtham bhūta-nairātmya-khyāpanārthañ-ca-āha : śūnyatā vidyate tu-atra iti.* MVKBT I.2

3. For full text see MVKBT I.2

4. *Lakṣaṇam saṅkleśa-vyavadānād-anyan-nāsti-iti-ataḥ saṅkleśa-vyavadāna-lakṣaṇapradarśanārtham-āha.* MVKBT I.2

5. *Abhūta-parikalpa-svabhāvaḥ saṅkleśo bhrānti-lakṣaṇatvāt.* Ibid

of illusory character in the sense that the forms of graspable and grasper (*grāhya-grāhaka-ākāra*) in which things appear (*prakhyāna*) do not belong to those things themselves (*sva-ātmani-avidyamāna*).[1] Emptiness of subject-object characterization, however, is the very form (*svarūpa*) of purity (*vyavadāna*).[2] Conversely, too, the very nature (*svabhāva*) of purity is such emptiness, for purity means the absence of subject-object duality (*dvaya-abhāva-svabhāva*).[3] Thus, in short, *abhūta-parikalpa* and *śūnyatā* respectively stand for *saṅkleśa* and *vyavadāna*. Hence the following equation may be made :

abhūta-parikalpa = *grāhya-grāhaka-vikalpa* = *saṅkleśa* = *saṃsāra*.
śūnyatā = *grāhya-grāhaka-vikalpa-abhāva* = *vyavadāna* = *nirvāṇa*.

In the state of *saṃsāra* one is under the illusion that the subject-object duality is a genuine characteristic of things,[4] and this exactly is one's bondage.

Sthiramati has drawn two analogies to help one understand the theory of *abhūta-parikalpa*, the imagination of the unreal. One is that of an illusory elephant made to appear by the working of *māyā*. He says: "the graspable-grasper discrimination is like the [unreal] form of an elephant in *māyā* in which there is no such form".[5] That is, *māyā* produces the form of an elephant so that a piece of wood, for example, will appear like an elephant. *Māyā*, which is one's power to produce such illusory forms, as such is devoid of the form of an elephant (*hasti-ākāra-śūnya-māyā*), for as such *māyā* is the power to produce such forms, not those forms themselves, nor does it exist in such forms. However, such forms are within *māyā* (...*māyāyām-iva hasti-ākāraḥ*), in the sense that their seeds (*bīja*) or rather the tendency (*vāsanā*) to create such forms, were already there within oneself. The form of an elephant does not belong to the piece

1. *Sva-ātmani-avidyamānena grāhya-grāhaka-ākareṇa prakhyānād-bhrānti-svarūpeṇa jñāyate.* Ibid

2. *Vyavadāna-svarūpa-pradarśanārtham-āha-Śūnyatā vidyate tu-atra-iti.* Ibid.

3. *Śūnyatā-svabhāvo hi vyavadānam dvaya-abhāva-svabhāvatvāt.* Ibid

4. *Yadi dvayam nāsti katham tasyām vidyamānāyām loko bhrānta iti āha—tasyām-api sa vidyate—iti.* Ibid

5. *Grāhya-grāhaka-vikalpo hasti-ākāra-śūnya-māyāyām-iva hasti-ākāra-ādayaḥ.* MVKBT I.2

of wood, either, which appears as an elephant. In other words, the piece of wood does not exist in the form in which it appears to exist, namely in the form of an elephant.

Then, the working of *abhūta-parikalpa* should be understood on the above analogy. *Abhūta-parikalpa* is one's power to produce unreal forms, namely the forms of subjectivity and objectivity. "It is called the *abhūta-parikalpa,* [the imagination of the unreal,] because by it, or in it, is imagined [=mentally constructed] the unreal pair. By the term abhūta is meant that it [=*abhūtaparikalpa*] does not exist as it is imagined, namely in [terms] of subjectivity and objectivity. By the term *parikalpa* is meant that the thing does not exist as it is imagined, [namely in the form of a subject or object]. Thus its definition that it is free of subject-object characterization, is made clear."[1] Thus the theory of *abhūta-parikalpa* is meant to shatter one's belief in the subject-object characterization of things. About what comes under *abhūta-parikalpa* Sthiramati continues:

> *Abhūta-parikalpa* includes the entire range of *citta* and *caitta* which are in accordance with *saṃsāra.* In particular, however, it means the graspable-grasper discrimination. There, the discrimination of the graspable refers to the consciousness which appears as non-living and living beings; and the discrimination of the grasper refers to the consciousness which appears as self and representation of consciousness.[2]

These words of Sthiramati may be explained as follows : The *abhūta-parikalpa* includes everything (*aviśeṣeṇa*) that is called mind and mental factors, under the influence of which one finds oneself in the state of *saṃsāra.* They cease to operate at the attainment of *nirvāṇa* (*nirvāṇa-paryavasānaḥ*). All such *citta* and *caittas* can be subsumed under the forms of subjectivity, and objectivity, and, therefore, *abhūta-parikalpa* particularly

1. *Abhūtam-asmin dvayam parikalpyate'nena vā-iti abhūta-parikalpaḥ. Abhūta-vacanena ca yathā-ayam parikalpyate grāhya-grāhakatvena tathā nāsti-iti pradarśayati. Parikalpa-vacanena tu-artho yathā parikalpyate tathā-artho na vidyate iti pradarśayati. Evam-asya grāhya-grāhaka-vinirmuktam lakṣaṇam paridīpitam bhavati.* MVKBT I.2

2. ... *saṃsāra-anurūpaś-citta-caitta aviśeṣeṇa-abhūta-parikalpaḥ. Viśeṣeṇa tu grāhya-grāhaka-vikalpaḥ. Tatra grāhya-vikalpo' arthasattva-pratibhāsam. Grāhaka-vikalpa ātma-vijñapti-pratibhāsam.* Ibid

means the *graspable-grasper* distinction (*grāhya-grāhaka-vikalpaḥ*). Graspable-discrimination (*grāhya-vikalpa*) refers to the form of objectivity under which consciousness appears as non-living and living beings (*artha* and *sattva*), and the grasper-discrimination refers to the form of subjectivity under which consciousness (*vijñāna*) appears (*pratibhāsa*) as self and representations of consciousness (*ātma* and *vijñapti*).[1]

Explaining the terms *grāhya* and *grāhaka* Sthiramati again says: "*Grāhya* means colour etc., and *grāhaka* means eye-consciousness etc.[2] This is an important clue to the understanding of the whole system. Colour etc., namely colour, taste, touch, smell and sound, are the forms under which things are experienced : they are mere forms of objectivity, and as such they are unreal (*abhūta*); eye-consciousness etc., namely the eight types of consciousnesses, are forms of an experiencing subject: they are mere forms of subjectivity, and as such they are unreal too. What I am trying to say is that unless colour etc. and eye-consciousness etc. are summarized respectively as forms of objectivity and subjectivity, their distinction into *grāhya* and *grāhaka*, and the subsequent denial of their reality will make no sense. Therefore Sthiramati's statement means:

> Colour etc. being mere forms under which things become knowable (*grāhya*), are mere imagination (*parikalpa*) and therefore unreal (*abhūta*), too. Similarly, eye-consciousness etc. being mere forms under which one becomes a knower (*grāhaka*), are mere imagination (*parikalpa*), and therefore unreal (*abhūta*), too.

Thus, as I have already made it clear, whenever something is denied reality, it is treated under the aspect of being a knowable (*grāhya*) or a knower (*grāhaka*).

The second of the two analogies mentioned above is that of a rope appearing under the form of a snake. The message of this analogy is that what is unreal (*abhūta*) in this case is the nature of the snake (*sarpa-svabhāva*) while the rope as such is real. Similarly, the forms of subjectivity and objectivity, under

1. This point will be further explained under MVK I.4
2. *Tatra grāhyam rūpādi. Grāhakam cakṣur-vijñānādi.* MVKBT I.2

which *abhūta-parikalpa* appear, are unreal, but not *abhūta-parikalpa* itself.[1] That is, *abhūta-parikalpa* as such, i.e. short of the forms of subjectivity and objectivity, is real. This statement has two meanings: (i) *abhūta-parikalpa*, namely, that one mentally constructs unreal forms, is an undeniably real fact of saṃsāric existence, although those forms are themselves unreal; (ii) what remains once the forms of subjectivity and objectivity have been negated, namely *śūnyatā*, otherwise called *tathatā*, is eternally (*sarvakālam*) real. Thus having exploded the myth of subject-object distinction two assertions can be made about any individual: (i) as long as he is in the state of *saṃsāra* he is subject to the imagination of the unreal (*abhūta-parikalpa*); (ii) in the state of *nirvāṇa* he realizes the emptiness (*śūnyatā*) of subjectivity and objectivity.[2]

Neither void nor non-void

Thus all that can be said with reference to any individual in the state of *saṃsāra* can be reduced to two statements : (i) an assertion of the imagination of the unreal and of the absolute state of emptiness; (ii) a negation of subjectivity and objectivity. To understand any individual these two statements, one affirmation and the other negation, have to be put together. Nothing is exclusively void (*śūnya*) nor exclusively non-void (*aśūnya*).[3] It is in avoiding these two extremes[4] that the Yogācārins claim to be holding a middle position.[5] Hence the next stanza says:

[MVK I.3] Neither void nor non-void :
So is everything described,
That indeed is the middle path,

1. *Grāhya-grāhaka-bhāvena virahitatā viviktatā hi-abhūta-parikalpasya śūnyatā. Na tu-abhūta-parikalpo'pi-abhāvaḥ yathā śūnya rajjuḥ sarpa-svabhāvena-atat-svabhāvāt sarvakālam śūnyā, na tu rajju-svabhāvena tathā-iha-api.* Ibid

2. *Yat punar-avaśiṣṭam tat-sat. Kim-punariha-avaśiṣṭam ? Abhūta-parikalpaḥ śūnyatā ca.* Ibid

3. *Sarvam na ekāntena śūnyam na ekāntena aśūnyam.* MVKB I.3

4. *antaḥ*, as in the title of the book, *Madhya-anta-vibhāga*.

5. *Sā ca madhyamā-pratipad yad sarvam na-ekāntena śūnyam na-ekāntena-aśūnyam.* MVKB I.3

For there is existence as well as non-existence,
And again existence.[1]

Commenting on this stanza Vasubandhu says :

On account of the existence of emptiness, on the one hand, and that of the imagination of the unreal, on the other, it is not void. And on account of the non-existence of the pair of graspable and grasper, it is not non-void, either. This description applies to everything whether conditioned or unconditioned. The term 'conditioned' goes for what is called the imagination of the unreal, while the term 'unconditioned' goes for what is called the emptiness. That indeed is the middle path, for, on the one hand, there is the existence of emptiness within the imagination of the unreal, and, on the other, the existence of the imagination of the unreal within the emptiness. It is therefore neither exclusively void nor exclusively non-void. This reading is thus in accordance with the scriptures such as *Prajñā-pāramitā*, [where it is said]: 'all this is neither void nor non-void.'[2]

The statement, "So is everything described",[3] deserves special attention. It implies that the description that it is "Neither void nor non-void" applies to every single being separately, not to reality in general. In other words, here there is an indication that the text is speaking about individual beings, not about a cosmic, monistic, reality. The Sanskrit term translated as "every" is *sarva*. It could also be translated as "all". In either case the term *sarva* stands for a multiplicity of beings. This observation of mine is confirmed by Vasubandhu's subsequent commentary. He says that the

1. *Na śūnyam na-api ca aśūnyam tasmāt sarvam vidhīyate*
Sattvād-asattvāt sattvac-ca madhyamā pratipac-ca sā. MVK I.3

2. *Na śūnyam śūnyatayā ca-abhūta-parikalpena ca. Na ca-aśunyam dvayena grāhyena grāhakena ca. Sarvam-saṃskṛtam ca-abhūta-parikalpākhyam, asaṃskṛtam ca śūnyatā-ākhyam. Vidhīyate nirdiśyate. Sattvād-abhūta-parikalpe, tasyām ca-abhūta-parikalpaśya sā ca madhyamā pratipat. Yat sarvam na-ekāntena śūnyam, na-ekāntena aśūnyam. Evam-ayam pāṭhaḥ prajñāpāramitātiṣu-anulomito bhavati—Sarvamidam na śūnyam na-api ca-aśūnyam-iti.* MVKB I.3

3. *Tasmāt. sarvam vidhīyate.* MVK I.3

term *sarvam* in the verse stands for everything whether "conditioned" (*saṃskṛta*) or "unconditioned" (*asaṃskṛta*). Division of the entire (*sarvam*) range of elements (*dharmāḥ*) into "conditioned" and "unconditioned" goes back to the time of the Buddha. Therefore, Vasubandhu's interpretation of the term *sarvam* as covering both the conditioned and the unconditioned elements implies that he retains the original analysis of reality into so many individual elements. Then it is to each of those individual elements that the description "neither void nor non-void" applies. Therefore, every individual element is envisaged as having two aspects, one positive (*aśūnya*) and the other negative (*śūnya*).

The terms *śūnya* and *aśūnya*, here translated respectively as "void" and "non-void", too, need explanation. Linguistically they are just opposites. However, in the present context they are not quite so. *Śūnya* evidently refers to the absence of subject-object characterizations. Then one could rightly expect *aśūnya* to mean the presence of such characterizations. That is not the case, though. Instead, it refers to the existence of that to which the subject-object characterizations are denied. In other words, *śūnya* means that something is devoid of subject-object characterizations, while *aśūnya* means that the same thing, although devoid of such characterizations, still exists. Similarly, according to the present stanza, everything (*sarvam*) conditioned (*saṃskṛta*) as well as unconditioned (*asaṃskṛta*) is devoid of subject-object characterizations,[1] but still is an existing reality, either as *abhūta-parikalpa* or as *śūnyatā*. The conditioned elements exist as *abhūta-parikalpa* while the unconditioned ones exist as *śūnyatā*.[2] *Abhūta-parikalpa*, as has been explained in the previous stanza, exists as an undeniable factor of *saṃsāra*, although the forms of subjectivity and objectivity, in which it manifests itself, do not exist.[3] Consequently, the conditioned elements,

1. *Na-śūnyam śūnyatayā ca-abhūta-parikalpena ca. Na ca aśūnyam dvayena grāhyena grāhakena ca. Sarvam saṃskṛtam ca-abhūta-parikalpa-ākhyam, asaṃskṛtam ca śūnyatākhyam.* MVKB I.3

2. *Sarvam saṃskṛtam ca-abhūta-parikalpākhyam, asaṃskṛtam ca śūnyatā-ākhyam* MVKB I.3.

3. *Abhūta-parikalpo'sti, dvayam tatra na vidyate.* MVK I.2

too, which make up the realm of *abhūta-parikalpa*,[1] are undeniable factors of *saṃsāra*, although the forms of subjectivity and objectivity, in which they manifest themselves, do not exist, and therefore are unreal (*abhūta*). The point at issue will be clearer if one remembers that "the *abhūta-parikalpa* includes everything that is called *citta* and *caitta* under the influence of which one finds oneself in the state of *saṃsāra*, and which cease to operate at the attainment of *nirvāṇa*".[2] That is, what is presently treated as "conditioned" should be referred to the same *citta-caitta* complex. So ultimately it is those *citta-caittas* that are described as *saṃskṛta-dharmas* and as *abhūta-parikalpa* and finally as both *śūnya* as well as *aśūnya* : they exist (*aśūnya*) as undeniable factors of *saṃsāra*, but are devoid (*śūnya*) of the forms of subjectivity and objectivity in which they manifest themselves.

Similarly, *śūnyatā* exists in the absolute sense of the term, but is eternally devoid of subject-object characterizations. Consequently, the unconditioned elements, which make up the realm of *śūnyatā*,[3] exist in the absolute sense of the term, but are eternally devoid of subject-object characterizations.

Thus everything (*sarvam*), whether conditioned (*saṃskṛta*) or unconditioned (*asaṃskṛta*), the former under the aspect of *abhūta-parikalpa* and the latter under the aspect of *śūnyatā*, is rightly described as "neither void nor non-void" (*na śūnyam na-api ca aśūnyam*).

Abhūta-parikalpa and *śūnyatā*, theoretically speaking, refer to mutually excluding modes of existence, namely *saṃsāra* and *nirvāṇa*. But in a concrete individual undergoing the *saṃsāra* experience those two modes co-exist, so to speak, *abhūta-parikalpa* overshadowing and obscuring (*āvaraṇa*) *śūnyatā*. An individual undergoing the state of *saṃsāra* combines in himself *abhūta-parikalpa* and *śūnyatā*, *saṃskṛta-dharmas* and *asaṃskṛta-dharmas*, *saṅkleśa* and *vyavadāna*, *saṃsāra* and *nirvāṇa*. All *dharmas*, *saṃskṛta* as well as *asaṃskṛta*, which constitute his being, are each *śūnya* as well as *aśūnya*, as explained above. At the dawn of *nirvāṇa*,

1. *saṃskṛtam ca-abhūta-parikalpākhyam*. MVKB I.3

2. . . .*nirvāṇa-paryavasānāḥ saṃsāra-anurūpāś-citta-caittā aviśeṣeṇa-abhūta-parikalpaḥ*. MVKBT I.2

3. *Asaṃskṛtam ca śūnyatā-ākhyam*. MVKB I.3

saṃskṛta-dharmas, which are the same as *citta-caittas* cease to exist, and for that matter so do *abhūta-parikalpa, saṅkleśa* and *saṃsāra.* It is this co-existence of *abhūta-parikalpa* and *śūnyatā,* a point already emphasized in stanza I.2, that Vasubandhu has in mind when he says: "On the one hand, there is the existence of emptiness within the imagination of the unreal, and, on the other, the existence of the imagination of the unreal within the emptiness."[1] Then by shedding the covering (*āvaraṇa*) of *abhūta-parikalpa* one attains the state of *śūnyatā,* which is the same as *nirvāṇa.*

Forms of the imagination of the unreal

The next stanza is a further inquiry into the particular forms of the imagination of the unreal. It has already been said that the imagination of the unreal expresses itself in two primary forms, namely the forms of subjectivity and objectivity. However, each of those primary forms may have different secondary forms. What are such secondary forms ? This is the question discussed in the next stanza. Vasubandhu calls it the "own-definition" (*svalakṣaṇa*) of the imagination of the unreal. The previous two stanzas gave a positive definition (*sal-lakṣaṇa*) and a negative definition (*asal-lakṣaṇa*) of the same imagination of the unreal. Positively it was defined (or rather described) as an existing reality,[2] and negatively as not having within itself the pair of subjectivity and objectivity.[3] However, what particular forms it takes was not clearly discussed, except that Vasubandhu in his commentary said that "the imagination of the unreal means the discrimination between the grasper and the graspable".[4] Hence, "thus having stated the positive and negative definition of the imagination of the unreal, now [the author] gives its own definition."[5] As for the distinction between the positive definition

1. See note 2 on p. 42.

2. *Idam sattvena lakṣyate iti sattvam-eva sal-lakṣaṇam. Abhūta-parikalpo vidyata iti-anena-abhūta-parikalpasya sattvam pradarśayati-iti-arthaḥ.* MVKBT I.4

3. *Evam-asattvena lakṣyate iti asattvam-eva-asal-lakṣaṇam. Tat punar-yad grāhya-grāhaka-bhāvena-asattvam-yasmād-abhūta-parikalpe dvayam nāsti tasmād-abhūtaparikalpo'pi dvayātmanā nāsti-iti-utkam bhavati.* MVKBT I.4

4. *Tatra-abhūta-parikalpo grāhya-grāhaka-vikalpaḥ.* MVKB I.2

5. *Evam abhūta-parikalpasya sal-lakṣaṇam-asal-lakṣaṇam ca khyāpayitva sva-lakṣaṇam khyāpayati.* MVKB I.4

and the own-definition Sthiramati says that the former is only a general (*sāmānya*) assertion while the latter is a particular (*viśeṣa*) one,[1] implying that the positive definition was concerned with only a general assertion of the reality of the imagination of the unreal, while the own-definition is going to give more particulars about the same imagination of the unreal.

Now, the first part of the stanza reads as follows:

> [MVK I.4] Under the appearance of things inanimate,
> Living beings, self and representations of consciousness
> Is born the consciousness.[2]

Commenting on these lines Vasubandhu says:

> In the form of colour etc. the consciousness appears as inanimate things, and in that of five senses it appears as living beings. These five senses refer to one's own as well as others' streams of existence. The appearance of consciousness as self is the same as defiled thought, because it is associated with self-delusion etc. The representations of consciousness are otherwise called the sixfold consciousness.[3]

According to Sthiramati this passage answers two questions. The first one is concerned with the possibility of having sense-knowledge. It has been said in the previous stanzas that although there is the imagination of the unreal, there is no graspable-grasper duality. How then could there be sense-knowledge, which necessarily presupposes the duality between graspable objects and grasping subjects ? This question, says Sthiramati, is answered by the present stanza saying that it is the *abhūta-parikalpa* itself which appears in the different forms of

1. *Ko viśeṣo'sti sal-lakṣaṇa-svalakṣaṇayoḥ ? Sal-lakṣaṇam hi sāmānyam. Svalakṣaṇam tu viśeṣaḥ.* MVKBT I.4

2. *Artha-sattva-ātma-vijñapti-pratibhāsam prajāyate Vijñāna. . .* MVK I.4

3. *Tatra-artha-pratibhāsam yad rupādi-bhāvena pratibhāsate. Sattva-pratibhāsam yat pañca-indrīyattvena-sva-para-santānayoḥ. Ātma-pratibhāsam kliṣṭam manaḥ, ātma-mohādi-samprayogāt. Vijñapti-pratibhāsam sad vijñānāni. Nāsti ca-asya-artha-iti artha-sattvapratibhāsasya-anākāratvāt, ātma-vijñapti-pratibhāsasya ca vitatha-pratibhāsatvāt. Tadabhāvāt tad-api-asad-iti yat grāhyam rūpadi, pañca-indrīyam, manaḥ, ṣaḍ-vijñāna-sañjñakam caturvidham tasya grāhyasyābhāvāt tadapi grāhakam vijñānam asat.* MVKB I.4

subjectivity and objectivity.[1] Here Sthiramati obviously means that the above said four appearances of consciousness, namely *artha*, *sattva*, *ātma* and *vijñapti*, and the consciousness itself, are different forms of subjectivity and objectivity in which the *abhūta-parikalpa* expresses itself. I shall return to this point later.

The second question which Sthiramati thinks the present stanza answers is the following. It has been positively said that there exists the imagination of the unreal. But its own-nature remains to be explained. It has also been said that there is no subject-object duality at all. If so it remains to be explained how one has still the passion for making a distinction between the graspable and the grasper, and how one can be led to believe that there is no duality.[2] These problems are solved, says Sthiramati, by the present stanza as follows. The own-nature of *abhūta-parikalpa* is consciousness (i.e. the *abhūta-parikalpa* is of the nature of consciousness). The same consciousness is to be understood together with its associates. However, primarily it is consciousness. The same consciousness, which is bound up with the appearances of *artha*, *sattva* etc., is itself the passion for the graspable-grasper distinction.[3] What Sthiramati says may be put in other words: *abhūta-parikalpa* for all practical purposes is the same as consciousness (*vijñāna*), including its associates (*samprayoga*), namely, *citta* and *caittas*. This consciousness, or more specifically, the *citta* and *caittas*, is always the consciousness of something, either *artha*, or *sattva* or *ātma* or *vijñapti*, and therefore appears as if split into two parts, one of subjectivity and the other of objectivity, and thus accounts for

1. *Yadi sva-lakṣaṇam-anākhyātam-atra kim syāt ? . . .grāhya-grāhaka-rahitatā-abhūta-parikalpa-mātratā-iti-uddiṣṭam. Tasya-abhūta-parikalpa-mātratāyām-indrīya-viṣaya-vijñānam yathā-vyavasthītam (tathā) na jñāyata (iti). Abhūta-parikalpa-pratibhāsa-bhedena tad-vyavasthiti-jñāpanārtham-abhūta-parikalpasya sva-lakṣaṇam khyāpayati.* MVKBT I.4

2. . . . *abhūta-parikalpo'sti-iti-anena tat-sattva-mātram jñāyate, na tu tat-svabhāvaḥ. Dvaya-abhave'pi yad grāhya-grāhaka-abhiniveśa-kāraṇam na jñāyate, dvayam ca nāsti-iti yataḥ pratīyate tad-api na-uktam-iti-ataḥ-tat-pratipādaṇārtham-āha.* Ibid

3. *Tatra vijñānasvabhāvo'bhūtaparikalpaḥ. Tac-ca vijñānam sa-samprayogam-abhipretam. Pradhānena tu vijñānam gṛhītam. Sa eva grāhya-grāhaka-abhīniveśo-artha-sattva-ādi-pratibhāsa-nibandhaḥ.* Ibid

one's passion for graspable-grasper distinction (*grāhya-grāhaka-abhiniveśa*), and leads one to believe that there is really the distinction between the subjects and objects.

Before proceeding further I must make one point clear. That consciousness appears in the form of different objects is the basic contention of the present stanza. This should not be understood to mean that there are no things other than consciousness. On the contrary, it means only that what falls within the range of experience are different forms of consciousness, while the things-in-themselves remain beyond the limits of experience. For example, when a rope is mistaken for a snake, it is the form of snake, which is being experienced, that can be explained as a mental form, while the rope itself remains outside that experience. That just the same is the message of the present stanza is clear from a similar example cited by Sthiramati which is as follows. One may mistake a stump for a man. There, one is projecting one's past experience of man on to the stump before one, and thus making oneself unable to recognize the stump as such. Similarly, says Sthiramati, 'the ignorant people mistake the different forms of consciousness for things other than consciousness, just as people with bad eyes mistake their own mental images for hair, egg etc.'[1]

- It is obvious that the present stanza is dealing with the ordinary categories of experience/thought, namely consciousness (*vijñāna*), non-living beings (*artha*), living beings (*sattva*), self (*ātma*), and representations of consciousness (*vijñapti*). Analyzing those categories the stanza says that they are different forms of subjectivity and objectivity, and as such being different appearances of consciousness itself they do not represent things in themselves. I shall now explain how those categories can be interpreted as different forms of subjectivity and objectivity. The central point is that they present themselves to thought/experience either as subject or as object of some experience. Thus, first there appears consciousness as the subject of all the

1. *Katham asati-arthādau vijñānam tad-abhāsam-udpadyate ? Na hi puruṣe asati sthāṇuḥ bhavati-iti. Na eṣah doṣaḥ. Artha-ādi-ābhāsam hi vijñānam bālāḥ vijñānāt pṛthag-artha-astitvena-abhiniviśante taimirikasya keśāṇdukādivat.* Ibid

other four categories.[1] That is, consciousness is invariably the consciousness of either self or ideas or living beings or non-living beings. Apart from being the subject of those other categories consciousness is nothing, and therefore it makes sense only as an experiencing subject. Again, self and the representation of consciousness are contrasted with living beings and non-living beings as subjects and objects. Self defined as defiled thought (*kliṣṭam manaḥ*, literally meaning impassioned thought)[2] is described as the subject of passions such as ego-delusion, ego-belief, ego-desire and ego-pride,[3] all these passions having living and non-living beings as their objects.[4] In other words, self is a bundle of passions which presuppose external beings as their objects. The representations of consciousness stand for the six-fold consciousness, namely the five sense-consciousnesses (*indriya-vijñānāni*) and the thought-consciousness (*mano-vijñānam*). Being consciousness none of them has any meaning without reference to the respective objects, either animate or inanimate. So they are essentially in the form of subjects. Finally, living and non-living beings are there as objects of either self, or one or another form of consciousness. By living being are meant those which are endowed with five senses. Such beings ultimately represent one's own as well as other people's streams of existence.[5] What is important here is that those "persons" (or streams of existence) are experienced only as objects of one's consciousness and passions. Similarly the non-living beings, which can be reduced to sense-data (i.e., colour etc.), are presented to consciousness through the senses.[6] As they appear, they, too, have the form of objects of consciousness, the latter appearing either as self or as representations of consciousness.

1. Cf. . . .*tad-grāhyam rūpadi, pañca-indriyam, manaḥ, ṣaḍ-vijñāna-sañjñakam catur-vidham tasya grāhyasya . . . tadapi grāhakam vijñānam* . . . Ibid.
2. *ātma-pratibhāsam kliṣṭam manaḥ*. MVKB I.4
3. *Ātma-pratibhāsam kliṣṭam manaḥ, ātma-mohādi-samprayogād-iti kliṣṭasya manasa ātma-mohena-ātmadṛṣṭyā-ātma-tṛṣṇayā-asmimānena ca nityam samprayuktatvāt, teṣām-ca ātma-ālambanatvād-yuktam ātma-pratibhāsatvam kliṣṭasya manasaḥ*. MVKBT I.4
4. Because underlying these passions (*kleśas*) is the I-consciousness as opposed to other objects.
5. *Sattva-pratibhāsam yat pañca-indriyattvena sva-para-santānayoḥ*. MVKB I.4
6. *Tatra artha-pratibhāsam yad-rūpādi-bhāvena pratibhāsate*. Ibid

The remaining part of the stanza under discussion, and its commentaries by Vasubandhu and Sthiramati, evaluate those categories and show how, under the aspects of subjectivity and objectivity, they are false and unreal:

> [MVK I.4 cont'd.] There is nothing as its [i.e. consciousness's] object,
> And thus that object being absent
> That [consciousness], too, is non-existent.[1]

What the author says here could be differently put as follows:

Consciousness makes sense only with reference to its object (*artha*).

There are no such objects.

Therefore there is nothing called consciousness either. Vasubandhu now in his commentary on the above lines examines and explains the minor premise of the argument, namely that there are no such objects. The objects (*artha*) referred to are evidently the categories of self, representations of consciousness, living beings and inanimate things, all of which have been spoken of in the former part of the stanza as appearances (*pratibhāsa*) of consciousness itself. Now, then, what is meant by saying that there are no such objects ? In what sense are those four objects absent ? Here is the answer given by Vasubandhu:

> The appearances of inanimate things as well as of living beings are devoid of form; likewise the appearances of self and representation of consciousness are not in the way they appear to be. This is why it is said that there is indeed nothing as its [i.e. consciousness's] object. That is, the four kinds of graspables—namely, (i) colour etc., (ii) the five senses, (iii) thought, and (iv) the sixfold consciousness—are absent. Thus the graspable being absent, the grasper, namely the consciousness, too, is non-existent.[2]

1. . . . *nāsti ca-asya-arthas-tad-abhāvāt tad-api-asat.* MVK I.4
2. *Nāsti-ca-asya-artha iti artha-sattva-pratibhāsasya-anākāratvāt, ātma-vijñapti-pratibhāsasya ca vitatha-pratibhāsatvāt. Tad-abhāvāt tadapi-asad-iti yat tad-grāhyam rūpādi, pañca-indriyam, manaḥ, ṣaḍ-vij ñāna-sañjñakam catur-vidham tasya grāhyasya-abhāvāt tadapi-grāhakam vijñānam-asat.* MVKB I.4

The main concern of this passage is to show in what sense the five categories of experience are unreal. And the whole thrust of the argument derives from contrasting consciousness as the grasper with the other four categories as the graspables. And the argument itself may be summarized as follows: graspability being a fake concept, grasperhood, too, does not make sense. How is then graspability a fake concept ?

First of all Vasubandhu distinguishes between inanimate and living beings on the one hand, and self and representations of consciousness on the other. Then he says that the former pair is absent/non-existent (*abhāva*) because they have no form. The Sanskrit term translated here as 'form' is *ākāra*. In the ordinary language it means 'form', or 'shape' or 'frame'. But in an epistemological context, such as the present one, it stands for the form in which a thing is perceived or grasped, and therefore can be better translated as 'objective frame' or 'objectivity'. That in the present context *ākāra* means 'objectivity' is clear from Sthiramati's subsequent commentary. He gives two interpretations:

(i) In the first instance, for him *ākāra* means 'the mode in which an object is grasped'.[1] In other words, for him *ākāra* means *prakāra*, this latter term being the one employed by Indian logicians to denote 'the way or mode in which an object is experienced.'[2] Sthiramati then says that both inanimate and living beings do not have such a *prakāra* (objectivity) in which they could be grasped. Why? Because they only appear in the form of graspables (*grāhyarūpeṇa prakhyānāt*).[3] Here are Sthiramati's own words:

> A form [*ākāra*] indeed is the mode in which an object [*ālambana*] is grasped, for example, as an impermanent thing etc. Neither of them [i.e. inanimate and living beings],

1. *grahaṇa-prakāraḥ*. See note 1 on p. 52.

2. For example Annambhatta's *Tarka-saṅgraha*, (Varanasi : The Chowkhamba Sanskrit Series, 1966), pp. 14-15, defines *true* experience as "that which presents the object in the *form* in which it really is" (*tad-vati tad-prakārako'nubhava yathārthaḥ*).

3. *sa* [*ākāraḥ*] *ca anayoḥ* [*artha-sattva-pratibhāsayoḥ*] *nāsti grāhya-rūpeṇa prakhyānāt*. MVKBT I. 4

however, has such a mode, because they only appear in the form of graspables. Therefore, the phrase 'because they have no form' means 'because they have no graspability'.[1]

This denial of *ākāratva* has to be understood in the light of, and on the model of, the denial of the pair (*dvayam*) in the second stanza. In the light of it, for my analysis of the denial of *dvaya* showed that "whenever reality is denied to something, it invariably refers to some form of subjectivity and objectivity" (see above p. 36), or that "whenever something is denied reality, it is treated under the aspect of being a knowable (*grāhya*) or a knower (*grāhaka*)" (see above p. 40). Therefore in the present case, too, the denial of *ākāratva* has to be understood with reference to forms of subjectivity and objectivity, and, as I have already explained, it definitely refers to the form of objectivity. Again, on the model of the denial of *dvaya*, for denial of *dvaya* means that neither *abhūta-parikalpa* nor *śūnyatā* has within itself the duality between subjectivity and objectivity, and that such a duality is altogether illusory just as the form of a magical elephant. Similarly, the denial of *ākāratva* (i.e. the form of objectivity, which is one of the above-mentioned pair, *dvaya*), too, should be understood to mean that neither appearances of consciousness as living and non-living beings, nor the things (no matter living or non-living) in themselves have *ākāratva*, and that *ākāratva* is altogether illusory as the form of a magical elephant.

(ii) A Second interpretation of *ākāra* given by Sthiramati is that "*ākāra* is the experience of subject. But no such experience of either of them [i.e. inanimate or living beings] is there. Therefore, they are formless in the sense that there is no perception of them."[2] These words of Sthiramati imply a down-

1. *Ākāro hi-ālambanasya-anityādi-rūpeṇa grāhaka-prakāraḥ. Sa anayor-nāsti grāhya-rūpeṇa prakhyānāt. Ato-anākāratvād-agrāhakatvād-iti arthaḥ.* MVKBT I.4. In this passage *agrāhakatvāt* has been translated as "because they have no graspability." *Grāhakatva* in normal situations would mean 'grasperhood' which does not fit in with the present context. As the suffix *ka* can also refer to objectivity it is here accordingly translated, as in the term *kāraṇaka*.

2. *Ālambana-saṃvedanam vā ākāraḥ. Tac-ca tayor nāsti iti upalabdhi-abhāvād anākāraḥ.* MVKBT I. 4.

right denial of experience of a thing, whether inanimate or living, as it is in itself. What is thought to be experienced is only the appearance (*pratibhāsa*) of consciousness (*vijñāna*), which under the aspect of knowable (*grāhya*) is as illusory as the form of a magical elephant, and therefore does not altogether exist (*atyanta-abhāva* Cf. TSN. 11).

Thus the above two interpretations of *ākāra* amount to the same conclusion, namely that the form in which a thing is thought to be grasped is purely imagined (*parikalpita*), and therefore is no sure guide to the thing-in-itself. It is in this sense, and only in this sense, that Vasubandhu's system can be called idealism. It by no means implies that there is nothing apart from ideas or consciousness.

Now coming to Vasubandhu's evaluation of the categories of self and the representations of consciousness, he has said that they are 'false appearances'. The Sanskrit term translated as 'false appearance' is *vitatha-pratibhāsa,* which literally means 'appearance of something in a false manner'. That means, the appearance of self and the representations of consciousness as objects (*artha*) of consciousness is false. Why ? Sthiramati explains: 'The other two objects, namely self and representations of consciousness manifest (*prakhyāna*) themselves as graspers (*grāhaka-rūpeṇa*), but take on the false appearance of graspables, and for that matter are absent (*abhāva*).[1] In other words self, and representations of consciousness stand for forms of subjectivity, as I have already explained above on pp. 48ff. Therefore, their appearance (*pratibhāsa*) as objects (*artha*) of consciousness (*vijñāna*) is false (*vitatha*), and for that reason (*kāraṇam*) is said to be absent, too. How their manifestation as graspers (*grāhaka*), too, are illusory is already made clear, for all forms of subjectivity have been described as altogether non-existent. Further, for them to be graspers there should be some objects which they can grasp. Living as well as non-living beings could be such graspable objects. But it has already been said that the graspability of living and non-living beings just does not exist. As graspable objects the living and non-living beings

1. *Natu-anyayor-grāhya-rūpeṇa prakhyānād-anākāraḥ; vitathapratibhāsatvam-eva-artha-abhāve kāraṇam-uktam.* MVKBT I.4

are altogether non-existent (*atyanta-abhāva*). Thus the graspable objects being absent, the term "grasping subjects" becomes meaningless and redundant. It is in this sense that self and representations of consciousness are said to be absent. Sthiramati says: "The graspable objects being absent, the appearances of both self and representations of consciousness, which manifest themselves as grasping subjects, are false."[1]

Sthiramati has one more explanation for the false appearance of self and representations of consciousness as graspables. He says:

> False appearance means the absence of the objects in the way they are imagined to be there by the consciousness. False appearance is thus owing to false basis [=object], just as a false rumour about the presence of a tiger etc. is owing to false basis.[2]

Thus there are things independent of consciousness, although they are not in the manner they are imagined by the grasping subject.

After having thus established the non-beingness (absence) of the categories of self, representations of consciousness, inanimate beings and living beings, the authors now call one's attention to consciousness, of which the former four are seemingly the objects. However, now that those objects (*artha*) are proved to be absent (*abhāva*), it is no longer sensible to call consciousness a subject.[3] Hence consciousness as a subject, too, is so much absent. It does not get at anything other than its own forms. In a way its own subjectivity itself is one of its own constructions. Sthiramati says:

> The objects being absent, there is no consciousness of them either. Consciousness is that which knows objects. Therefore in the absence of objects there cannot be the act of knowing as well. Thus, since objects are absent, consciousness, too, as a knowing subject, is non-existent.[4]

1. *Grāhya-abhāve dvayor-ātma-vijñapti-pratibhāsayor-grāhaka-ākāreṇa prakhyānāt vitatha-pratibhāsatvam.* MVKBT I.4
2. *Yathā vijñānena-arthaḥ parikalpyate tathā-arthasya-abhāvo vyāghrādi-śruti-iva vitatha-ālambanatvād-vitatha-pratibhāsatā.* Ibid.
3. *Artha-abhāvād-vijñātṛtvena vijñānam-asat.* MVKBT I.4
4. *Artha-abhāvāt-tad-vijñānam-asat. Vijānāti-iti-vijñānam grāhya-abhāve vijānanā-api ayuktam. Tasmād-artha-abhāvād-vijñātṛtvena vijñānam-asat.* Ibid.

The above analysis could be summarized as follows. The categories of consciousness, self, representations of consciousness, living beings and inanimate beings, insofar as they fall within the range of experience, are all but subjective constructions, and for that reason unreal, too. Those categories are experienced as one or other form of subjectivity and objectivity, and as such do not represent the things-in-themselves (things in their suchness). The things-in-themselves (i.e. the things in their suchness) are beyond the range of experience, because they do not have the forms of subjectivity and objectivity, under which alone experience is possible. Those categories, subjective forms as they are, are experienced either as subject or as objects. Categories of inanimate and living beings, insofar as they are objects of experience are absent/unreal, because they do not have objectivity (*anākāratvāt*). Categories of self and the representations of consciousness insofar as they are objects of experience, are likewise only mentally constructed forms and are therefore unreal, having nothing to do with things-in-themselves. Self and representations of consciousness insofar as they are subjects of experience, too, are mentally constructed forms, and therefore unreal, and as such are false appearances of consciousness. Consciousness itself insofar as it is subject of experience is unreal and non-existent. Thus, in short, whatever is referred to as subject or object is mere subjective construction, and therefore unreal; things-in-themselves are neither subjects nor objects.

Summarizing the discussion so far stanza I.5 says:

[MVKI.5] Therefore its being the imagination of the unreal
Remains established.[1]

For Vasubandhu the meaning of these lines are so clear that he does not bother to elaborate it. According to Sthiramati's commentary the term "its" (*asya*) stands collectively for the four appearances of consciousness mentioned in the previous stanza.[2] The term "therefore" (*ataḥ*) refers to what has been

1. *Abhūta-parikalpatvam siddham-asya bhavati-ataḥ*. MVK I.5
2. *Abhūta-parikalpatvam-ca teṣām caturṇām vijñānānām siddham.* MVKBT I.5

said in the previous stanza, namely that 'the objects being absent, the knowing consciousness, too, is non-existent'.[1] Thus the meaning of the above lines turns out to be as follows :

> On the basis of what has been said in the previous stanza
> It becomes established that the four objective categories,
> Namely, *artha, sattva, ātma* and *vijñapti*,
> Insofar as they are thought to be objects,
> Are but imagination of the unreal.

According to Sthiramati the term "therefore"(*ataḥ*) may refer also to what is subsequently said in the same stanza, namely,

> [MVK I.5 cont'd] For it is not so,
> It is not altogether absent, either.[2]

commenting on which Vasubandhu says,

> For its existence is not the way it appears to be. It is not totally absent, either, because there is the production of illusion only.[3]

Here the pronoun "it" evidently refers to the fourfold appearance of consciousness. It appears to be objects (*artha*) of consciousness, which it is not (*na tathā*). It is not altogether absent, either (*na ca sarvathā-abhāvaḥ*). Why not ? "Because there is the production of illusion-only" says Vasubandhu. Illusion (*bhrānti*) does not mean the absence of the appearance of a particular form, says Sthiramati, but the absence of its essence (*ātmatvena-abhāva*).[4] For example, when a rope appears in the form of a snake, that it appears in that form is a fact, while it does not have the essence of a snake. Similarly that there are appearances of consciousness as objects is an undeniable fact, while they do not really exist as objects. In

1. *Ata iti anantaroktād-hetor-artha-abhāvāt-tadapi-asad-iti.* Ibid
2. *Na tathā sarvathā-abhāvāt.* MVK I.5
3. *Yasmān-na tathā-asya bhāvo yathā pratibhāsa utpadyate. Na ca sarvathā abhāvo bhrānti-mātrasya-utpādāt.* MVKB I.5
4. *ātmatvena-abhāvo na tu yad-ākāreṇa pratibhāsate tena bhrāntir-ucyate māyā-vat.* MVKBT I.5

other words, there is illusion of objects,[1] although there is no objectivity itself. Why should one recognize the existence of illusion at all ? Vasubandhu himself has raised this question: "why not admit the absence of that illusion itself ?"[2] His answer is, "For otherwise there would be neither bondage nor liberation, which would imply the denial of the facts of defilement and purity."[3] This is, according to Vasubandhu, the interpretation of the final part of the stanza, which says,

[MVK I.5 cont'd.] From its cessation results liberation.[4]

The entire discussion can be summarized as follows: That there is the imagination of the unreal, which gives rise to the illusion that there are graspable, enjoyable, objects,[5] is a fact. And this has to be accepted as a fact, so that the distinction between *saṃsāra* and *nirvāṇa* may be explained: cessation of the imagination of the unreal, and of the consequent illusion of objectivity, explains *nirvāṇa/mukti*, and the non-cessation (*aparikṣiṇa*) of the same explains *saṃsāra/bandha*.[6] Facts of defilement and purity, too, are similarly explained: state of *saṃsāra/bandha* is characterized by defilement (*saṅkleśa*) while that of *nirvāṇa/mukti* is characterized by purity (*vyava dāna*).[7] "Therefore", concludes Sthiramati, "the imagination of the unreal as well as the absence of the pair [of subjectivity and objectivity] should necessarily be recognized".[8]

1. *Bhrānti-vijñānasya sad-bhāvān-na sarvathā-abhāva. Ibid.*
2. *Kim-artham punas-tasya* [*bhrāntimātrasya*] *abhāva eva na iṣyate* ? MVKB I.5
3. *Yasmād-anyathā na bandho na mokṣaḥ prasidhyed-iti saṅkleśa-apavāda-doṣaḥ syāt.* MVKB I.5
4. . . *Tat-kṣayān-muktir-iṣyate.* MVK I.5
5. *grāhya-grāhakatvena bhrāntir-udbhāsitā*. . MVKBT I.5 *grāhya-grāhaka-pratibhāsam-utpadyate.* Ibid
6. *Tat-kṣayān-muktir-iṣyate. Tasmin-ca-aparikṣīṇe bandha iti-arthād-uktam bhavati.* Ibid
7. . . *evam sati nityaḥ saṅkleśa syāt. Tathā ca nirvāṇa-abhāvaḥ. Evam ca bhrānti-mātrasya-api-abhāve saṅkleśa-abhāvo nityam-ca vyavadānam prasajyate.* MVKBT. I.5
8. *Ato'vaśyam-abhūta-parikalpa-bhāvo'bhyupagantavyo dvaya-abhāvaś-ca.* MVKBT. I.5

Thus, observes Sthiramati, on the one hand denying the graspable-grasper duality, and, on the other, asserting the fact of the imagination of the unreal, the present stanza is simply restating what has already been said in MVK I.2: "There exists the imagination of the unreal; however there is no pair".[1]

The imagination of the unreal in relation to the three natures

The next stanza relates the idea of the imagination of the unreal to that of the three natures, namely, the absolutely accomplished, the other-dependent and the imagined. According to Vasubandhu the very purpose of this stanza is to show that the idea of the imagination of the unreal includes that of the three natures. He says: "Thus having stated the own-definition of the imagination of the unreal, now the [author] states its inclusive definition. It shows, how, there being only the imagination of the unreal, there could be the inclusion of the three natures."[2] The stanza reads:

[MVK I.6] The imagined, the other-dependent,
And the absolutely accomplished,
Are derived respectively from
The objects, the imagination of the unreal,
And the absence of the pair.[3]

In other words, the imagined, the other dependent, and the absolutely accomplished natures refer respectively to the objects (*artha*), the imagination of the unreal (*abhūta-parikalpa*) and the absence of the pair (*dvaya-abhāva*) of subjects and objects. So Vasubandhu has the following commentary on this stanza:

> The object is the imagined nature, the imagination of the unreal is the other-dependent nature, and the absence of the

1. *Evam grāhya-grāhaka-abhāvāt-tat-pratibhāsa-vijñāna-sad-bhāvāc-ca yat-pūrvam pratijñātam, abhūta-parikalpo'sti dvayam tatra na-vidyate* (I.2), *iti tat-prasiddham-iti-pradarśayan-āha-* MVKB I.5

2. *Evam-abhūta-parikalpasya sva-lakṣaṇam khyāpayitvā saṅgraha-lakṣaṇam khyāpayati. Abhūta-parikalpa-mātre sati yathā trayāṇām svabhāvānām saṅgraho bhavati.* Ibid. I.6

3. *Kalpitaḥ para-tantraś-ca pariniṣpanna-eva ca.*
Arthād-abūta-kalpāc-ca dvaya-abhāvāc-ca deśitāḥ. MVK I.6

graspable-grasper duality is the absolutely accomplished nature.[1]

This is an explanation of the three natures in terms of the imagination of the unreal. Sthiramati puts it clearly as follows:

> That the imagination of the unreal is lacking in the graspable-grasper duality has already been said. But it is not just the absence of such duality. The same imagination of the unreal is, moreover, the other-dependent, because it depends on causes and conditions. The same imagination of the unreal, again, is the imagined, because it manifests itself in the forms of graspables and graspers, forms which do not exist within the imagination of the unreal itself. Also, the same imagination of the unreal is the absolutely accomplished, because it is lacking in the graspable-grasper duality. Thus the three natures are included in the same imagination of the unreal. Thus, by referring to the imagination of the unreal, is shown that reality which should first be known, then abandoned, and finally realized.[2]

What the three natures stand for is now quite clear :

First, there is the fact of the imagination of the unreal, which in effect is the act of discriminating between subjects and objects. It is this act of discrimination between subjects and objects that is described as the other-dependent nature, "because", says Sthiramati, "its birth depends on causes and conditions".[3] It means that one is forced to discriminate between subjects and objects because of the forces (*saṃskāras*) and

1. *Arthaḥ parikalpitaḥ svabhāvaḥ. Abhūta-parikalpaḥ paratantraḥ svabhāvaḥ. Grāhya-grāhaka-abhāvaḥ pariniṣpannaḥ svabhāvaḥ.* MVKB I.6

2. *Atra hi-abhūta-parikalpasya dvaya-rahitatā grāhya-grāhaka-abhāva uktaḥ. Na tu dvayasya abhāva-mātram. Evam-abhūta-parikalpa-eva hetu-pratyaya-pāratantryāt paratantraḥ. Sa eva grāhya-grāhaka-rūpeṇa sva-ātmani-avidyamānena prakhyānāt parikalpitaḥ. Sa eva grāhya-grāhaka-rahitatvāt pariniṣpannaḥ. Evam abhūta-parikalpe trayaḥ svabhāvaḥ saṅgṛhītaḥ. Etena-abhūta-parikalpam-anūdya parijñeyam, parijñāya prahatavyam, parijñāya sākṣāt-kartavyam ca vastu sandarśitam bhavati* MVKBT I.6

3. *Para-tantraḥ, para-vaśaḥ, hetupratyaya-pratibaddha-janmakatvāt.* MV-KBT I.6

habits (*vāsanās*) of one's past deeds (*karma*), which function as the causes (*hetu*)and conditions (*pratyaya*) of the imagination of the unreal.

Secondly there are the appearances of the same imagination of the unreal as graspable and grasper (*grāhya-grāhaka-pratibhāsam*). It is such appearances of the graspables and graspers that are called the imagined nature. "For", says Sthiramati, "the graspable as well as the grasper are devoid of own-nature, and therefore unreal too. However, they are imagined to be existing, and therefore called the imagined. Again, although substantially non-existent, still they do exist from the practical point of view, and therefore are said to have own-nature."[1] What exactly, then is the imagined nature ? It is the objects (*artha*),[2] or rather those which are thought to be objects of consciousness. Here the reference is clearly to the fourfold appearance of the consciousness referred to in stanza I. 4. Hence Sthiramati says, "Here *artha* stands for colour etc., eye etc., self and the representations of consciousness. They do not exist within the imagination of the unreal, and thus being non-existent they are called the imagined nature."[3]

Thirdly, there is that state of the same imagination of the unreal, which is lacking in the duality between subjects and objects. It is this subject-object distinctionless state that is called the absolutely accomplished nature, "because", says Sthiramati, "this state of existence is unconditioned and unchangeably accomplished".[4]

The negative definition further explained

The negative definition (*asal-lakṣaṇa*) of the imagination of the unreal, namely that it is lacking in subject-object duality,

Abhūta-parikalpah para-tantra-svabhāvaḥ iti, parair-hetu-pratyayais-tantryate, janyate, na tu svayam bhavati iti paratantraḥ. Ibid

1. *Grāhyam grāhakam ca svabhāva-śūnyatvād-abhūtam-api astitvena iti parikalpyata ucyate. Sa punar-dravyato'san-api vyavahārato'sti iti svabhāva ucyate.* Ibid

2. *Arthaḥ parikalpitaḥ svabhāvaḥ.* MVKB I.6

3. . .*artho'tra rūpādayas-cakṣurādaya-ātma vijñaptayaś-ca kalpitena svabhāvena-abhūta-parikalpe nāsti-iti-asan parikalpitaḥ svabhāva ucyate.* MVKBT I.6

4. *Yā-abhūta-parikalpasya dvaya-rahitatā sa pariniṣpanna-svabhāvaḥ, tasya-asaṃskṛtatvāt, nirvikāratvena pariniṣpannatvāt.* Ibid.

has already been stated. Now the question is how one can realize it. The next stanza answers this question. Introducing it Vasubandhu says, "Now is shown a definition which can be used as an instrument in comprehending the negative definition of the same imagination of the unreal."[1] Sthiramati further comments, "The imagination of the unreal, unaware of the negative definition, works in favour of the defilement of *kleśa*, *karma* and *janma*. Hence the present stanza to show an instrument of knowing the negative definition."[2] The stanza says:

[MVK I.7] Depending upon perception
There arises non-perception,
And depending upon non-perception
There arises non-perception.[3]

Vasubandhu interprets these lines as follows:

> Depending upon the perception that there are only representations of consciousness, there arises the non-perception of knowable things. Depending upon the non-perception of knowable things, there arises the non-perception of the mere representations of consciousness, too. Thus one understands the nagative definition of graspable and grasper.[4]

This is rather the intellectual process whereby one attains to the realization of the emptiness of subjectivity and objectivity. First, one realizes that what have been taken to be objects are only representations of consciousness. This realization of mere-representations shatters one's belief in objectivity. Then the realization that there is no objectivity makes one give up one's belief in subjectivity as well, for this latter term makes sense only with reference to objectivity. Absence of subjectivity means

1. *Idānīm tasmin-eva-abhūta-parikalpe'sal-lakṣaṇa-anupraveśa-upāya-lakṣaṇam paridīpayati.* MVKB I.7
2. *Aparijñāta-asal-lakṣaṇo hi-abhūta-parikalpaḥ kleśa-karma-janma saṅkleśāya sampravartate.* MVKBT I.7
3. *Upalabdhim-samāśritya nopalabdhiḥ prajāyate*
Nopalabdhim samāśritya nopalabdhiḥ prajāyate. MVK I.7
4. *Vijñapti-mātra-upalabdhim niśritya-artha-anupalabdhirjāyate. Artha-anupalabdhim niśritya vijñapti-mātrasya api-anupalabdhirjāyate. Evam-asallakṣaṇam grāhya-grāhakayoḥ praviśati.* MVKB I.7

that there are not even mere-representations of consciousness, because consciousness is meaningful only as a knowing subject. Thus one finally realizes the emptiness of graspability and grasperhood.

Sthiramati, too, makes the same point in a different way:

> It [i.e. the object] is mere-representation of consciousness. That is, the consciousness, which has no supporting object, due to the maturing of its own seeds, appears in the form of colour etc. There is no object like colour etc. actually existing. Depending on such perception of the grasper, one comprehends the non-perception of the graspable...Just as the mind, knowing that the imagined-graspable does not exist outside the consciousness, comprehends the absence of the graspable, so on the basis of the absence of the graspable, the absence of mere-consciousness, too, is obtained. In the absence of graspables, grasperhood does not make sense. For, the conception of grasper is relative to that of the graspable ... For the graspable and the grasper are never independent of each other.[1]

"Thus", concludes Sthiramati, "one comprehends the negative definition, not of the imagination of the unreal, but of the imagined forms, namely the forms of the graspable and the grasper".[2]

The next stanza is almost a repetition of the previous one in another fashion. The first half of the stanza reads:

> [MVK I. 8] Therefore it remains established
> That perception has the same nature
> As non-perception.[3]

1. *Idam-vijñapti-mātram-ālambana-artha-rahitam sva-bījaparipākād rūpādi-ābhāsam vijñānam pravartate na tu rūpādiko'rtho' sti-iti-evam grāhaka-upalabdhim niśritya grāhya-anupalabdhim praviśati..Yathā na vijñānād bahiḥ parikalpitam grāhyam-asti-iti vijñapti-mātratā-balena mano grāhya-abhāvam praviśati,* tathā *grāhya-abhāva-balena vijñapti-mātrasya-api abhāvam-pratipadyate. Na grāhya-abhāve grāhakatvam yujyate. Grāhyam apekṣya tad-grāhakasya vyapasthāpanāt. ..Grāhya-grāhakayoḥ paraspara-nirapekṣatvāt.* MVKBT I

2. *Evam-asal-lakṣaṇam grāhya-grāhakayoḥ parikalpita-rūpayoḥ praviśati, na-abhūtaparikalpasya-iti darśanam bhavati.* Ibid

3. *Upalabdhes-tataḥ siddhā nopalabdhi-svabhāvatā.* MVK I.8

Wherefore? "Because", says Vasubandhu, "there being no perceivable things, there is no possibility of having perception either".[1] It must be particularly noted that Vasubandhu is speaking about the absence of "perceivable objects" (*upalabhya-artha-abhāva*), not of things-in-themselves. There could well be things-in-themselves, independently of the perceiving subject, but they are not perceivable. And what are thought to be perceived are not things as they are, but only one's own mental constructions. Hence the second half of the stanza:

> [MVK I. 8 cont'd.] Therefore the sameness
> Of non-perception and perception
> Should be recognized.[2]

Wherefore? "Because", says Vasubandhu, "perception as such is not obtained".[3] He means that a perception is properly so called (*upalabdhir-upalabdhitvena*) only when it reaches real objects existing independently of the perceiving subject. As there is no perception that reaches real objects, i.e. things-in-themselves, no perception can be properly so called. Hence what is usually called perception is in fact non-perception. Why then is it called perception at all? Vasubandhu continues his commentary, "Though not having the own-nature of perception, still it is called perception because there are the appearances of unreal objects."[4] That is, the so-called perceptions perceive the unreal objects (*abhūta-artha-pratibhāsa*), and thus the name 'perception' is somehow justified, too. What is ultimately conveyed by this stanza is that, as Sthiramati notes, "to say that one does not perceive objects is the same as to say that one perceives only representation of consciousness."[5]

The next stanza is a further look at the contents of the imagination of the unreal. Vasubandhu calls it the classification

1. *Upalabhya-artha-abhāve upalabdhyayogāt.* MVK I.8
2. *Tasmāc-ca samatā jñeyā nopalambha-upalambhayoḥ.* MVK I.8
3. *Upalabdhir-upalabdhitvena-asiddhā*
4. *Abhūta-artha-pratibhāsatayā tu-upalabdhir-iti-ucyate' nupalabdhi-svabhāvā-api satī.* MVKB I.8
5. *Artha-anupalambhasya vijñapti-mātratā-upalambhasya ca-satvād-aviśeṣataḥ.* MVKBT I.8

definition (*prabheda-lakṣaṇam*). Introducing the first half of the stanza he says, "Now follows the classification-definition of the same imagination of the unreal".[1] The first half of the stanza reads:

> [MVK I.9] The imagination of the unreal
> Is *citta* as well as *caittas*,
> Belonging to all three worlds.[2]

Commenting on it Vasubandhu says that the three worlds refer to "the distinction between the worlds of passion, forms, and formless beings".[3] That the imagination of the unreal (*abhūta-parikalpa*) includes whatever is called 'mind' and 'mental' in western thought has already been repeatedly said. The above lines are a clear statement of the same point: the imagination of the unreal is nothing but the mind (*citta*) and the mental factors (*caittas*), no matter to which of the three modes of existence they belong.

Introducing the second half of the stanza Vasubandu says, "Now follows the synonym-definition".[4] It says how *citta* and *caittas* operate, and therefore serves as a synonymous description of the imagination of the unreal. Hence the name 'synonym-definition' (*paryāya-lakṣaṇam*). It reads as follows:

> [MVK I.9 cont'd.] There, perception of objects is consciousness, And perception of their qualities is mental factors.[5]

Vasubandhu then comments :

> Consciousness is perception of just the objects. The mental factors, namely, feeling etc., are the perception of the qualities of the same objects.[6]

1. *Tasya-eva-idānīm-abhūta-parikalpasya prabheda-lakṣaṇam khyāpayati.* MVKB I.9
2. *Abhūta-parikalpaś-ca citta-caittas-tridhātukāḥ.* MVK I.9
3. *Kāma-rūpa-ārūpya-avacara-bhedena.*
4. *Paryāya-lakṣaṇam khyāpayati.* MVKB I.9
5. *Tatra-artha-dṛṣṭir-vijñānam tad-viśeṣe tu caitasāḥ.* MVK I.9
6. *Tatra-artha-mātre dṛṣṭir-vijñānam. Arthaviśeṣe dṛṣṭis-caitasāḥ vedanā-dayaḥ.* MVKB I.9

Here one or two terminological clarifications are required. First of all, what are referred to as consciousness (*vijñāna*) and mental factors (*caitasāḥ*) are respectively the mind (*citta*) and mental factors (*caittāḥ*) mentioned in the first half of the same stanza. Secondly, what are referred to as objects (*artha*) and their qualities (*viśeṣa*) are respectively what are otherwise called *bhūta* and *bhautikas*. *Bhūtas* are just the objects (*artha-mātra*) in the sense that they do not refer to the qualities (*viśeṣas*, characteristics) such as being pleasant, unpleasant etc., while *bhautikas* are such qualities. Perception of *bhūta/artha-mātra* is what is called *vijñāna/citta*, while perception of their *bhautikas/artha-viśeṣa* is called *cetasa/caitta*.[1] In both cases it is just the imagination of the unreal (*abhūta-parikalpa-mātra*), for the object (*artha*) perceived (*dṛṣṭa*), no matter whether it is *bhūta/artha-mātra* or *bhautika/artha-viśeṣa*, is only imaginary or rather mentally constructed (*parikalpita-svabhāva*). So Sthiramati says, '*Citta* and *caittas* operate with reference to the own-nature and qualities of the things which though unreal are imaginable. *Citta* and *caittas*, which are respectively the perception of the own-nature and qualities of objects, are themselves the imagination of the unreal, and therefore are synonyms of the latter.'[2]

The store-consciousness and the active consciousness

The next stanza introduces the distinction between the store-consciousness (*ālaya-vijñāna*) and the active consciousness (*pravṛtti-vijñāna*). They are both viewed as functions of the imagination of the unreal, and in that sense Vasubandhu has named this stanza the activity-definition (*pravṛtti-lakṣaṇam*) of *abhūta-parikalpa*. Introducing the stanza he says, "[The next verse] states the activity-definition."[3] The stanza reads:

1. ...*mātra-śabdo viśeṣa-nirāsārthaḥ. Tena-agṛhīta-viśeṣa vastu-svarūpamātra-upalabdhir-iti-arthaḥ...tatra-āhlādaka-paritāpakatvaviśeṣo yas-tasya bhāvasya yat-saumanasyādisthānam tad-grahaṇam vedanā. Strī-puruṣa-vyavahāra-lakṣaṇo yo'rtha-viśeṣas-tad-grahaṇam sañjñā. Evam-anye 'pi yathā-yogam yojyaḥ.* MVKBT I.9

2. *Abhūta-parikalpya-vastunaḥ svabhāva-viśeṣa-parikalpanayā citta-caittānām pravṛttatvāt. Artha-svarūpa-viśeṣa-dṛṣtiś-citta-caitta-abhūta-parikalpaś-ca-iti par - yāya - antarbhūtaḥ.* MVKBT I.9

3. *Pravṛtti-lakṣaṇam ca khyāpayati.* MVKB I.10

[MVK I. 10] One is the source-consciousness,
And the other is the enjoyment-consciousness,
There, the mental factors are
Enjoyment, determination and motivation.[1]

Vasubandhu commenting on this stanza says:

> The store-consciousness being the source of other consciousnesses is called the source-consciousness. The active consciousness, which has the latter as its source, is called the enjoyment-consciousness. Enjoyment refers to feelings etc., determination to concept, and motivation to the conditioning forces such as volition, attention etc., of consciousness.[2]

Sthiramati places this stanza and the following one in the context of life-process. *Pravṛtti* for him means process/movement. When it is applied to life, he recognizes two levels of movement: (i) movement from one moment to the next forming a series of moments which is responsible for defilements and enjoyments in the present life; (ii) movement from one life to the next, which is responsible for the defilements of *kleśa, karma* and *janma*. The present stanza, says Sthiramati, "deals with the former type of movement, leaving the latter for the next stanza.

The concept of movement involves that of cause-effect relationship. In Buddhism, causality means, to put it rather naively, one moment giving way to the next, or, in technical terms, the rising of one moment depending on the previous one (*pratītya-samutpāda*). In any case such a view of causality presupposes the distinction between the causal moment and the resultant moment. There being only the imagination of the unreal (*abhūta-parikalpa-mātra*) how could one account for the distinction between cause and result (*hetu-phala-prabhedam*)? This, according to Sthiramati, is the concern of the present stanza.[3]

1. *Ekam pratyata-vijñānam dvitīyam aupabhogikam*
Upabhoga-pariccheda-prerakas-tatra caitasāḥ. MVK I.10

2. *Ālaya-vijñānam-anyeṣām vijñānānām pratyayatvāt pratyaya-vijnānam. Tat-pratyayam pravṛtti-vijñānam-aupabhogikam. Upabhogo vedanā. Paricchedaḥ sañjñā. Prerakāḥ saṃskārā vijñānasya cetanā-manaskārādayaḥ.* MVKB I.10

3. *Abhūta-parikalpa-mātre'nyasya ca-abhāve hetu-phala-prabhedam na vijñāyata iti tad-pratipādanārtham pravṛtti-lakṣaṇam-ca khyāpayati.* MVKBT I.10

According to him this stanza must be interpreted so as to mean that it is the imagination of the unreal itself that appears as both cause and result (*hetuphal-bhāvena*).[1] That is, the imagination of the unreal on the one hand appears as the store-consciousness, which functions as the causal source (*hetu-pratyaya*) of the active consciousnesses;[2] the same imagination of the unreal appears on the other hand as the resultant active-consciousness.[3] The sevenfold active consciousness is called enjoyment consciousness (*aupabhogikam vijñānam*) because it leads to enjoyment (*upabhoga-prayojakatvāt*).[4] The mental factors (*caitasa/caitta*), too, are part of the resultant consciousness.[5]

Thus what the whole stanza is trying to establish is that every sort of consciousness, whether *ālaya-vijñāna* or *pravṛtti-vijñāna* or *caitta*, is an expression of the same imagination of the unreal. The imagination of the unreal, transforming itself into various types of consciousness, each involving the subject-object distinction, keeps one's empirical life going from moment to moment. A stream of consciousness is what constitutes the stream of saṃsāric existence, and this is made possible by the continuous imagination of the unreal forms of subjectivity and objectivity.

The life-circle

Now it remains to explain in terms of the same imagination of the unreal how one moves from one life to the next (*janma-antara-pravṛtti*). This is done in the next two stanzas, which according to Vasubandhu, "state the defilment-definition"[6] of the imagination of the unreal. It shows how by the operation of the imagination of the unreal the defilements (*saṅkleśa*), namely *kleśa*, *karma* and *janma*, bring about the sufferings of the world.[7]

1. *Anena hetu-phala-bhāvena-abhūta-parikalpa iti lakṣaṇam.* MVKBT I.10
2. *Tatra-ekam-iti-ālaya-vijñānam śeṣāṇām vijñānānām hetu-pratyayabhāvena hetur-iti pratyaya-vijñānam.* Ibid.
3. *Dvitīyam-aupabhogikam..phalam iti vakya-śeṣaḥ.* Ibid
4. *Sapta-vidham pravṛtti-vijñānam-upabhoga-prayojakatvāt aupabhogikam.* Ibid
5. *Tatra vijñāne ye caitasās-te'pi tat-phalam-iti sambandhaḥ.* Ibid
6. *Saṃkleśa-lakṣaṇam-ca khyāpayati.* MVKB I.11
7. *Kleśa-karma-janma-saṅkleśā yathā pravartamānā jagataḥ parikleśāya bhavanti tat-saṅkleśa-lakṣaṇam.* MVKBT I.11

Thus it shows "how, although there is no substantial self, solely from the imagination of the unreal there arises the *saṃsāra*".[1] The stanzas under reference may be translated as follows:

[MVK I.11-12] The world is oppressed/defiled[2]
(1) By being concealed,
(2) By being raised,
(3) Be being led,
(4) By being seized,
(5) By being completed,
(6) By being trebly determined,
(7) By enjoying,
(8) By being attracted,
(9) By being bound,
(10) By being orientated, and
(11-12) By being subjected to suffering.[3]

This clearly is the Yogācārin's version of the twelve links (*nidāna*) of the chain of dependent origination (*pratītya-samutpāda*), which explain the ever-reverting process of *saṃsāra*. The Sanskrit word translated here as "world" is *jagat*. This term literally means "moving" or "going". So it is just another word for *saṃsāra*, meaning "going round". Sthiramati says, "*Jagat* is that which keeps going".[4] Just like the term *saṃsāra*, the term *jagat*, too, although it ordinarily refers to the world as a whole, for all practical purposes refers to the individual beings who constitute that world. Therefore the above-described process of oppression/defilment (*saṅkleśa*) by the twelve-linked

1. *Yathā-ca asati-api-ātmani abhūta-parikalpa-mātrāt saṃsāraḥ prajāyate iti pradarśanārtham khyāpayati.* Ibid.

2. Sthiramati points out that the verb *kliśyate* in this context may be taken either to mean *pīḍyate* (is oppressed) or to mean *na vyavadāyate* (is made impure): "*kliśyata iti..pīḍyata iti arthaḥ. Kliśyata iti na vyavadāyata iti-apare*" MVKBT I.11. Sthiramati personally seems to prefer the first meaning, namely, *pīḍyate.*

3. *Chādanād-ropaṇāc-ca nayanāt samparigrahāt*
Pūraṇāt tri-paricchedād-upabhogāc-ca karṣanāt. MVK I.11
Nibandhanād-ābhimukhyād duḥkhanāt kliśyate jagat. MVK I.12

4. *Gacchati-iti jagat.* MVKBT.. I.12

process of dependent-origination should be understood as applying to each individual undergoing the experience of *saṃsāra*. Vasubandhu interprets those twelve links as follows:

There,

(1) 'by being concealed' means 'by being impeded by ignorance from seeing things as they are',

(2) 'by being raised' means 'by the installation of the impressions of deeds on consciousness by the conditioning forces',

(3) 'by being led' means' 'by being taken by consciousness to the place of re-birth',

(4) 'by being seized' means '[by being seized] by the *nāma* and *rūpa* of egohood,

(5) 'by being completed' means '[by being completed] by the six organs',

(6) 'by being trebly determined' means '[by being trebly determined] by contact',[1]

(7) 'by enjoying' means 'by feeling',

(8) 'by being attracted' means '[by being attracted] by the desire for a new existence the seeds of which have already been sown by previous deeds',

(9) 'by being bound' means '[by being bound] by the inclinations towards sense-pleasure etc., which are conducive to a new birth of the consciousness',

(10) 'by being orientated' means 'by making the deeds of former existence tend to manifest their matured fruits in a new existence',

(11-12) 'by being subjected to suffering' means '[by being subjected] to birth, old age and death'.

By all these is the world oppressed/defiled.[2]

1. Here 'contact' (*sparśa*) means 'sensation' which is trebly determined (*pariccheda*) by *indriya*, *viṣaya* and *vijñāna*: (See MVKBT I.1)

2. *Tatra-*

Chādanād—avidyayā yathā-bhūta-darśana-avabandhanāt.

Ropaṇāt—saṃskārair-vijñāne karma-vāsanāyāḥ pratiṣṭhāpanāt.

Nayanāt—vijñānena-upapatti-sthāna-saṃprāpaṇāt.

Samparigrahaṇāt—nāma-rūpeṇa-ātmabhāvasya.

pūraṇāt—ṣaḍ-āyatanena.

[The same stanza continues :]

[MVK I.12 cont'd.] The oppressives/defilements,
All proceeding from the imagination of the unreal,
Could be classified
Either into three groups,
Or into two groups,
Or into seven groups.[1]

Vasubandhu's commentary on these lines reads as follows:

The classification of the oppressives/defilements into three groups is as follows:

1. Oppressive opressors, namely ignorance, desire and inclinations;
2. Deed-oppressives, namely conditioning forces and existence/birth;
3. Birth-oppressives, namely the remaining members.

The classification of the oppressives/defilements into two groups is as follows:

1. Causal oppressives/defilements which include the groups of oppressive oppressors, and deed-oppressives;
2. Resultant oppressives which are the same as the birth-oppressives.

The classification of the oppressives/defilements into seven groups refer to the seven kinds of causes such as:

1. cause of error, namely ignorance,
2. cause of sowing of seeds, namely conditioning forces,
3. cause of direction, namely consciousness,
4. cause of seizure, namely *nāma-rūpa* and the six bases,
5. cause of enjoyment, namely contact and feeling,

Tri-paricchedāt—sparśena.
Upabhogāt—vedanayā.
Karṣaṇat—Tṛṣṇayā karma-ākṣiptasya punar-bhavasya.
Nibandhanāt—upādānair-vijñānasya-utpatti-anukūleṣu kāmādiṣu.
Ābhimukhyāt—bhāvena kṛtasya karmaṇaḥ punar-bhave vipākadānāya-abhimukhī-karaṇāt.
Duḥkhanāt—jātyā jarā-maraṇena ca parikliśyate jagat.

1. *Tredhā dvedhā ca saṅkleśaḥ saptadhā-abhūtakalpanāt* VK I.12

6. cause of attraction, namely desire, inclination and existence,
7. cause of unrest, namely birth, old age and death.

All these oppressives/defilements operate due to the imagination of the unreal.[1]

What is to be particularly noticed here is the fact that the entire *saṅkleśa*, which is just another name for *saṃsāra*,[2] is traced to the imagination of the unreal.[3] This is so, because, as already explained, the experience of *saṃsāra/saṅkleśa* is ultimately the passion for graspable-grasper distinction,[4] which depends entirely on the imagination of the unreal.[5] Sthiramati derives the same conclusion in a different way:

> All these oppressives/defilements operate due to the imagination of the unreal, because the oppressives/defilements depend on *citta* and *caittas*, about which it has been said:
>
> The imagination of the unreal
> Is *citta* as well as *caittas*
> Belonging to all three worlds. (MVK I.9)[6]

1. *Tredhā saṅkleśaḥ—kleśa-saṅkleśaḥ, karma-saṅkleśaḥ janma-saṅkleśaś-ca. Tatra kleśa-saṅkleśo'vidyā-tṛṣṇopādānāni. Karma-saṅkleṣaḥ saṃskārā-bhavaś ca. Janma-saṅkleśān śeṣāṇi-aṅgāni.*

   Dvedhā saṅkleśaḥ—Hetu-saṅkleśaḥ phala-saṅkleśaś-ca. Tatra hetu-saṅkleśaḥ kleśa-karma-svabhāvair-aṅgaiḥ. Phala-saṅkleśas-ca śeṣaih.

   Saptadhā saṅkleśaḥ saptavidho hetuḥ : viparyāsa-hetuḥ, ākṣepa-hetuḥ, upanaya-hetuḥ, parigraha-hetuḥ, upabhoga-hetuḥ, ākarṣaṇa-hetuḥ, udvega-hetuś-ca. Tatra viparyāsa-hetur-avidyā. Akṣepa-hetuḥ saṃskārāḥ. Upanaya-hetur-vijñānam. Parigraha-hetur-nāma-rūpa-ṣaḍ-āyatane. Upabhoga-hetuḥ sparśa-vedane. Ākarṣaṇa-hetus-tṛṣṇopādānābhāvaḥ. Udvega-hetur-jāti-jarā-maraṇe.

   Sarvaś-ca-eṣa saṅkleśo'bhūta-parikalpāt pravartata iti. MVKB I.12
2. See the equation above on page 38
3. *Sarvasca eṣasaṅkleśo'bhūta-parikalpāt pravartate.* MVKB I.12

   Also, *Tredhā dvedhā ca saṅkleśaḥ saptadhā-abhūta-parikalpanāt.* MVK I.12
4. For example, see above pp. 38 ff
5. *Abhūta-parikalpo grāhya-grāhaka-vikalpaḥ.* MVKB I.2
6. *Sarve-ca-ete saṅkleśā abhūta-parikalpāt pravartante iti citta-caitta-āśrayatvāt saṅkleśasya. Uktam hi tat, abhūta-parikalpaś-ca citta-caittas-tridhātukaḥ (Ka. 1.9) iti.* MVKBT I.12

The summary-meaning of the imagination of the unreal

Vasubandhu now winds up the discussion on the imagination of the unreal by recalling the various definitions of it:

> The ninefold definition, giving the summary-meaning of the imagination of the unreal, has [now] been explained. Those definitions are, namely, positive definition, negative definition, own-definition, inclusive definition, instrumental definition, classification-definition, synonym-definition, activity-definition and the defilment-definition.[1]

3. *The Emptiness*

From the next stanza onwards one has the discussion on the emptiness (*śūnyatā*), which has already been described as "that state of the imagination of the unreal which is lacking in the form of being the graspable and grasper."[2] Introducing the next stanza Vasubandu says, "Thus having explained the imagination of the unreal, the author now shows how the emptiness should be understood."[3]

[MVK I.13] About the emptiness
One should summarily know
Its definition,
Its synonyms along with their meaning,
Its classification,
And the reason[4] for its classification.[5]

1. *Piṇḍārthaḥ punar-abhūta-parikalpasya navavidham lakṣaṇam paridīpitam bhavati. Sal-lakṣaṇam, asal-lakṣaṇam, sva-lakṣaṇam, saṅgraha-lakṣaṇam, asallakṣaṇa-anupraveśa-upāya-lakṣaṇam, prabheda-lakṣaṇam, paryāya-lakṣaṇam, pravṛttilakṣaṇam, saṅkleśa-lakṣaṇañ -ca.* MVKB I.12

2. MVKB I.2 See above page 30 and note 1 for the text.

3. *Evam abhūtaparikalpam khyāpayitvā yathā śūnyatā vijñeyā tan-nirdiśati.* MVKB I.13

4. The term translated here as 'reason' is *sādhanam*, which ordinarily means 'a proof'. However, as Sthiramati has pointed out, in the present context it means 'reason' (*yukti*): *sādhanam śūnyatāprabheda-pradarśane yuktiḥ.* MVKBT I.13

5. *Lakṣaṇam-ca-athaparyāyas-tadartho bheda eva ca*
Sādhanam-ca-iti vijñeyam śūnyatāyāḥ samāsataḥ. MVK I.13

This is just an enumeration of the various topics that are going to be dealt with in the subsequent stanzas. First of all the author attempts a definition of the emptiness. "How the definition of the emptiness is to be understood ?"[1]

[MVK I.14] The negation of the pair
Is indeed the assertion of such negation;
This is the definition of the emptiness.[2]

That is, when one denies the existence of the pair of subject and object, it amounts to the assertion that there is no such pair. In other words, to say that there is the absence of the pair (*dvaya-abhāvaḥ*) is the same as to say that there is the presence of such absence (*abhāvasya bhāvaḥ*). Thus, by emptiness is meant the positive state of existence in which there is no place for the duality between subjects and objects. Vasubandhu comments,

> There is the negation of the pair of the graspable and grasper. The definition of emptiness then, is the assertion of that negation. Thus, it is shown how the emptiness is to be defined in negative terms. And, what those negative terms are,[3]

is further stated:

[MVK I.14 cont'd.] It is neither [total] assertion,
Nor [total] negation.[4]

"Why not [total] assertion ? Because there is the negation of the pair of subject and object. Why not [total] negation ? Because there is the assertion of the negation of that pair. This indeed is the definition of the emptiness. Therefore, with reference to the imagination of the unreal"[5] the emptiness is:

1. *Katham lakṣaṇam vijñeyam* ? MVKB I.14
2. *Dvaya-abhāvo hi-abhāvasya bhāvaḥ śūnyasya lakṣaṇam.* MVK I.14
3. *Dvaya-grāhya-grāhakasya-abhāvaḥ. Tasya ca-abhāvasya bhāvah śūnyatāyāḥ lakṣaṇam-iti-abhāva-svabhāva-lakṣaṇatvam śūnyatāyāḥ paridīpitam bhavati. Yaś-ca-asau tad-abhāva-svabhāvaḥ sa*—MVKB I.14
4. *Na bhāvo na-api ca-abhāvaḥ.* MVK I.14
5. *Katham na bhāvaḥ ? Yasmād dvayasya-abhāvaḥ. Katham na-abhāvaḥ ? Yasmād dvaya-abhāvasya bhāvaḥ. Etac-ca śūnyatāyāḥ lakṣaṇam. Tasmād-abhūta-parikalpāt*—MVKB I.14

[MVK I.14 cont'd.] Neither different [from the imagination of the unreal],
Nor identical [with the imagination of the unreal].[1]

Vasubandhu explains it as follows:

> If different, it would imply that the 'universal' [*dharmatā*] is other than the particular thing [*dharmas*], which is unacceptable. For example, 'impermanence' is not other than the impermanent things, and the state of suffering is not other than suffering itself. If identical, there would be no place for purifying knowledge, nor would there be the commonplace knowledge. Thus is shown a definition which states that emptiness is that which is free from being different from thatness.[2]

Thus, *śūnyatā* stands to *abhūta-parikalpa* just as *dharmatā* stands to *dharma*, or *anityatā* to *anityadharma*, or *duḥkhatā to duḥkha*. The terms of these pairs are not quite different from each other, nor quite identical with each other. Similarly *śūnyatā* and *abhūta-parikalpa* are neither quite different (*na-pṛthak*) from each other, nor quite identical (*na-eka*) with each other. They are instead just two different modes of existence of the same individual: *śūnyatā* refers to one's mode of existence in the state of *nirvāṇa*, while *abhūta-parikalpa* refers to one's mode of existence in the state of *saṃsāra*. Thus both *śūnyatā* and *abhūta-parikalpa* refer to the same individual. They are not, however, identical with each other. If, for example, *śūnyatā* were identical with *abhūta-parikalpa*, it would mean either that one is always in the state of *saṃsāra*, characterized by *abhūta-parikalpa* and that, therefore, the idea of purifying knowledge (*viśuddhi-ālambanam jñānam*), which is believed to lead one to the state of *nirvāṇa*, would make no sense; or that one is always in the state of *nirvāṇa*, and that, therefore, commonplace/empirical/conventional knowledge

1. *Na-pṛthaktva-eka-lakṣaṇam*. MVK I.14

2. *Pṛthaktve sati dharmād-anya dharmatā-iti na yujyate, anityatā-duḥkhatā-vat. Ekatve sati viśuddhi-ālambanam jñānam na syāt sāmānya-lakṣaṇam-ca. Etena tattva-anyatva-vinirmuktam lakṣaṇam paridīpitam bhavati.* MVKB I.14

(*sāmānya-lakṣaṇam jñānam*), which is characteristic of *saṃsāra* experience cannot occur at all.[1] *Śūnyatā*, then is the bare reality (*tattvam*), characterized neither as subject nor as object. It should be defined as nothing other than thatness.[2]

The next question is, "how is the synonym [of emptiness] to be understood?"[3] Hence the next stanza:

[MVK I.15] Suchness, the extreme limit of existence,
The uncaused, absoluteness,
The source-reality:
These are summarily the synonyms of emptiness.[4]

The next stanza explains, "how is the meaning of these synonyms to be understood ?"[5]

[MVK I.16] The synoyms respectively mean [that the emptiness is]
Never otherwise,
Never falsified,
Never admitting a cause,
The object intuited by the sages,
And [that it is]
The source of the powers of the sages.[6]

Vasubandu interprets the above two stanzas as follows:

The emptiness is called suchness in the sense that it is never otherwise insofar as it remains ever the same way. It is called the extreme limit of existence in the sense that it is never falsified, because it is never an object of doubt. It is called the uncaused, because it does not admit for itself any cause, for it is far from having any cause whatsoever. It is called the

1. Cf. MVKBT I.14
2. *Śūnyatā..tattva-anyatva-vinirmukta-lakṣaṇā.* MVKBT I.14
3. *Katham paryāyo vijñeyaḥ ?* MVKB I.15
4. *Tathatā bhūtakotiś-ca-animittam paramārthatā*
Dharma-dhātuś-ca paryāya śūnyatāyāḥ samāsataḥ. MVK I.15
5. *Katham paryāya-artho vijñeyaḥ ?* MVKB I.16
6. *Ananyathā-aviparyāsa-tan-niroddha-ārya-gocaraiḥ*
Hetutvāc-ca-ārya-dharmāṇām paryāyārtho yathākramam. MVK I.16

absoluteness/the ultimate object, because it is the object of the knowledge of the sages, meaning that it is the object of the ultimate knowledge. It is called the source-reality, because it is the source of the powers of the sages, meaning that the powers of the sages have their origin depending upon it: here the term *dhātu* is used in the sense of *hetu*, indeed.[1]

As I have already pointed out here there is no attempt to describe emptiness in terms of consciousness, which would justify the interpretation of the Yogācāra system as idealism.[2]

Next, "how is the classification of the emptiness to be understood".[3]

[MVK I.17] It is defiled and purified;[4]

"So is its classification. In what condition is it defiled, and in what condition is it purified?"[5]

[MVK I.17 cont'd.] It is with and without impurities.[6]

That is, "when it is with impurities, then it is defiled, and when it is rid of the impurities then it is purified."[7] Here the emptiness is considered as defiled (*saṅkliṣṭā/samalā*) and pure (*viśuddhā/prahīṇamalā*). However, this classification of the emptiness raises a problem, which Vasubandhu formulates as follows: "Getting rid of the impurities once associated with it [i.e. emptiness]

1. *Ananyathārthena tathatā, nityam tathā-iti kṛtvā. Aviparyāsā-rthena bhūta-koṭiḥ, viparyāsa-avastutvāt. Nimitta-noirodhārthena animittatvam, sarva-nimitta-abhāvāt. Ārya-jñāna-gocaratvāt paramārthaḥ, parama-jñāna-viṣayatvāt. Ārya-dharma-hetutvād dharma-dhātūḥ, arya-dharmāṇām tadālambana-prabhavatvāt. Hetu-artho hi-atra dhātu-arthaḥ.* MVKB I.16

2. See above page 6.

3. *Katham śūnyatāyāḥ prabhedo jñeyaḥ ?* MVKB I.17

4. *Saṅkliṣṭā ca viśuddhā ca.* MVK I.17

5. *Iti-asyāḥ prabhedaḥ. Kasyām-avasthāyām saṅkliṣṭā, kasyām-viśuddhā ?* MVKB I.17

6. *Samalā nirmalā ca sā.* MVK I.17

7. *Yadā saha malena vartate tadā saṅkliṣṭā. Yadā prahīṇamalā tadā viśuddhā.* MVKB I.17

implies that it [i.e. emptiness] is changing in character. How is it then that it is still not impermanent? Because its"[1]—

[MVK I.17 cont'd.] Purity is understood
As the purity of elemental water,
Gold and space.[2]

That is, elemental water (*abdhātu*), gold, and space are pure by nature. However, they can be made impure by the addition of foreign matter. Such foreign matter cannot, however, change their inner nature, but can only externally cover it, so to speak. Moreover, to recover their original, pure, nature, one needs only to remove that foreign matter, which will not imply any change in the character of water or gold or space. Similarly, the stanza argues, the factors which are thought to constitute the impurities of the emptiness are only externals or accidentals (*āgantuka*) which do not affect it substantially. Nor does the removal of these accidental impurities (*āgantuka-malāḥ*) imply any change in the character (*dharma*) of the emptiness. Vasubandhu, interpreting the above lines says, "[The purity of the emptiness is recovered] by shaking off the accidental impurities, which does not mean a change in its own-nature".[3]

The next stanza is trying to classify the emptiness from another point of view. Introducing it Vasubandhu says,

> Here is another classification according to which there are sixteen kinds of emptiness:
>
> (1) emptiness of internal [elements],
> (2) emptiness of external [elements],
> (3) emptiness of internal as well as external [elements],
> (4) emptiness of the great,
> (5) emptiness of emptiness,
> (6) emptiness of the absolute object,
> (7) emptiness of the conditioned [elements],

1. *Yadi samalā bhūtva nirmalā bhavati, katham vikāra-dharmiṇītvādanityā na bhavati? Yasmād-asyāḥ*—MVKB I.17

2. *Abdhātuka-naka-ākāsā-śuddhivac-chuddhir-iṣyate.* MVK I.17

3. *Āgantuka-mala-apagamāt, na tu tasyāḥ svabhāva-anyatvam-bhavati.* MVKB I.17

(8) emptiness of the unconditioned [elements],
(9) emptiness of the ultimate [element],
(10) emptiness of the eternal [element],
(11) emptiness of the unforsaken [element],
(12) emptiness of nature,
(13) emptiness of defining marks,
(14) emptiness of every power,
(15) emptiness of negation,
(16) emptiness of negation as own-nature.[1]

This enumeration of the sixteen kinds of emptinesses is an attempt to show that all kinds of characterizations are bound to be only approximations, when they are applied to things in themselves. There are different elements (*dharmas*), but their characterizations as internal (*adhyātma*), external (*bāhya*) etc., are empty of meaning. The elements in their suchness are just things (*vastūni*) without any qualification. Their multiplicity is accounted for not by different predications, but merely by numerical distinctions. "That all elements are of non-dual form, is the general definition of emptiness. The multiplicity is shown on account of the numerical multiplicity of things, not otherwise."[2] This observation of Sthiramati is important. Right in the beginning of this chapter it was made clear that emptiness essentially consists in the absence of the duality between subjects and objects. In other words, emptiness means that nothing can be characterized as subject or object. A strict application of this concept of emptiness will demand that all characterizations of things as such and such are to be avoided. For, any characterization of a thing implies attribution of some kind of objectivity to that thing. For example, when one says, "This is good", one is characterizing "this" as "good". In so

1. *Ayam-aparaḥ prabhedaḥ—ṣoḍaśavidhā śūnyatā. Adhyātma-śūnyatā, bahirdhā-śūnyatā, adhyātma-bahirdhā-śūnyatā, mahā-śūnyatā, śūnyatā-śūnyatā, paramārtha-śūnyatā, samskṛta-śūnyatā, atyanta-śūnyatā, anavarāgra-śūnyatā, anavakāra-śūnyatā, prakṛti-śūnyatā, lakṣaṇa-śūnyatā, sarva-dharma-śūnyatā, abhāva-śūnyatā,abhāva-svabhāva-śūnyatā ca.* MVKB I.18

2. *Sāmānya-lakṣaṇam śūnyatāyāḥ sarva-dharmasya-advaya-svarūpatvam. Nānyathā nānātvam śakyate darśayitum-iti-ato vastu-nānātvena tan-nānātvam darśayati.* MVKBT I.18

doing one is first of all envisaging a distinction between the subject "this" and its predicate "good", which is just another form of subject-object distinction. Secondly, one is claiming that one has experienced "this" as "good", which again, presupposes the distinction between the experiencing subject and the experienced object. Thus the characterization of "this" as "good" violates the definition of emptiness as the absence of duality in two ways: first by making a distinction between the subject (i.e. "this"), and the predicate (i.e. "good"), and secondly by making a distinction between the experiencing subject, and the experienced object. This applies to all the sixteen characterizations mentioned by Vasubandhu. All those characterizations may be valid and useful from a commonplace (*saṃvṛti/sāmānya-lakṣaṇa/vyāvahārika*) point of view. But in the abolute state of existence one cannot think of any characterizations which will distinguish the individual things (*vastūni*) from one another, although they are numerically different things (*vastu-nānātvam*).

"All those kinds of emptiness should be briefly understood".[1] Hence the next four stanzas.

[MVK I. 18] There is the emptiness of the enjoyer,
Emptiness of the enjoyed,
Emptiness of the body [of the enjoyer and enjoyed],
Emptiness of the basic thing,
Emptiness of that by which it [i.e. the emptiness of the enjoyer etc.] is perceived,
Emptiness of the way in which it is perceived, and
Emptiness of that for which it is perceived.[2]

Here the first six kinds of emptinesses correspond to the first six of the sixteen emptinesses enumerated above by Vasubandhu, He, therefore, says:

1. *Sā-eṣā samāsato veditavyā.* MVKB I.18
2. *Bhoktṛ-bhojana-tad-deha-pratiṣṭā-vastu-śūnyatā*
Tac-ca yena yathā dṛṣṭam yad-artham tasya śūnyatā. MVK I.18

Here, the emptiness of the enjoyer means the emptiness of the internal senses etc., the emptiness of the enjoyed means the emptiness of the external elements, the emptiness of their bodies, namely the *śariras* which are the basis of both the enjoyer and the enjoyed, means the emptiness of the internal and the external elements. The basic thing means the universe which is the basis [of the enjoyer, the enjoyed and their bodies]. Its emptiness is called the emptiness of the great because of the vastness of the universe. The emptiness of the internal senses etc. is perceived by the knowledge of emptiness, whose emptiness is called the emptiness of emptiness. The emptiness of internal senses is perceived as the absolute object, whose emptiness is called the emptiness of the absolute object.[1]

The last kind of emptiness mentioned in the above stanza (I.18) covers the last ten kinds of emptinesses on Vasubandhu's list. Explaining it Vasubandhu says,

The emptiness of that for which the Bodhisattva attains [the emptiness of the internal senses etc.] is the [final] kind of emptiness. For what, indeed, is the emptiness of the internal senses etc. attained ?[2]

This question is answered as follows :

[MVK I.19] For the attainment of the twofold prosperity.[3]

That is, for the attainment of "the conditioned as well as the unconditioned fortune".[4] The emptiness of the conditioned as well as the unconditioned fortune corresponds respectively

1. *Tatra bhoktṛ-śūnyatā adhyātmikāni-āyatanānyārabddhā, bhojana-śunyatā bāhyāni. Tad-dehas-tayor-bhokrtṛ-bhojanayor-yad-adhiṣṭhānam śarīram tasya śūnyatā-adhyātma-bahirdha śūnyatā-iti-ucyate. Pratiṣtā-vastu bhājana-loka, tasya vistīrṇa-tvāc-chunyatā maha-śūnyatā-iti-ucyate. Tac-ca-adhyātmika-āyatanādi yena śūnyam dṛṣṭam śūnyatā-jñānena, tasya śūnyatā śūnyatā-śūnyatā. Yathā ca dṛṣṭam paramārtha-ākāreṇa tasya śūnyatā paramārtha-śūnyatā.* MVKB I.18

2. *Yadartham-ca bodhisatvaḥ prapadyate tasya ca śūnyatā. Kimartham-ca prapadyate ?* MVKB I. 18-19

3. *Śubha-dvayasya prāptyartham.* MVK I.19

4. *Kuśalasya saṃskṛtasya-asamṣkṛtasya ca.* MVKB I.19

to "the emptiness of the conditioned" and "the emptiness of the unconditioned" on Vasubandhu's list.

[MVK I.19 cont'd.] For the everlasting benefit of the living beings.[1]

That is "for the ultimate benefit of the living beings"[2], the emptiness of which has been referred to by Vasubandhu as "the emptiness of the ultimate element".

[MVK I.19 cont'd.] And for not leaving the *saṃsāra*,[3]

That is, if one does not perceive the emptiness of the internal senses etc., then "not seeing the emptiness of the eternal *saṃsāra*, one, being depressed, would rather leave the world."[4] The emptiness of 'not leaving the *saṃsāra*' has been referred to as "the emptiness of the eternal [element]".

[MVK I.19 cont'd.] For the non-cessation of fortune.[5]

"Even in the absolute state of *nirvāṇa* there is something that one does not give up, the emptiness of which is called the emptiness of the unforsaken."[6]

[MVK I.20] For the purity of the lineage.[7]

"Lineage means nature, for it belongs to one's own-nature."[8] Its emptiness has been referred to as "the emptiness of nature".

1. *Sadā sattva-hitāya ca.* MVK I.19
2. *Atyanta-sattva-hitārtham.* MVKB I.19
3. *Saṃsāra-atyajanārtham.* MVK I.19
4. *Anavarāgrasya hi saṃsārasya śūnyatām-apaśyan khinnaḥ saṃsāram parityajate.* MVKB I.19
5. *Kuśalasya-akṣayāya.* MVK I.19
6. *Nirupadhiśeṣe nirvāṇe'pi yan-na-avikirati notsṛjati tasya śūnyatā anavakāra-śūnyatā-iti-ucyate.* MVKB I.19
7. *Gotrasya ca viśudhyartham.* MVK I.290
8. *Gotram-hi prakṛtiḥ, svābhāvikatvāt.* MVKB I.20

[MVK I.20 cont'd.] For attaining the defining marks.[1]

That is, "for attaining the marks that are characteristic of great men."[2] Its emptiness has been referred to as "the emptiness of defining marks".

[MVK I.20 cont'd.] And for the purity of the powers of an enlightened one.
Does the Bodhisattva attain the emptiness of internal senses etc.[3]

Namely, for the purity of the powers such as "strength, fearlessness, special endowments etc.",[4] the emptiness of which has been referred to as "the emptiness of every power". "Thus, indeed, the fact of the fourteen kinds of emptiness should be known."[5]

The last two kinds of emptiness are still to be explained, which the next stanza does. "What other kinds of emptiness are still there?"[6]

[MVK I.21] The negation of *pudgala* and *dharmas*,
Is indeed one kind of emptiness there,
The existence of that negation in it [i.e. in the enjoyer etc.]
Is another kind of emptiness.[7]

Vasubandhu explains this stanza as follows:

> The negation of *pudgala* and *dharmas* is one emptiness. Another kind of emptiness is the existence of that negation in the above said enjoyer etc. These two kinds of emptiness are explained at the end in order to make the definition of the

1. *Lakṣaṇa-vyañjana-āptaye.* MVK I.20
2. *Mahāpuruṣa-lakaṣaṇānām sa-anuvyañjanānām-prāptaye.* MVKB I.20
3. *Śuddhaye Buddha-dharamāṇām bodhisattvaḥ prapadyate.* MVK I.20
4. *Balavaiśāradya-āveṇikādīnām.* MVKB I.20
5. *Evam tāvac-caturdaśānām śūnyatānām vyavasthānam veditavyam.* MVKB I.20
6. *Kā punar-atra śūnyatā ?* MVKB I.21
7. *Pudgalasya-atha dharmāṇām-abhāvaḥ śūnyatā-atra hi*
   Tadabhāvasya sad-bhāvas-tasmin sā śūnyatā-aparā, MVK I.21

> emptiness clear: in order to avoid the exaggeration of *pudgala* and *dharmas* the emptiness is explained, on the one hand, as the negation of *pudgala* and *dharmas*, and in order to avoid the underestimation of their negation the emptiness is explained, on the other hand, as having the negation of [*pudgala* and *dharmas*] for its own-nature. This is how the classification of emptiness is to be understood.[1]

Here, as it is clear from Sthiramati's commentary, *pudgala* and *dharma* stand respectively for the subjective (*bhoktṛ-sammata*) and objective (*bhogya-sammata*) aspects of experience. These two aspects are merely imaginary (*kalpita-lakṣaṇa*). Therefore they are to be negated, and their negation is one kind of emptiness. However, their negation does not mean nihilism. On the contrary, it points to a positive state of existence which cannot be characterized either as *pudgala/bhoktṛ* or as *dharma/bhogya*. This positive state of existence, which has negation for its own-nature (*abhāva-svabhāva*) is the last and final sort of emptiness.[2]

These two kinds of emptiness have to be put together to construct a complete definition of emptiness. Why ? Sthiramati answers as follows:

> If *śūnyatā* as the negation [of *pudgala* and *dharmas*] is not mentioned [in the definition], it would mean that there is indeed the existence of *pudgala* and *dharmas*, which in fact are only of imagined forms. If, on the other hand, *śūnyatā* as having the negation [of *pudgala* and *dharmas*] for its own-nature is not mentioned, it would mean that there is not even the emptiness. Such negation of the emptiness itself

1. *Pudgala-dharma-abhāvaś-ca śūnyatā. Tad-abhāvasya ca sad-bhāvastasmin yathokte bhoktrādau sā anyā śūnyatā-iti śūnyatā-lakṣaṇa-ākhyānaartham dvividhām-ante śūnyatām vyavasthāpayati-abhāva-śūnyatām-abhāva-svabhāvaśūnyatām-ca, pudgala-dharma samāropasya tac-chūnyatā-apavādasya ca parihārārtham yathākramam. Evam śūnyatāyāḥ prabhedo vijñeyaḥ.* MVKB I.21

2. *Tatra-adhyātmikeṣu-āyataneṣu vipāka-vijñāna-svabhāveṣu bālānām bhoktṛsammateṣu bhoktṛ-pudgalasya kalpitalakṣaṇānām ca cakṣurādīnām-abhāvas-tadabhāvasya ca sad-bhāvo'adhyātma-śūnyatā.* . MVKBT I.21

would mean the existence of the same *pudgala* and *dharmas*.[1]

Therefore, it is necessary that the definition of the emptiness includes both *abhava-śūnyatā* and *abhāva-svabhāva-śūnyatā* as well.

Of the four topics mentioned in stanza I.13, the last one, namely, 'the reason for the classification of *śūnyátā*', now remains to be discussed. This is what the next stanza does by showing why *śūnyatā* has to be classified into defiled (*saṅkliṣṭā*) and purified (*viśuddhā*), a classification mentioned in stanza I.17. "How is the reason [for such clasification] to be understood ?"[2]

[MVK I.22] If it were not [ever] defiled,
Then all living beings would be [ever] liberated;
If it were not [ever] purified,
Then all efforts for liberation would be futile.

The meaning of this stanza is clear enough: it is necessary to distinguish between the defiled and the purified aspects of the emptiness, in order to explain the distinction between *saṃsāra* and *nirvāṇa*. One is in the state of *saṃsāra* when one experiences reality, which is otherwise called emptiness, as defiled, and one is in the state of *nirvāṇa* when one experiences the same reality as pure. So, *śūnyatā* is considered defiled or purified depending upon whether it is looked at from the sphere of *saṃsāra* and *nirvāṇa*. Interpreting the above stanza Vasubandhu says :

If the emptiness of elements would not be defiled by the accidental and secondary defilments, even when no remedy is applied, then, since there are no defilements whatsoever, all living beings would become liberated without any effort at all. Again, if it would not become purified, even when some

1. *Yadi-abhāva-śūnyatā nocyeta parikalpita-svarūpayor-dharma-pudgalayor-astitvam-eva prasajyeta. Yadi-abhāva-svabhāva-śūnyatā nocyeta śūnyatāyāḥ abhāva eva prasajyeta. Tad-abhāvāc-ca pudgala-dharmayoḥ pūrvavad bhāvaḥ syāt.* MVKBT I.21

2. *Katham sādhanam vijñeyam?* MVKB I.22

3. *Saṅkliṣṭā-ced bhaven-na-asau muktās-syuḥ sarva-dehinaḥ*
Viśuddhā ced bhaven-na-asau vyāyāmo niṣphalo bhavet. MVK I.22

> remedy is applied, then the efforts towards liberation would prove fruitless.[1]

In other words, the fact that some are not liberated while others are, shows that the emptiness is looked at as defiled and purified.

However, *śūnyatā*, considered in itself, is neither defiled nor purified. It is defiled or purified only with reference to the way it is looked at. As Sthiramati says:

> There, the defilement is on account of the inclusion of the *saṅkleśa-dharma*, and the purity is on account of the grasping of the *viśuddhi-dharma*. On the contrary, neither defilement nor purity issues directly from *śūnyatā*, for the substance [*dharmatā*] depends for its manifestation on its attributes [*dharmas*].[2]

What Sthiramati means by these words may be expressed differently as follows: A substance (*dharmatā*, reality) as such is not perceived, but only in accordance with the attributes (*dharmas*) imposed on it by the perceiver. If attributes of defilements are imposed on it, then it will be perceived as defiled (*saṅkliṣṭa*), and if attributes of purity are imposed on it, then it will be perceived as purified (*viśuddha*). It then follows that the distinction between the defiled and purified modes of emptiness is only an epistemological one, and that the emptiness in itself is neither defiled nor purified. This is explicitly stated in the next stanza, which Vasubandhu introduces with the conjunction "however"[3] to suggest its contrast from the previous stanza.

> [MVK I.23] It is neither defiled nor undefiled,
> Also, it is neither purified nor unpurified;[4]

1. *Yadi sarva-dharmāṇām śūnyatā āgantukair-upakleśair-anutpanne'pi pratipakṣe na saṅkliṣṭā bhavet, saṅkleśa-abhāvād-ayatnata eva muktāḥ sarva-sattvā bhaveyuḥ. Atha-utpanne'pi pratipakṣe na viśuddhā bhavet, mokṣārthamārambho niṣphalo bhavet.* MVKB I.22

2. *Atra saṅkleśadharma-upādānāt saṅkleśo, viśuddhi-dharma-grahaṇād viśuddhiḥ. Na tu śūnyatāyāḥ sākṣāt saṅkleśo viśuddhir-vā-iṣyate, dharma-paratantratvād-dharmatāyāḥ.* MVKBT I.22

3. *Evam-ca kṛtvā.* MVKB I.23

4. *Na kliṣṭā na-api vā-akliṣṭā śuddhā-asuddhā na ca-eva sā* MVK I.23

"How is it that it is neither defiled nor unpurified ? It is so by its very nature."[1]

[MVK I.23 Because of the shining nature of citta;[2] cont'd]

Evidently, this line does not fit in with the context, because it abruptly suggests *citta* to be another name for *śūnyatā*, the absolute state of reality. Nowhere before, not even on the list of the synonyms of *śūnyatā*[3] was *citta* mentioned as another name for *śūnyatā*. On the contrary Vasubandhu has always used the term *citta* to mean *ālaya-vijñāna*, or in conjunction with *caitta*. Therefore, the present line sounds very much out of context. It is, therefore, difficult to believe that this is part of the original text. S. Yamaguchi, in his edition of *Madhyānta-vibhāga-tīkā* (Nagoya 1934) does not in fact consider it as part of the original stanza. Th. Stcherbatsky treats it as a Scriptural quotation cited by Vasubandhu.[5] It is quite possible, indeed, that the original line is lost, and that the present one is only a Scriptural quotation occurring in Vasubandhu's commentary, as Stcherbatsky's translation suggests Even so the problem about considering *citta* as another name for *śūnyatā* remains unsolved. Is it possible that Vasubandhu really means that *citta* is another name for *śūnyatā*? No, because it would contradict his other passages which treat *citta* only as *ālaya-vijñāna*, which operates only on the saṃsāric sphere. So, how is one to understand the present line? Sthiramati, as if sensing the problem, says that the term *citta* in the present context should be taken to mean *citta-dharmatā*.[6] This interpretation

1. *Katham na kliṣṭā na-api ca-aśuddhā? prakṛtyā-eva.* MVK I.23
2. *Prabhāsvaratvāc-cittasya.* MVK I.23
3. Cf. MVK I.15-16; (see above pages 75-76)
4. Cf. R. C. Pandeya, ed., *Madhyānta-vibhāga-śāstra*, (Delhi, Varanasi, Patna : Motilal Banarsidass, 1971), p. 49, note 4.
5. Cf. Th. Stcherbatsky, trans., *Madhyānta-vibhāga: Discourse on Discrimination between Middle and Extremes*, (Bibliotheca Buddhica XXX, 1936; reprint, Calcutta : Indian Studies, Past and Present, 1971), p. 215. The reference is possibly to *Aṅguttara-nikāya* 1.10 : *Prabhāsaram idam cittam..*
6. *Atra ca citta-dharmatā-eva citta-śabdena-uktā, cittasya-eva malalakṣaṇatvāt.* MVKBT I.23

solves the problem partly, for any element (*dharma*) in its abstract state (*dharmatā*) is for the Yogācārins another name for the absolute state of *śūnyatā*. Consequently, the element *citta*, in its abstract state of existence is no more the phenomenal intellect nor the *ālayavijñāna*, but is the absolute state of *śūnyatā*. It is just like the case of *abhūta-parikalpa* which, once it is rid of the subject-object characterizations, turns out to be identical with *śūnyatā*.[1] Thus, Sthiramati's interpretation of *citta* as *citta-dharmatā* somehow solves the problem at issue. However, it may be still asked how the attribute 'shining' (*prabhāsvara*) can be validly applied to *citta*, which here means *citta-dharmatā*/*śūnyatā*, for the explanation of the different kinds of *śūnyatā* (stanzas 18-22) implied that no attribute whatsoever can validly be applied to the thing-in-itself, for which the term *śūnyatā* stands.[2] If so, how can the attribute 'shining' (*prabhāsvara*) be meaningfully applied to *citta-dharmatā*/*śūnyatā*. A possible answer to this question may be that Vasubandhu, while quoting a traditional passage, does not take the attribute 'shining' in its literal sense, but only in its metaphorical sense of 'par excellence.' However, I feel that the entire line under discussion can be interpreted in a much simpler way. That 'the *citta* is of shining nature' can be understood literally to mean that *citta*, i.e. *ālaya-vijñāna*,[3] is of shining nature (*prabhāsvara*) so that it leaves its reflections on the things around, which consequently would look different from what they really are. Then the first three lines of the present stanza would mean the following:

Śūnyatā is neither defiled nor undefiled,
Also, it is neither purified nor unpurified,
It is neither defiled nor unpurified
Because the defilements and impurities,
Which are attributed to *śūnyatā*,

1. *Śūnyatā tasya abhūta-parikalpasya grāhya-grāhaka-bhāvena virahitatā*. MVKB I.2; see above pages 29 ff

2. See above pages 78ff

3. In fact in one of the Tibetan versions of this stanza the term used is *sems*, which means *ālaya-vijñāna*. Cf. Th. Stcherbatsky, op. cit., p. 215, note 162.

Are only reflections from *citta*,
Which is otherwise called *ālaya-vijñāna*.
This latter is shining in nature, and, therefore,
Can cause its own defiled and impure contents to reflect on *śūnyatā*,
Which will consequently appear as defiled and unpurified.

The final line of the same stanza explains "how is it [i.e. *śūnyatā*] neither undefiled nor purified ?[1]

[MVK I.23 cont'd.] Because of the accidental character of the defilements.[2]

That is, the defilements attributed to *śūnyatā* are only some accidentals which by no means affect it substantially. So the *śūnyatā* never really gets defiled or impure. Consequently the removal of those defilements, which means only a change in the perceiver, rather than in the perceived *śūnyatā*, cannot be said to be an undefiling or purification of *śūnyatā*

"Thus, the above-mentioned classification of emptiness [into defiled and purified] is justified."[3]

Finally Vasubandhu summarises the discussion on the emptiness as follows:

There, the summary-meaning of emptiness is to be understood under two heads: one, the definition [of emptiness], and the other, the establishment [of the same definition]. There, definition is, again, twofold: positive and negative. The positive definition is likewise twofold: one, [the assertion that emptiness is] neither assertion nor negation, two, [the assertion that emptiness is] that which is free from being different from thatness. By the establishment [of definition] is to be understood the establishment ofsynonyms of emptiness

1. *Katham na-akliṣṭā na śuddhā ?* MVKB I.23
2. *Kleśasya-āgantukatvataḥ.* MVK I.23
3. *Evam śūnyatāyāḥ uddiṣṭaḥ prabhedaḥ sādhito bhavati.* MVKB I.23

etc. There, by the fourfold introduction of the emptiness the following four definitions of it are intended : its own-definition, operative-definition, defilement-purity-definition and rationality-definition; these definitions help one respectively to get rid of uncertainty, fear, indolence and doubt.[1]

1. *Tatra śūnyatāyāḥ piṇḍārtho lakṣaṇato vyavasthānataś-ca veditavyaḥ. Tatra lakṣanato bhāva-lakṣaṇato'bhābva-lakṣaṇataś-ca. Bhāva-lakṣaṇam punarbhāva-abhāva-vinirmukta-lakṣaṇataś-ca tatva-anyatva-vinirmukta-lakṣaṇataś-ca. Vyavasthānam punaḥ paryāyādi-vyavasthānato veditavyam. Tatra-etayā caturprakāra-deśanayā śūnyatāyāḥ sva-lakṣaṇam, karma-lakṣaṇam, saṅkleśa-vyavadāna-lakṣaṇam, yukti-lakṣaṇam-ca udbhāvitam bhavati : vikalpa-trāsa-kausīdya-vicikitsānpasāntaye.* MVKB I. (conclusion)

Chapter Three

A TREATISE ON THE THREE NATURES (*TRI-SVABHĀVA-NIRDEŚA*)

1. Introduction

Tri-svabhāva-nirdeśa is a small treatise of thirty eight stanzas concentrating on the doctrine of three natures. A theoretical explanation of the doctrine of three natures, it sheds light on many otherwise obscure points of Vasubandhu's view of reality. It states clearly what each of the three natures stands for.

What interests me most in this text is that the entire doctrine of three natures hinges on the subject-object duality. That is, the text explains each of the three natures with reference to the subject-object duality. Thus, for example,

(i) *pariniṣpanna-svabhāva* (the absolutely accomplished nature) is that state of existence in which the indivudual is characterized neither as a subject nor as an object;

(ii) *paratantra-svabhāva* (the other-dependent nature) is that state of existence in which the individual is bound to see things as distinguished into subjects and objects of experience;

(iii) *parikalpita-svabhāva* (the imagined nature) is that state of existence in which the individual is seen as an object or subject of experience.

In other words, every individual in his absolutely accomplished state of existence (*pariniṣpanna-svabhāva*) is neither a subject nor an object of experience, but is reality as such (*tathatā*); then he slips into the unfortunate situation called *saṃsāra*, where he is led to find himself as the suject enjoying all else as objects of experience: this state of existence being conditioned by the forces of one's own past deeds and habits, is called the other-dependent (*paratantra-svabhāva*); the forms of sujectivity and objectivity that are projected on to the things by the individual in the other-dependent state of existence, are the imagined nature (*parikalpita-svabhāva*).

Of the three natures only *pariniṣpanna* and *parikalpita* have any ontological pretensions. The former is the absolute state of existence, while the latter is the saṃsāric (phenomenal) state of existence. The *paratantra svabhāva*, on the contrary, refers essentially to the very act of projecting the forms of subjectivity and objectivity, which every individual in the saṃsāric state is bound to do. Hence it is variously called as *parikalpa* (the act of imagination), *abhūta-parikalpa* (the act of imagining the unreal forms), or simply as *asat-kalpa* (the act of imagining the non-existent). My point is further confirmed by the fact that the terms *pariniṣpanna* and *parikalpita* are past participles indicating something concretely accomplished, while the term *parikalpa* is only a verbal noun referring to an action.

However, in the last analysis, *pariniṣpanna-svabhāva* alone has any ontological status. *Para-tantra-svabhāva* is but a characteristic with which one's saṃsāric existence is marked, and *parikalpitasvabhāva* refers to the imaginary forms of subjectivity and objectivity superimposed on things. Therefore, *para-tantra-svabhāva* and *parikalpita-svabhāva* are both far from being ontological, while *pariniṣpanna-svabhāva* is the ontological mode of things.

2. The Three Natures

With these introductory remarks I shall now analyse the text. I may start with a summary of stanzas 1-5 as follows:

There are three natures such as the other-dependent (*paratantra*), the imagined (*parikalpita*) and the absolutely accomplished (*pariniṣpanna*) (Stanza 1). The other-dependent is *citta* which imagines (i.e. mentally constructs) the non-existent (*asat-kalpa*) forms of subjectivity and objectivity (stanza 5); it manifests itself (*khyāti*)(stanzas 2, 3 and 4) under the double form (*khyāti-dvayātmanā*) (stanza 4) of subjectivity and objectivity.

The imagined (*parikalpita*) is the form in which the other-dependent manifests itself (*yathā khyāti sa kalpitaḥ*) (stanza 2); the form in which the latter manifests itself is evidently the dual form (*dvayātmanā*) of subjectivity and objectivity; therefore it follows that the imagined nature (*parikalpita-svabhāva*) refers to the forms of subjectivity and objectivity; its reality depends entirely on its cause (i.e. the other-dependent nature, which is the same as *citta*) and therefore is mere imagination (*pratyaya-adhīna-vṛttitvāt-kalpanā-mātra-bhāvataḥ*) (stanza 3), and as such it is totally non-existent (*yathā ca kalpayati-artham tathā-atyantam na vidyate*) (stanza 5).

The absolutely accomplished nature (*pariniṣpanna-svabhāva*) is the perpetual absence (*sadā-avidyamānatā*) of the form in which the other-dependent manifests itself (*tasya khyātur-yathā-ākhyānam yā sadā-avidyamānatā*) (stanza 3); it has already been said that the form in which the other-dependent manifests itself is the dual form of subjectivity and objectivity; therefore it follows that wherever there is the perpetual absence of the forms of subjectivity and objectivity, there is the absolutely accomplished nature of things; in other words, in the realm of the absolutely accomplished nature of things the subject-object distinction does not apply at all; therefore, the absolutely accomplished nature is characterized on the one hand by the absence of the imagination of unreal forms (*tasya asatkalpasya kā nāstitā*) and on the other hand it is the very non-duality (*advaya-dharmatā*) of subjectivity and objectivity (stanza 4); further, the absolutely accomplished nature can never be otherwise (*pariniṣpanna-svabhāvo' nanyathātvataḥ*) (stanza 3).

What I want to point out here is this : what Vasubandhu describes as imaginary (*kalpita*) or merely mental construction (*kalpanā-mātrabhāva*) or non-existent (*asat*) or unreal (*abhūta*) or phenomenal (*prātibhāsika*) is just the subject-object duality, and not by any means the plurality of beings. Therefore there is no sufficient reason to call his system monism. Again, what Vasubandhu traces to thought (*citta*) or imagination (*parikalpa*), is the same subject-object distinction, not the things in themselves; the latter are there independent of any mental activity by any being. Therefore, again, there is no sufficient reason to call his system idealism.

A literal translation of stanzas 1-5 would be as follows:

[TSN. 1] The imagined,
The other-dependent, and

The absolutely accomplished:
These are the three natures,
Which should be thoroughly known by the wise.[1]

[TSN. 2] That which appears is the other-dependent,
For it depends on causal conditions;
The form in which it appears is the imagined,
For it is merely an imagination.[2]

[TSN. 3] The perpetual absence of the form
In which the other-dependent appears,
Is to be understood as
The absolutely accomplished nature,
For it is never otherwise.[3]

[TSN. 4] What is it that appears ?
It is the imagination of the non-existent.[4]
How does it appear?
In the form of duality.
What will result from its non-existence ?
There will be the state of non-duality.[5]

[TSN. 5] What is meant by the imagination of the non-existent ?
It is thought,
For by it (the subject-object duality) is imagined.
The form in which it imagines a thing,
Never at all exists as such.[6]

1. *Kalpitaḥ paratantraś-ca pariniṣpanna eva ca*
Trayaḥ svabhāva dhīrāṇām gambhīra-jñeyam-iṣyate. TSN. 1
2. *Yat-khyāti paratantro'sau yathā khyāti sa kalpitaḥ*
Pratyaya-adhīna-vṛttitvāt-kalpanā-mātra- bhāvataḥ. TSN. 2
3. *Tasya khyātur-yathā-ākhyānam yā sadā-avidyamānatā*
Jñeyaḥ sa pariniṣpanna-svabhāvo'nanyathātvataḥ. TSN. 3
4. *Abhūta-parikalpa*, translated as 'the imagination of the unreal', appearing in MV, is here replaced by *asat-kalpa*, translated as 'the imagination of the non-existent'. Both terms, however, stand for the same concept.
5. *Tatra kim khyāti-asatkalpaḥ katham khyāti dvayātmanā*
Tasya kā nāstitā tena yā tatra'dvayadharmatā. TSN. 4
6. *Asat-kalpo'tra kaś-cittam yatas-tena hi kalpyate*
Yathā ca kalpayati-artham tathā-atyantam na vidyate. TSN. 5

3. The Other-dependent Nature

Thus, after having explained what each of the three natures refers to, Vasubandhu now takes up a short analysis of the *para-tantra-svabhāva*, which he said is the same as *citta*.[1] This analysis runs through the next four stanzas. The contents of these stanzas have been discussed elsewhere[2] under the title of eight-fold consciousness. So Vasubandhu is not introducing any new topic here. But the present context has something special to say. For the eight-fold consciousness is discussed here under the title *paratantra-svabhāva*, thereby showing that the latter includes nothing more than the eight-fold consciousness. It could be said, therefore, that *paratantra-svabhāva* stands for what in the Western terminology 'mind' and 'mental activity' stand for. Consequently, just as mind and mental activities are not things by themselves, so *paratantra-svabhāva*, too, is not a thing by itself. It rather indicates a disposition or a tendency or a characteristic or an activity of an individual in a particular mode of existence, namely, *saṃsāra*.

Now, the translation of the four stanzas under reference:

[TSN. 6] The *citta* takes on two modes, as cause and effect,
It is then respectively called
The store-consciousness and the active consciousness,
The latter being seven-fold.[3]

[TSN. 7] The first is called *citta*, meaning 'collected',
Because in it are collected the seeds
Of defilements and habits;
The second, however, is called *citta*,
Because it acts in diverse ways.[4]

1. TSN. 5
2. See below Chapt. 4, see 3.
3. *Tad-hetu-phala-bhāvena cittam dvi-vidham iṣyate*
Yad-ālaya-ākhyam vijñānam pravṛtti-ākhyam ca saptadhā. TSN.6
4. *Saṁkleśa-vāsanā-bījais-citatvāc-cittam-ucyate*
Cittam-ādyam dvitīyam tu citra-ākāra-pravṛttitaḥ. TSN.7

[TSN. 8] Collectively [i.e. as a collection of store-consciousness and seven active consciousnesses]
It is the imagination of the unreal [forms of subjectivity and objectivity];
That, too, is said to be three-fold :
Maturing, caused and phenomenal.[1]

[TSN. 9] Of them, the first, [namely the maturing one,]
Is the basic consciousness,
Because its nature is to become matured;
The others, [namely the caused and the phenomenal ones],
Are the active consciousness,
For, the latter for its reality, depends
On the knowledge of the perceived-perceiver distinction.[2]

Thus it becomes clear that *paratantra-svabhāva* looked at from one angle is the same as *citta* (stanza 6), and, looked at from another angle it is the same as the imagination of the unreal forms of subjectivity and objectivity (*abhūta-kalpa* or *abhūta-parikalpa* or *asat-kalpa*) (stanza 8). In other words, *para-tantra-svabhāva* is treated here under two titles : *citta* and *abhūta-parikalpa.*

The title *citta* says, what the *paratantra-svabhāva* is, so to say, namely that it includes all sorts of consciounesses and the mental associates (Stanzas 6-7), and the title *abhūta-parikalpa* says, how it functions, namely by constructing and projecting the subjective forms of subjectivity and objectivity (stanza 8). The *abhūta-parikalpa* has three stages of development : maturing (*vaipākika*), caused (*naimittika*) and phenomenal (*prātibhāsika*). The *vaipākika* stage evidently refers to the *ālaya*-(or *mūla*-) *vijñānā.* What the other two stages, *naimittika* and *prātibhāsika*, refer to becomes clear in the light of a parallel passage from *Triṃśatika*, which says that the transformation of consciousness happens in three stages: *vipāka*, *manana*, and *vijñaptir-viṣayasya* (maturing, thinking

1. *Samāsato'bhūtakalpaḥ sa ca-eṣa trividho mataḥ*
Vaipākikas-tathā naimittiko'anyaḥ prātibhāsikaḥ. TSN.8
2. *Prathamo mūla-vijñānam tad-vipākātmakam yataḥ*
Anyaḥ pravṛtti-vijñānam dṛśya-dṛg-vitti-vṛttitaḥ. TSN.9

and representation of consciousness of objects).[1] Here, too, *vipāka* stands for *ālaya-vijñāna.*[2] And, *manana* and *vijñaptir-viṣayasya* in the last analysis turn out to be respectively self-consciousness and object-consciousness.[3] Correspondingly, in the present case *naimittika* and *prātibhāsika,* too, have to be understood as self-consciousness and object-consciousness. That *naimittika* refers to self-consciousness is further suggested by a different reading in one of the Tibetan versions of the text, which has *āhaṅkārika,* which literally means self-consciousness, instead of *naimittika.*[4] Then it is quite reasonable to argue that *prātibhāsika,* just as its counterpart *vijñaptir-viṣayasya,* refers to object-consciousness. Thus it is more or less certain that *naimittika* and *prātibhāsika* in the present context correspond respectively to self-consciousness (*manana*) and object-consciousness (*vijñaptir-viṣayasya*) in *Triṃśatikā.* It may be further asked, however, why self-consciousness is described as *naimittika* (caused), and object-consciousness as *prātibhāsika* (phenomenal). The answer to this question would make the correspondence between the two sets of concepts (*naimittikā* and *prātibhāsika* on the one hand, and *manana* and *vijñaptir-viṣayasya* on the other) complete. What I am trying to point out is the fact that the description in *Triṃśatikā* has emphasized the caused (*naimittika*) nature of *manana* (or *mano nāma vijñāna*) on the one hand, and the phenomenal (*prātibhāsika*) nature of *vijñaptir-viṣayasya* on the other: it is clearly said there that the *manana* has *ālaya-vijñāna* for its *āśraya* and *ālambana,*[5] and that the *vijñaptir-viṣayasya* (i.e. the remaining six active consciousnesses) manifests itself, as it were, under certain circumstances.[6] However, this distinction should not be stretched too far. For, in the last analysis Vasubandhu holds that both self-consciousness and object-consciousness are caused

1. ..*pariṇāmaḥ sa ca tridhā*
Vipāko mananākhyaś-ca vijñāptir-viṣayasya ca. Triṃś 1-2
2. *Tatra-ālaya-ākhya vijñānam vipākaḥ sarva-bījakam.* Ibid. 2
3. See below Chap. 4, Sec. 3.
4. See S. Mukhopadhyaya, *The Trisvabhāva-nirdeśa of Vasubandhu, Sanskrit Text and Tibetan Versions Edited with an English Translation, Introduction, and Vocabularies,* (Calcutta: Visvabharati, 1939), p. 2, note 5.
5. ..*tad-āśritya pravartate*
Tad-ālambanam mano-nāma vijñānam mananātmakam. Triṃś. 5
6. *Pañjānām mūlavijñāne yathā-pratyayam-udbhavaḥ.* Ibid. 15
Mano-vijñāna-saṃbhūtiḥ sarvadā ... Ibid. 16

as well as phenomenal. What the distinction ultimately says may be this : self-consciousness is caused *entirely from within* by the working of the 'unconscious', namely *ālaya-vijñāna*, while object-consciousness emerges *not entirely from within*, but depending upon various conditions, external as well as internal.

There is one more significant remark to be made in this contexts : active consciousness, whether it is self-consciousness or object-consciousness, invariably depends on "the knowledge of perceiver-perceived distinction".[1] It is worth noticing that *paratantra-svabhāva*, no matter whether it is considered as *citta* or *abhūta-parikalpa*, ends up in active consciousness (*pravṛtti-vijñāna*). And this active consciousness rests on the distinction between perceiver and perceived, a distinction, unreal (*abhūta* or *asat*) as it is, supplied by the *para-tantra-svabhāva*. In other words, *paratantra-svabhāva*, which is essentially the act of imagining the unreal forms (*abhūta-parikalpa*), constructing and projecting the unreal forms of subjectivity and objectivity, paves the way for active consciousness.

4. Different, Yet Non-different

In the next few stanzas Vasubandhu shows how the three natures are different from each other, but at the same time non-different from each other. This is shown mostly by applying the same terms to all three natures, but with different meanings or senses. So apparently the description turns out to be a play on words, although behind those words there are certain basic convictions of Vasubandhu. The central point seems to be that an individual going through the three natures, does not ever lose his continuity of existence, only he is assuming different modes of existence. So it is the same individual, but different modes of existence. Again, the difference is more a question of the way in which one looks at things, than any substantial change of being : one in *pariniṣpanna-svabhāva* looks at things as they are (*yathā-bhūta*), while one in *para-tantra* and *parikalpita-svabhāvas* looks at them as subjects and objects. This in turn means that the distinction between *nirvāṇa* and *saṃsāra* is basically only a

1. . .*pravṛtti-vijñānam dṛśya-dṛg-vitti-vṛttitaḥ*. TSN.9

matter of view-point : one in the state of *nirvāṇa* views things as they are in themselves, while one in the state of *saṃsāra* is bound to view them as endowed with the forms of subjectivity and objectivity. Hence, the attainment of *nirvāṇa* turns out to be a matter of enlightenment (*buddhatā*). That *nirvāṇa* and *saṃsāra* are ontologically the some reality, was already declared by *Laṅkāvatāra-sutra*.[1] Now Vasubandhu in the present text is only stating the same thesis in his own way :

[TSN. 10] The profundity of the three natures
Is indeed recognized, because
The defiled and the pure are each
Existent as well as non-existent,
Dual as well as unitary;
Also because
The three natures are not mutually different
In definition.[2,3]

Here "the defiled" (*saṅkleśa*, literally meaning, defilement) refers, as will be said later in stanza 17, to the *para-tantra-svbhāva* and *parikalpita-svabhāva* together, while "the pure" (*vyavadāna*, literally meaning, purity) refers to *pariniṣpanna-svabhāva*. So what the stanza says is this : the three natures are all

(i) existent as well asnon-existent,
(ii) dual as well as unitary, and
(iii) not mutually different in definition,

and are, therefore, not really different from each other. How this is so, is explained in the stanzas that follow.

1. *Saṃsāra-nirvāṇa-samatā*. Lanka. p. 42, line 7.

2. The term 'definition' (*lakṣaṇa*) appearing here and in the subsequent stanzas need not be taken in the strict logical sense, but only as meaning 'description'.

3. *Sad-asattvāt-dvaya-ekatvāt-saṅkleśa-vyavadānayoḥ*
Lakṣaṇa-abhedataś-ca-iṣṭā svabhāvānām gambhīratā. TSN.10

Existent and non-existent

[TSN. 11] The imagined nature is said
To be defined both as existent and as non-existent,
For, on the one hand it is grasped as existent,
While, on the other,
It is totally non-existent.[1]

That is, one in the state of *saṃsāra* takes imagined nature as something really existing by itself, while in fact it is only one's own imagination, and therefore totally non-existent (*atyanta-abhāva*). As I have already explained,[2] by imagined nature is meant the subject-object duality. This subect-object duality, although it is one's own mental construction, is understood by one as something that exists independently of one's mental activity. Thus as an invariable factor of saṃsāric experience it exists, but not otherwise.

[TSN. 12] The other-dependent nature is said
To be defined both as existent and as non-existent,
For, it exists as an illusion,
It does not exist, though, in the form in which it appears.[3]

The other-dependent nature is the act of imagination whereby one projects the unreal forms of subjectivity and objectivity.[4] Thus, as an act of imagination it is a reality, illusory as it is, and in that sense it exists, too. But the way it expresses itself, namely the forms of subjectivity and objectivity, is totally non-existent (*atyanta-abhāva*), as was said in the previous stanza. In other words, the imagination of the unreal forms (*abhūta-parikalpa*) is a fact of saṃsāric existence, although those forms

1. *Svatvena gṛhyate yasmād-atyanta-abhāva eva ca*
Svabhāvaḥ kalpitas-tena sad-asal-lakṣaṇo mataḥ. TSN.11
2. See above, pp. 91-92
3. *Vidyate bhrānti-bhāvena yathā-akhyānam na vidyate*
Paratantro yatas-tena sad-asal-lakṣaṇo matah. TSN.12
4. See above, p. 91

have no extramental reality. This was stated already in MVK. I. 2, which along with Vasubandhu's commentary on it, I paraphrased as follows :[1]

> There exists the imagination of the unreal,[2]
> Namely the discrimination
> Between the graspable and the grasper.[3]
> However, there is no pair,[4]
> such as the graspable and the grasper.[5]

[TST. 13] The absolutely accomplished nature is said
To be defined both as existent and as non-existent,
For, it exists as a state of non-duality,
It is also the non-existence of duality.[6]

Here evidently Vasubandhu is playing with words. All that he is saying in this stanza is that the absolutely accomplished nature is unaffected by the duality between subject and object. This same fact he expresses in negative as well as positive terms so that one can say that the absolutely accomplished nature exists as well as does not exist : it exists as non-duality, and it does not exist as duality.

Dual and unitary

Thus after having shown how all three natures are both existent as well as non-existent, Vasubandhu now proceeds to explain how they are also both dual (*dvaya*) as well as unitary (*eka*).

[TSN. 14] The nature that is imagined by the ignorant is said
To be both dual and unitary,

1. See above, p. 31
2. *Abhūta-parikalpo'sti.* MVK. I.2
3. *Tatra-abhūta-parikalpo grāhya-grāhaka-vikalpaḥ.* MVKB. I.2
4. *Dvayam tatra na vidyate.* MVK I.2
5. *Dvayam grāhyam grāhakam ca.* MVKB. I.2
6. *Advayatvena-yac-ca-asti dvayasya-abhāva-eva ca*
   Svabhāvas-tena niṣpannaḥ sad-asal-lakṣaṇo mataḥ. TSN.13

For, as it is imagined
A thing has two forms,
But as those two forms do not exist,
It is unitary.[1]

That is, the imagined nature is real only for the ignorant (*bālāḥ*), for it is just their mental creation. They imagine it as divided into subjects and objects, and in this sense the imagined nature is dual (*dvaya*). But as already established,[2] subject-object duality has no extra-mental reality, and therefore the imagined nature is unitary (eka).

[TSN. 15] The other-dependent nature is said
To be dual as well as unitary,
For, it appears in dual form,
While it has an illusory unity as well.[3]

That is, the other-dependent nature, which is just the imagination of the unreal (*abhūta-parikalpa*) forms of subjectivity and objectivity, can be described in terms of duality as well as unity. As said above, it appears in the forms of duality[4] between subjectivity and objectivity,[5] and therefore can be described as dual. But in itself it is only a unitary act of imagining the illusory forms, and therefore, as MVK declares, there is no duality within it.[6] Thus in this latter sense it can be described in terms of unity, too.

[TSN. 16] The absolutely accomplished nature is said
To be dual as well as unitary,
For, on the one hand,
It is by nature the absence of duality,

1. *Dvaividhyāt-kalpita-arthasya tad-asatva-eka-bhāvataḥ*
Svabhāvaḥ kalpito balair-dvaya-ekatvātmako mataḥ. TSN.14
2. *Yathā-ca kalpayati-artham tathā-atyantam na vidyate.* TSN. 5
3. *Prakhyānād-dvaya-bhāvena bhrāntimātra-ekabhāvataḥ*
Svabhāva paratantra-ākhyo dvaya-ekatva-ātmako. TSN. 15
4. *Katham khyāti? dvayātmanā.* TSN.4
5. *Dvayam grāhyam grāhakam ca.* MVKB. I.2
6. *Dvayam tatra na vidyate.* MVK. I.2

And, on the other hand,
It is in the nature of unity without duality.[1]

This stanza, too, is mostly a play on words, even a poor play on words. The message of the whole stanza is just that the absolutely accomplished nature is absolute unity without any taint of duality. This Vasubandhu expresses in two ways, namely,

(i) that it is negation of duality (*dvaya-abhāva-svabhāva*), and

(ii) that it is unity without duality (*advaya-eka-svabhāva*).

Thus he somehow manages to describe the absolutely accomplished nature in terms of duality (i.e. *dvaya-abhāva-svabhāva*), and also in terms of unity (i.e. *advaya-eka-svabhāva*). But from stanza 10 one expected him to show that the absolutely accomplished nature is both dual and unitary, which he fails to do. The text itself is very ambiguous, having two different, contradictory, readings :[2]

(i) *Mahāyāna-sūtra-alaṅkāra* and one of the Tibetan versions read '*dvaya-bhāva-svabhāva*' instead of '*dvaya-abhāva-svabhāva*', the former reading being obviously unacceptable.

(ii) Another Tibetan version reads it '*dvaya-abhāva*', which in meaning is not substantially different from '*dvaya-abhāva-svabhāva*'. This latter phrase is the one reconstructed by S. Mukhopadhyaya,[3] and I have accepted it for my interpretation.

The next stanza further clarifies the distinction between the defiled (*saṅkleśa-lakṣaṇa*) and pure (*vyavadāna-lakṣaṇa*) already mentioned in stanza 10.

[TSN. 17] What is to be known as being defined
As defilement are the imagined and the other-dependent natures,

1. *Dvaya-abhāva-svabhāvatvād-advaya-eka-svabhāvataḥ*
Svabhāvaḥ pariniṣpanno dvaya-ekatva-ātmako mataḥ. TSN.16
2. S. Mukhopadhyaya, op.cit., p. 3, n.6
3. Ibid.

While the absolutely accomplished nature
Is recognized as the definition of purity.[1]

What is conveyed by this stanza is simply that (i) the imagined nature (*parikalpita-svabhāva*) and other-dependent nature (*paratantra-svabhāva*) are defined as (i.e., characterized by) defilement (*saṅkleśa-lakṣaṇam*), while (ii) the absolutely accomplished nature is defined as (i.e. characterized by) purity (*vyavadāna-lakṣaṇam*). The text, of course, has this second part in a different way. Instead of saying that the absolutely accomplished nature is defined as purity, it says in effect that the absolutely accomplished nature is the definition of purity (*vyavadānasya lakṣaṇam*). It implies that purity is defined as the absolutely accomplished nature rather than the other way round. However, I feel that Vasubandhu is not very serious about this change of words: whether he says that the absolutely accomplished nature is defined as purity, or that purity is defined as the absolutely accomplished nature, he should be meaning the same thing, because with reference to the absolute state of existence, which the absolutely accomplished nature refers to, one cannot possibly make a clear distinction between the subject and predicate of a statement.

However, by distinguishing the three natures into just two groups, namely, *saṅkleśa-lakṣaṇa* and *vyavadāna-lakṣaṇa*, the present stanza makes an important point. It thereby suggests that although one can speak of *three* natures, as a matter of fact there are only *two* of them: *parikalpita and paratantra*, which are *saṅkleśa-lakṣaṇa* on the one hand, and *pariniṣpanna*, which is *vyavadānalakṣaṇa* on the other. In other words, by describing both *parikalpita-svabhāva* and *paratantra-svabhāva* equally as *saṅkleśa-lakṣaṇa*, Vasubandhu is somehow admitting that the distinction between *paratantra-svabhāva* and *parikalpita-svabhāva* is not to be taken too seriously, but only in an operational sense. I have already pointed this out above on page 91.

1. *Kalpitaḥ paratantraś-ca jñeyam saṅkleśa-lakṣaṇam*
Pariniṣpanna iṣṭas-tu vyavadānasya lakṣaṇam. TSN.17

Not mutually different in definition

So far Vasubandhu has been trying to show that each of the three natures can be described as both existent and non-existent on the one hand, and as both dual and unitary on the other. Now in the next four stanzas he says how the three natures are not mutually different in definition (*abhinna-lakṣaṇa*). This discussion is only an extension of, or conclusion from, the above one, and says that all three natures being describable using the same terms such as 'existent and non-existent' and 'dual and unitary', cannot be mutually different in definition :

[TŚN. 18] The absolutely accomplished nature
Is to be understood
As not different in definition from the imagined nature,
For, the latter being in the nature of unreal duality,
Is by nature the absence of that duality.[1]

Stanza 3 described the absolutely accomplished nature as the perpetual absence (*sadā-avidyamānatā*) of the dual form,[2] and stanza 5 described it as the very state of non-duality (*advaya-dharmatā*).[3] Now the present stanza shows that the duality of the imagined nature is unreal (*asat*), and that, therefore, the imagined nature, too, "is by nature the absence of that duality". Thus Vasubandhu is showing that the absolutely accomplished nature and the imagined nature are not different from each other in definition, both being defined as 'the absence of duality'. However, what Vasubandhu is trying to get across should be that in the final analysis there is only the absolutely accomplished nature, the imagined one being only a misconstruction of it. In other words, one should not understand that those two natures are two separate levels of reality, but as one and the same reality, which is essentially non-dual, but mis-

1. *Asad-dvaya-svabhāvatvāt-tad-abhāva-svabhāvataḥ*
Svabhāvāt-kalpitāj-jñeyo pariniṣpanno'bhinna-lakṣaṇaḥ. TSN.18
2. See above, page 93
3. See above, page 93

constructed as having two forms, namely subjectivity and objectivity.

The next stanza is making the same point as above in another way. It says how the imagined nature is not different from the absolutely accomplished one, while the previous stanza puts it the other way round.

[TSN. 19] The imagined nature, too,
Is to be understood
As not different in definition from the absolutely accomplished one,
For, the latter being in the nature of non-duality,
Is by nature the absence of duality.[1]

The next two stanzas show how the other-dependent nature and the absolutely accomplished nature are not mutually different in definition. Here, too, the absence of duality is the point of comparison.

[TSN. 20] The absolutely accomplished nature
Is to be understood
As not different in definition from the other-dependent nature,
For, the latter being non-existent in the form in which it appears,
Is by nature the non-existence of that form.[2]

Here the emphasis is on the form in which the other-dependent nature manifests itself (*yathā-ākhyānām*). It is this form that makes the other-dependent somehow different from the absolutely accomplished one. But this form being just imaginary (*kalpita*), and therefore non-existent (*asat*), the stanza says, the difference between those two natures turns out to be nil. What is the form in which the other-dependent manifests itself ? Stanza 4

1. *Advayatva-svabhāvatvād-dvaya-abhāva-svabhāvataḥ*
Niṣpannāt-kalpitaś-ca-eva vijñeyo'bhinna-lakṣaṇaḥ. TSN.19
2. *Yathā-ākhyānām-asad-bhāvāt-tathā'satva-svabhāvataḥ*
Svabhāvāt-para-tantrākhyān-niṣpanno'bhinna-lakṣaṇaḥ. TSN.20

above says that the form in which the other-dependent appears is duality,[1] and also that from the non-existence (*nāstitā*) of that form there results the state of non-duality (*advaya-dharmatā*),[2] which is the same as the absolutely accomplished nature. Thus the present stanza is only another version of stanza 4.

A remark that I made above[3] about the reality of the other-dependent nature becomes all the clearer in the present stanza, namely, that the other-dependent nature is only the act of imagining the unreal forms of subjectivity and objectivity, and that therefore it has no reality apart from those forms, which are the same as the imagined nature (*parikalpita-svabhāva*). Further, what I said about the non-difference between the absolutely accomplished nature and the imagined nature, namely that they are not just non-different, but one and the same reality,[4] applies also to the non-difference between the absolutely accomplished nature and the other-dependent nature. That is, the latter two natures are not two separate realities, not even two separate levels of reality, but just one reality, the other-dependent nature being only an operational form of the absolutely accomplished one.

The next stanza repeats differently what was said in the previous one :

[TSN. 21] The other-dependent nature, too,
Is to be undrstood
As not different in definition from the absolutely accomplished one,
For, the former being in the nature of non-existent duality,
Is by nature non-existent in the form in which it appears.[5]

1. *Katham khyāti ? dvayātmanā.* TSN.4
2. *Tasya kā nāstitā tena yā tatra'dvaya-dharmatā.* TSN.4
3. See above, page 91
4. See above, page 104
5. *Asat-dvaya-svabhāvatvāt-yathā-ākhyāna-asvabhāvataḥ/-ākhyāna-abhāvataḥ*
Niṣpannāt-paratantro' pi vijñeyo-'bhinna-lakṣaṇaḥ. TSN.21

5. How to Evaluate and Understand the Three Natures ?

In the next five stanzas Vasubandhu discusses the three natures from a practical point of view, first in terms of convention (*vyavahāra*), and then in terms of understanding (*praveśa*). How are the three natures to be explained in terms of convention (*vyavahāra*) ? And how does one treading the path towards enlightenment come to realize the reality or unreality of each nature ? These are the two questions Vasubandhu is going to discuss briefly now. Introducing them he says :

[TSN. 22] For the sake of proficiency
A particular order of the natures
Is recommended, which takes into account
The conventions [about them], and
How one understands them.[1]

Here Vasubandhu is suggesting a particular order (*krama-bheda*) of considering the three natures (*svabhāvānām*), which he thinks will be convenient for those who want to acquire proficiency (*vyutpatti*) in the science of the three natures. The term *krama-bhedaḥ*, here translated as 'a particular order', ordinarily would mean 'a change in the order', which obviously does not fit in with the context. To be sure, here Vasubandhu does not at all introduce any detectable 'change of order' in dealing with the three natures. Hence I have taken the term *bheda* to mean 'particularity' or 'speciality', rather than 'change' or 'difference'. To attach the term *bheda* to nouns to indicate that what is under reference is something particular or special or different, is not unusual in Sanskrit literature. Thus, for example, '*artha-bheda*' would mean 'a particular thing' or 'a particular meaning'. Similarly, in the present case *krama-bheda* means the *particular order*, in which Vasubandhu is going to speak of the three natures. This is suggested also by a different reading in one of the Tibetan versions. It reads *krama bhāva* instead of *krama-bheda*.[2]

1. *Krama-bhedaḥ svabhāvānām vyavahāra-adhikārataḥ*
Tad-praveśa-adhikārāc-ca vyutpattyartham vidhīyate. TSN. 22
2. See S. Mukhopadhyaya, op. cit. p. 4, n. 4

The former reading can be very well taken to mean 'the apparent order' in which the three natures are going to be treated.

Vasubandhu adopts this particular order in dealing with the three natures, in the first place, with a view to helping those who want to acquire proficiency (*vyutpatti*) in this matter. Secondly, the order is based on two considerations : (i) how the three natures are to be explained in terms of convention (*vyavahāra-adhikārataḥ*), and (ii) how one can gradually come to realize the facts about the three natures (*praveśa-adhikārataḥ*).

How can one explain the three natures in terms of convention (*vyavahāra-adhikārataḥ*) ? The answer is

[TSN. 23] The imagined nature is essentially of conventional values
The other, [namely the other-dependent nature],
Is essentially that which brings about such conventional values
And the third, [namely the absolutely accomplished nature],
Is the nature freed of all conventional values.[1]

The term *vyavahāra*, literally meaning 'behaviour' or 'activity' or 'usage', is a technical term used in philosophy to mean 'convention' or 'practice'. Thus the phrase *vyavahāra-satya* would mean 'truth which has only a conventional or practical application.' Similarly, in the present staza Vasubanhu is considering the natures from a conventional or practical point of view. And this enables him to make the idea of the three natures much clearer than ever before. Thus the picture of the three natures, that comes out of the present stanza, is as follows :

The imagined nature, which has already been established as none other than the subject-object distinction, is only a conventional reality. That means, it is what the common man out of ignorance takes for granted. However, as long as he is in the state of *saṃsāra*, it is not only useful for him, but also is the very

1. *Kalpito vyavahāra-ātmā vyavahartṛ-ātmako'paraḥ*
Vyavahāra-samuccheda-svabhāvas-ca-anya iṣyate. TSN. 23

râison d'etre of his existence in the state of *saṃsāra*. For, as I have already explained,[1] on the one hand, the basic experience of *saṃsāra* is that of subject-object distinction, and, on the other hand, all other experiences in the state of *saṃsāra* can be reduced to that basic experience. Therefore, the imagined nature, namely the subject-object distinction, is real for all practical and conventional purposes. However, it is totally unreal except from a practical or conventional point of view. Hence, it is essentially of conventional values (*vyavahāra-ātmā*).

The other-dependent nature is that which is responsible for the creation of the conventional values (*vyavahartṛ*). In the final analysis it turns out to mean that the other-dependent nature is that which creates the imagined nature which is essentially of conventional values. What is it that creates the imagined nature along with its conventional values ? It is obviously the imagination of the unreal (*abhūta-parikalpa*) forms of subjectivity and objectivity. In other words, the imagined nature, as well as its conventional values, is the creation of the imagination of the unreal (*abhūta-parikalpa*). It has already been repeatedly pointed out that the other-dependent nature is the same as the imagination of the unreal (*abhūta-parikalpa*), which in turn consists essentially in imagining the unreal (or rather conventional) forms of subjectivity and objectivity. Thus the other-dependent nature is essentially the creator of the conventional values (*vyavahartṛ-ātmā*) of the imagined nature.

Now, the absolutely accomplished nature is free of all conventional values (*vyavahāra-samuccheda-svabhāva*), for, it is beyond the realm of the imagined distinction between subject and object, to which the conventional values are attached. That is, the absolutely accomplished nature is real in the absolute sense of the term, not merely from the conventional point of view.

The next two stanzas are concerned with the order in which one comes to realize the three natures.

[TSN. 24] First, the other-dependent nature,
Which is essentially the absence of duality
Is understood;

1. See, for example, above, pp. 12 ff.

Then, the unreal duality,
Namely, the duality that is mere imagination,
Is understood.[1]

Again, the emphasis is obviously on the falsity of duality between subject and object, and, therefore, the real knowledge of the three natures is obtained only when they are understood (*praviśyate*) in their non-dual, unitary, aspect. Accordingly, the meaning of the above stanza may be expressed as follows:

First, one has to understand
that the duality in which the other-dependent appears,
is unreal;
this will lead one to understand
that the subject-object duality,
which constitutes the imagined nature,
too, is unreal.

It may be recalled that in stanzas 11-16 Vasubandhu has been trying hard to establish that all three natures can be understood in terms of non-duality and unity. Now, therefore, it is easy for him to say that one aspiring for buddhahood should understand, or more literally, penetrate (*praviś*), the non-dual, unitary, aspect of the three natures. Perhaps it was to come to this point that he took pains first to explain how all three natures can be understood in terms of non-duality and unity.

Vasubandhu continues, referring to the realization of the absolutely accomplished nature :

[TSN. 25] Then is understood
The absolutely accomplished nature,
Which is positively the absence of duality,
For, that very nature is then said
To be both existing and non-existing.[2]

1. *Dvayā-bhāva-ātmaka-pūrvam para-tantraḥ praviśyate*
Tataḥ praviśyate tatra kalpa-mātram-asad-dvayam. TSN. 24
2. *Tato dvaya-abhāva-bhāvo niṣpanno'tra praviśyate*
Tathā hi-asau-eva tadā asti-nāsti-iti ca-ucyate. TSN. 25

It has already been explained how the absolutely accomplished nature is "positively the absence of duality" (*dvaya-abhāva-bhāva*) (see above, for example, TSN. 16), and how it is "both existing and non-existing" (*asti-nāsti-iti ca ucyate*) (see above TSN. 13).

The next stanza is a clear summary of the discussion on the three natures in terms of 'existence and non-existence' on the one hand, and 'duality and unity' on the other :

[TSN. 26] All these three natures
Depend for their definition
On [the concept of] non-duality;
For, [with reference to the imagined nature],
There is the unreality of duality,
[With reference to the other-dependent nature],
It is not in the dual form in which it appears,
And, [with reference to the absolutely accomplished nature],
It is by its nature the absence of that duality.[1]

In other words, all the three natures can be defined it terms of non-duality : the imagined nature is non-dual, because it consists of unreal / imaginary (*abhūta* / *parikalpita*) distinction between subject and object (*abhāvāt*) ; the other-dependent is non-dual, because it does not exist in the dual form in which it manifests itself (*a-tathā-bhāvāt*); the absolutely accomplished nature is non-dual, because it is by its very nature the absence of duality between subjectivity and objectivity (*tad-abhāva-svabhāvataḥ*).

6. How Real and Unreal Are the Three Natures ?

In the next four stanzas Vasubandhu makes use of an illustration to explain further the reality (or unreality) of the three natures. The illustration is as follows. A magician, for example, can by the working of certain incantations (*mantra-vaśāt*) make his magical power (*māyā*) appear (*khyāti*) in the form (*ākāra*) of an

1. *Trayo-api-ete svabhāvā hi advaya-ālamba-lakṣaṇāḥ*
Abhāvād-atathā-bhāvāt-tad abhāvasvabhāvataḥ. TSN. 26

elephant (hastī), which form he will subsequently superimpose on a piece of wood (*kāṣṭha*), so that the latter will be mistaken for an elephant. Similarly, says Vasubandhu, one can by the working of the 'unconscious' (*ālaya-vijñāna* or *mūla-vijñāna* or *mūla-citta*) make one's mental power, namely the power to imagine unreal forms (*asat-kalpa*), appear in the form of duality (*dvayātmanā*), which form one will subsequently superimpose on things, so that the latter will be mistaken for subjects and objects.

[TSN. 27] It is like the magical power,
Which by the working of incantations
Appears in the nature of an elephant;
There is altogether no elephant at all,
But only its form.[1]

The term, here translated as 'magical power' is *māyā-kṛtam*. Literally it would mean 'something made of (or by) magical power', or simply 'something illusory'. However, when it is compared to its counterpart '*asat-kalpa*' occurring in stanza 29, it becomes clear that by the term *māyā-kṛtam* Vasubandhu means nothing other than the magical power. He is comparing one's power to imagine unreal forms (*asat-kalpa*) with the magician's magical power to create unreal forms.

My traslation of the present stanza bagins with the phrase "It is like". The Sanskrit term for that is the correlative conjunction *yathā*. This latter term should have been accurately translated as "just as", although for convenience's sake I have translated it as "it is like". Therefore, I want to remind myself that the present stanza having begun with the correlative conjunction *yathā* ("just as...), is not complete, grammatically as well as conceptually, without its correlative stanza below (namely, TSN. 29) which begins with the correlative *tathā* ("so...). This latter stanza describes the appearance of subject-object duality exactly on the same lines as the appearance of the elephant described in the present stanza. I will discuss the details of this correlation later when I come to stanza 29. Before that there

1. *Māyā-kṛtam mantravaśāt-khyāti hasti-ātmanā yathā*
Ākāra-mātram tatra-asti hastī nāsti tu sarvathā. TSN. 27

is one more stanza to be analyzed, in which Vasubandhu gives an interpretation of the above illustration :

[TSN. 28] The elephant stands for the imagined nature,
Its form for the other-dependent nature,
And, that which remains when the elephant has been negated,
Stands for the absolutely accomplished nature.[1]

The magical elephant, as its reality is totally imaginary, is of imagined nature (*svabhāvaḥ kalpitaḥ*); its form (*ākṛti*), as it depends on magical power and incantation, is of other-dependent nature; when the imaginary elephant has been negated one sees the real thing, for example, a piece of wood upon which the form of the elephant was superimposed; this real thing, as it is absolutely free of all mental constructions, stands for the absolutely accomplished nature.

The next stanza, to which I referred above as the correlative of TSN. 27, describes the appearance of subject-object reality on the same lines as the appearance of the magical elephant :

[TSN. 29] So, the imagination of the unreal
By the working of the basic thought
Appears in the nature of duality;
There is altogether no duality at all,
But only its form.[2]

Just as (*yathā*) the magical power appears in the nature of an elephant described above in TSN. 27, so (*tathā*) the imagination of the unreal (*asat-kalpa*, which is the same as the creative mind having the power to imagine unreal forms), by the working of basic thought (*mūlacitta*, i.e., *ālaya-vijñāna* or *mūlavijñāna*), appears (*khyāti*) in the nature of duality (*dvaya-ātmanā*); this duality is totally non-existent (*dvayam atyanto nāsti*), but is only a mental form (*tatra-asti-ākṛti-mātrakam*), just as the magical elephant

1. *Svabhāvaḥ kalpito hastī para-tantras-tad-ākṛtiḥ*
Yas-tatra hasti-abhāvo'sau pariniṣpanna iṣyate. TSN. 28

2. *Asat-kalpas-tathā khyāti mūla-cittād-dvaya-ātmanā*
Dvayam-atyanto nāsti tatra-asti-ākṛti-mātrakam. TSN. 29

being totally non-existent (*hasti nāsti tu sarvathā*) is only mental (or rather magical) form. To make the correspondence between TSN. 27 and 29 clear, I present them side by side as follows:

TSN. 27:	TSN. 29:
Just as the magical power	So the imagination of the unreal
(*yathā māyā-kṛtam*)	(*tathā asat-kalpaḥ*)
By the working of incantations	By the working of the basic thought
(*mantra-vaśāt*)	(*mūla-cittāt*)
Appears in the nature of an elephant,	Appears in the nature of duality;
(*khyāti hasti-ātmanā*);	(*khyāti dvaya-ātmanā*);
There is altogether no elephant,	There is altogether no duality,
(*hasti nāsti tu tatra sarvathā*),	(*dvayam atyanto nāsti tatra*),
But only its [mental] form.	But only its [mental] form.
(*ākāra-mātram tatra-asti*).	(*asti-ākṛti-mātrakam*).

This parallel presentation of these two stanzas brings out the points of comparison between the two cases at issue. I will return to those points after discussing the next stanza in which Vasubandhu himself makes a list, so to say, of those points:

[TSN. 30] The basic consciousness is like the incantations,
Suchness is like the piece of wood,
The [subject-object] discrimination is like the form of the elephant.
And the duality is like the elephant.[1]

That is, just as the incantations in the case of magic operate as the efficient cause in producing the magical elephant, so does the basic consciousness (*mūla-vijñānam*) in producing the duality between subject and object; just as the piece of wood (*kāṣṭha*) in the case of magic is what remains when all mental constructions are removed, so the same applies to the case of the suchness (*tathatā*); just as the form of the elephant in the case of magic

1. *Mantravan-mūlavijñānam kāṣṭhavat-tathatā matā*
Hasti-ākāravad-eṣṭavyo vikalpo hastivad-dvayam. TSN. 30

is only a mental form (or construction), so is the subject-object discrimination (*vikalpa*); just as the elephant in the case of magic is altogether unreal, so is the subject-object duality (*dvayam*) in ordinary experience. Now it may be useful to make a diagram of all the points of comparison between the instances of the magically appearing elephant on the one hand, and the phenomenally appearing subject-object duality on the other, as they come out of the four stanzas above :

	magical appearance of elephent	phenomenal appearance of subject-object duality	
mantra (incantation)	*mūlacitta/ ālayavijñāna/ mūlavijñāna* (unconscious)		(the efficient source)
	māyā (magical power)	*asatkalpa/ abhūta-parikalpa* (creative imagination/ mind)	(the material source)
PARATANTRA	*hasti-ātmanā/ hasti-ākāra/ hasti-ākṛti* (mental form, or construction, of elephant)	*dvaya-ātmanā/ vikalpa* (mental form or construction, of subject-object duality)	(the resultant form)
PARIKALPITA	*hasti* (magically manifested elephant)	*dvaya* (phenomenally manifested duality between subject and object)	

	magical appearance of elephant	phenomenal appearance of subect-object duality
PARINIṢPANNA	*hasti-abhāva/ kāṣṭha* (piece of wood)	*dvaya-abhāva/ tathatā* (suchness)

The picture of the three natures emerging from the above analysis is as follows. What is precisely described as the other-dependent nature (*para-tantra-svabhāva*) is the mental form (*ākāra* or *ākṛti*, call it mental construction or concept or idea) of the subject-object duality (*vikalpa* or *dvaya-ātmatā*). It is a transformed mode (*pariṇāma*) of the mind,[1] which is the faculty of imagining the unreal forms of subjectivity and objectivity (*asat-kalpa* or *abhūta-parikalpa*). Seeds of these forms are already there embedded in the 'unconscious' (*ālaya-vijñāna*). Thus the three terms, *ālaya-vijñāna*, *abhūta-parikalpa* and *vikalpa*, are not quite the same, but are closely interconnected with each other. One may roughly and safely say that although strictly speaking *para-tantra-svabhāva* refers only to the *ākāra* of *vikalpa* (the conceptual form of the discrimination between subject and object), in a less strict sense it covers whatever is meant by 'mind' in the Western thought. It can sometimes mean the very disposition of an individual in the state of *saṃsāra*, whereby he is bound to discriminate between subject and object; sometimes it can mean the very mental act of discriminating (*vikalpa*) between subject and object; sometimes it can mean strictly the metal conception (*ākāra*) of subject-object duality (*vikalpa*).[2] The imagined nature

1. See below, pp. 128 ff

2. It may be recalled that MV. has a different version of the inter-relation between the three terms, *ālaya-vijñāna*, *abhūta-parikalpa* and *vikalpa*. There *abhūta-parikalpa* is described on the one hand as *grāhya-grāhaka-vikalpa* (MVKB. I. 2), and, on the other, as *para-tantra-svabhāva* (MVKB. I. 6). Again, MV. I. 9-10 gives the impression that *ālaya-vijñāna* is a subdivision of *abhūta-parikalpa*.

refers to a thing as it is experienced. In the case of magic, the piece of wood experienced under the aspect of an elephant illustrated the imagined nature. Strictly speaking, here too, it is the elephant so experienced that is described as the imagined nature (*svabhāvaḥ kalpito hasti*, TSN. 28). Similarly, in the ordinary experience things experienced under the aspects of subjects and objects are in a less accurate sense the imagined nature, and the duality (*dvayam*) between subjectivity and objectivity so experienced is in the strict sense the imagined nature (*hastivad-dvayam*).

Here it may be noted that the distinction between the other-dependent nature and the imagined nature is so narrow that it is difficult to put it in so many words. The other-dependent nature refers to the subject-object distinction as a mental form (*ākāra*), a concept, an idea, a mental reality. The imagined nature refers to the same distinction as an extra-mental structure in which things are believed to exist. In other words, the subject-object distinction considered as an abstract concept or form (*ākāra*) is other-dependent nature, while the same distinction considered as, or mistaken for, an extra-mental dimension of things is imagined nature. This is what the distinction between *hasti-ākṛti* and *hasti* mentioned in the stanza suggests: *hasti-ākṛti* says Vasubandhu, stands for the other-dependent nature, while *hastī* stands for the imagined nature.[1]

That the term *ākāra* stands for the conceptual form in which something is perceived, has already been explained elsewhere.[2]

The absolutely accomplished nature is the thing as such (*tathatā*), free of the subject-object-duality structure that was superimposed on it. It is like the piece of wood underlying the magical appearance of the elephant. Just as once the superimposed form of the elephant is removed the piece of wood reveals itself, so once the superimposed form of subject-object duality is removed the thing as such (*tathatā*) reveals itself. Just as the negation of the superimposed form of the elephent (***hasti-abhāva***) resuls in the revelation of the real thing, namely the piece of wood,

1. *Svabhāaḥ kalpito hastī para-tantras-tad-ākṛtiḥ*. TSN. 28
2. See above, pp. 51ff

so the negation of subject-object duality (*dvaya-abhāva*) reveals the thing in itself, which is the absolutely accomplished nature. As MVKB clearly puts it, the absolutely accomplished nature is the negation of the grasper-graspable duality.[1]

Now there is an important question calling for an answer : in what relation does the absolutely accomplished nature stand to the imagined ? Or, in what relation does the thing as such (*tathatā*, suchness) stand to the thing as empirically perceived ? Negatively, the relation in which the absolutely accomplished nature stands to the imagined nature is not like that in which the soul stands to the body in Western tradition. For, in the latter case both soul and body are considered to be real, while in the former case only the absolutely accomplished nature is considered real, the imagined nature being totally-unreal (*nāsti-tu sarvathā*, TSN. 27; *atyanto nāsti*, TSN. 28). The distinction between body and soul is considered to be real or extra-mental; while that between the imagined nature and the absolutely accomplished nature is only a matter of understanding/misunderstanding. To talk about the imagined nature and the absolutely accomplished nature does not imply that they are two realities; on the contrary there is only one reality viewed from two different angles : viewed as endowed with subject-object forms, it is called imagined nature, and viewed in itself (i.e. as such), it is called the absolutely accomplished nature. Thus the distinction between those two natures depends on the way in which one looks at a thing; while the distinction between body and soul is never thought to depend on the perceiver.

Kant's distinction between noumenon and phenomenon seems to be closer to the distinction between the absolutely accomplished nature and the imagined nature. For Kant noumenon is the thing-in-itself, unqualified by any category of experience, and, therefore, even beyond the reach of experience; while phenomenon is the thing as it appears to the perceiver, necessarily qualified by the categories of experience superimposed by the perceiver. Similarly, the absolutely accomplished nature is the thing as such, unqualified by the mental forms of subjectivity

1. *Grāhya-grāhaka-abhāvaḥ pariniṣpannaḥ svabhāvaḥ*. MVKB. I. 6

and objectivity, the only categories of experience recognized by Vasubandhu, and, therefore also beyond the reach of ordinary, saṃsāric, experience; while the imagined nature is the thing as it appears to the ordinary perceiver, necessarily qualified by the categories of subjectivity and objectivity superimposed by the perceiver. Both for Kant as well as Vasubandhu, the mode in which a thing is experienced, depends on the perceiver, who of necessity imposes his subjective forms on the thing-in-itself. A difference between Kant's position and that of Vasubandhu is this : according to the former one never comes to realize the noumenon, the thing-in-itself, while according to the latter one definitely comes to realize the absolutely accomplished nature in the state of enlightenment (*Buddhānām gocaraḥ*, Viṃś. 21).

7. Towards the Realization of the Reality

The rest of the treatise deals with more practical aspects of the doctrine of three natures.

> [TSN. 31] In comprehending the truth of things
> All three definitions have to be taken together,
> [Although methods of] knowledge, rejection and attainment
> Are to be employed respectively.[1]

First of all, the three definitions referred to here are the three natures, namely the imagined, the other-dependent and the absolutely accomplished. Then, the term translated here as 'truth of things' is *artha-sattva*. Discussing the concept of *mūla-tattva* in MV. III I have explained why the term *tattva* has to be understood as meaning 'truth'.[2] Further, in the same chapter it was said that the basic truth about things is that they take on three natures, namely the imagined, the other-dependent and the absolutely accomplished.[3] Or, more precisely, "the threefold nature is the basic truth about things."[4] This makes the former

1. *Artha-tattva-prativedhe yugapal-lakṣaṇa-trayam*
Parijñā ca prahāṇam-ca prāptiś-ca-iṣṭā yathā-kramam. TSN. 31
2. See above, pp. 19ff
3. *Tatra mūla-tattvam svabhāvas-trividhaḥ, parikalpitaḥ para-tantraḥ pariniṣpannaś-ca*. MVK. and MVKB. III. 3
4. Ibid.

half of the present stanza intelligible. In other words, if the three natures are the basic truth about things, then it is obvious that to understand the truth about things, one has to take all those three natures together. Or, rather, as the stanza has it, the three-fold definition should be taken together in order to comprehend the truth of things.

However, in dealing with the three natures one's approach has to differ from nature to nature. In the case of the imagined nature one must acquire a correct knowledge (*parijñā*) of it, for it is sheer ignorance that makes one believe that there is such a nature. In the case of the other-dependent nature one must reject/destroy/stop it; as already said, the other-dependent nature is essentially the act of imagining the subject-object duality, or the very mental imagination of such duality; the mental act or imagination should be stopped, so that one can be free of the subject-object idiosyncrasy, and of the consequent *saṃsāra*; thus the other-dependent nature should be approached by rejecting it or destroying it or stopping (*prahāṇa*) it. In the case of the absolutely accomplished nature one must aim at attaining it, or rather realizing it (*prāpti*), for attaining the absolutely accomplished nature constitutes the state of enlightenment or *nirvāṇa*. Thus, knowledge (*parijñā*), rejection (*prahāṇa*) and attainment (*prāpti*) are respectively the methods one should employ in approaching the three natures.

The next stanza is a further explanation of the three concepts of *parijñā*, *prahāṇa* and *prāpti* :

[TSN. 32] There, knowledge is non-perception,
Rejection/destruction is non-appearance,
Attainment, effect by perception,
Is direct realization.[1]

Correct knowledge (*parijñā*) of the imagined nature would mean the non-perception (*anupalambha*) of subject-object duality, which constituted the imagined nature. That *anupalambha*

1. *Parijñā anupalambho'tra hānir-akhyānam-iṣyate*
Upalambha-nimittā tu prāptiḥ sākṣāt-kriyā-api sā. TSN. 32

refers to the non-perception of subject-object duality is clearly said in the next stanza.[1] That is, as a result of the correct understanding of the imagined nature one will cease to perceive, or rather to believe in, the subject-object duality. Now, the rejection or destruction (*hāniḥ*) of the other-dependent nature means the non-appearance (*akhyāna*) of the mental forms of subjectivity and objectivity (*dvaya-ākāro vigacchati* as the next stanza puts it). It may be remembered that right in the beginning of this treatise it was said that the other-dependent nature is that which appears in the form of subject-object duality.[2] This appearance of the other-dependent nature has to be made to cease, and that is done by stopping the imagination of the unreal subject-object duality (*asat-kalpa* or *abhūta-parikalpa*). Finally, attainment of the absolutely accomplished nature means the direct realization (*sākṣāt-kriyā*) of that nature. This is effected by perception (*upalambha-nimittā*), as the text says. Perception of what ? It means the perception that there is no subject-object duality. Or it may be a reference to MCK. I. 7 which says that 'the perception (*upalabdhi*) that there is only mental representations will lead to the non-perception (*anupalabdhi*) of objectivity, which in turn will lead to the non-perception of subjectivity as well, thus finally effecting the realization of the absolutely accomplished, non-dual, nature.'[3] Here the realization of the absolutely accomplished nature is ultimately effected by the perception (*upalambha-nimittā*) that there is no subject-object duality.

As already suggested, the next stanza is providing a clearer explanation of the previous one :

[TSN. 33] By the non-perception of duality
The form of duality disappears;
The non-duality resulting from its disappearance
Is then attained.[4]

1. *Dvayasya-anupalambhena*... TSN. 33
2. *Yat-khyāti para-tantro'sau. TSN.* 2; *Katham khyāti? dvaya-ātmanā.* TSN. 4
3. *Upalabdhim samāśritya nopalabdhiḥ prajāyate*
Nopalabdhim samāśritya nopalabdhiḥ prajāyate. MVK. I. 7
Read it along with Vasubandhu's *bhāṣya*, and my analysis above, pp. 61ff
4. *Dvayasya-anupalambhena dvaya-ākāro vigacchati*
Vigamāt-tasya niṣpanno dvaya-abhāvo'dhigamyate. TSN. 33

From this stanza it is now clear that (i) the non-perception (*anupalambha*) mentioned in the previous stanza means the non-perception of duality (*dvayasya-anupalambha*), (*ii*) the non-perception (*akhyāna*) mentioned in the previous stanza means the disappearance of the form of duality (*dvaya-ākāro vigacchati*), meaning the cessation of the appearance of the mental forms of subjectivity and objectivity, and that (iii) the direct realization (*sākṣāt-kriyā*) mentioned in the previous stanza means the attainment of the state of non-duality (*dvaya-abbāvo' dhigamyate*), namely the absolutely accomplished nature.

A clear distinction between duality (*dvaya*) and the form of duality (*dvaya-ākāra*), made also in this stanza, is worth noticing. I have already explained the importance of this distinction in understanding the distinction between the imagined nature and the other-dependent nature.[1]

Vasubandhu once again refers to the example of the magical appearance of the elephant to show that the way it disappears revealing the real piece of wood behind it exemplifies the process by which the subject-object illusion is undone, and the absolutely accomplished nature is realized :

[TSN. 34] It is just as the case of magic,
In which the non-perception of the elephant,
The disappearance of its form, and the perception of the piece of wood
Take place all at once.[2]

Vasubandhu is hinting that, although the non-perception of duality, the disappearance of the form of duality, and realization of the absolutely accomplished nature are theoretically distinguishable processes, in actuality they take place all at once instantaneously. Further,

1. See above, p. 117.
2. *Hastino'nupalambhaś-ca vigamaś-ca tad-ākṛteḥ*
Upalambhaś-ca kāṣṭhasya māyāyām yugapad-yathā. TSN. 34

Here the term *māyāyām* I have translated as 'in the case of magic'.

[TSN. 35] The attainment of liberation becomes effortless
By getting rid of misunderstanding,
Intellectually seeing the meaninglessness,
And following the three-fold knowledge.[1]

Here, too, the three points advocated as means of easily (*ayatnataḥ*) attaining liberation (*mokṣāpatti*) are probably to be taken with reference to the three natures. Thus, 'getting rid of misunderstanding' will mean 'getting rid of misunderstanding about the imagined nature'. The reality of the imagined nature rests on one's misunderstanding that the subject-object duality is real in its own right. Therefore one's first step towards liberation has to be the getting rid of this misunderstanding. Here the term translated as misunderstanding is *viruddha-dhi*. Its literal translation would have been 'opposite understanding' or 'contrary thought'. However, as the term 'misunderstanding' sounds more fitting in the context, I have preferred it.

'Intellectually seeing the meaninglessness' (*buddhyā vaiyyarthya-darśana*) has to be understood with reference to the other-dependent nature, which is meaningless in the sense that being just the mental forms of subjectivity and objectivity it has no reality other than mental. In one of the Tibetan versions the term *vaiyyarthya* is replaced by *nairātmya*, which suggests that one must 'intellectually see the non-substantiality' of the other-dependent nature. This latter version is quite understandable, because the forms of subjectivity and objectivity, which are the constituents of the other-dependent nature, are literally non-substantial (*nairātmya*).

Finally 'following the threefold knowledge' (*jñānatraya-anuvṛtti*) applies to the absolutely accomplished nature. The three knowledges are *cintā-mayā-paññā*, *suta-mayā-paññā* and *bhāvanā mayā-paññā* mentioned in *Digha Nikāya* (33) and *Visuddhi Magga* (XIV).[2]

The next stanza is just a slightly different, but clearer, version

1. *Viruddha-dhī-vāraṇatvād buddhyā vaiyyarthya-darśanāt*
Jñāna-traya-anuvṛtteś-ca mokṣa-āpattir-ayatnataḥ. TSN. 35

2. See, Nyanatiloka, *Buddhist Dictionary : Manual of Buddhist Terms and Doctrines*, rev. and enl. ed., (Colombo : Frewin and Co., Ltd., 1972) p. 122.

of MVK. I.7,[1] and includes what Vasubandhu said there in interpretation of that verse.

[TSN. 36] Through the perception
That there is only thought,
There arises the non-perception of knowable things;
Through the non-perception of knowable things,
There arises the non-perception of thought, too.[2]

This is exactly what Vasubandhu said in interpretation of MVK. I. 7: "Depending upon the perception that there are only representations of consciousness, there arises the non-perception of knowable things. Depending upon the non-perception of knowable things, there arises the non-perception of mere representations of consciousness, too".[3] The meaning of this text, and for that matter also of the present stanza, I have already explained above, which in summary is as follows : the realization that the objects of one's experience are only the representations of one's own consciousness, makes one realize that one does not perceive real, knowable objects, or rather that what one comes to know are not real objects, but only one's own mental representations. This realization that one's experience does not reach real objects, makes one realize that one is no more a knowing subject or an experiencer, and that therefore even the representations of one's own consciousness make no sense. Thus, in short, one no more entertains the belief in the objectivity of things, nor in the subjectivity of oneself. As Sthiramati says, " In the

1. Quoted above on page 121, note 3

2. *Citta-mātra-upalambhena jñeya-artha-artha-anupalambhatā*
Jñeya-artha anupalambhena syāc-citta-anupalambhatā. TSN. 36

3. *Vijñapti-mātropalabdhim niśritya-artha-anupalabdhir-jāyate. Artha-anupalabdhim niśritya vijñapti-mātrasya-api-anupalabdhir-jāyate. Evam-asal-lakṣaṇam grāhya-rāhakayoḥ praviśati.* MVKB. I. 7

absence of graspable objects, a grasping subject makes no sense. For, the conception of a grasping subject is relative to that of a graspable object. . . .For, the graspable and the grasper are never independent of each other."[1]

Thus there is the non-perception of subjectivity and objectivity (*dvayor-anupalambhaḥ*). What of it ? Vasubandhu says :

> [TSN. 37] From the non-perception of duality
> There arises the perception of the essence of reality;
> From the perception of the essence of reality
> There arises the perception of unlimitedness.[2]

From the non-perception of duality (*dvaya-anupalambhena*), that is, once the idiosyncrasy for subject-object duality is destroyed, one comes to realize the essence of reality (*dharma-dhātu*). This realization of reality will reveal the unlimitedness (*vibhutva*) of things. The term *vibhutva* is usually employed to mean 'infinity', or 'unlimitedness' or 'all-pervasiveness'.[3] In the present context it may mean 'the state unlimited by subject-object categories'. Therefore, "perception of unlimitedness" (*vibhutva-upalambhatā*) can very well be taken to mean the perception that things, including oneself, are beyond subject-object considerations, and that, therefore, one should no more remain bound by such considerations.

Thus, finally,

> [TSN. 38] The wise man, having perceived the unlimitedness,

1. *Na grāhya-abhāve grāhakatvam yujyate. Grāhyam-apekṣya tadgrāhakasya vyavasthāpanāt . . . grāhya-grāhakayoḥ paraspara-nirapekṣatvāt.* MVKBT I. 7

2. *Dvayor-anupalambhena dharma-dhātu-upalambhatā*
Dharma-dhātu-upalambhena syād-vibhutva-upalambhatā. TSN. 37

3. For example *Nyāya-sūtra* defines *vibhutva* as *Sarva-mūrtta-dravya-saṃyogitvam vibhutvam.*

And seeing the meaning of oneself and others,
Attains the unsurpassed enlightenment,
Which is in the nature of the three bodies.[1]

Thus everybody, not only Gautama the Buddha, if he only realizes the voidness (*śūnyatā*) of subjebt-object duality, can attain to the height of enlightenment (*anuttarām bodhim*) including the triple-body characteristics.

1. *Upalabdha-vibhutvaś-ca sva-para-artha-prasiddhitaḥ*
Prāpnoti-anuttarām bodhim dhīmān kāya-traya-ātmikām. TSN. 38

Chapter Four

A TREATISE IN THIRTY STANZAS (*TRIṂŚATIKĀ*)

1. Introduction

Triṃśatikā, a treatise in thirty stanzas, is the epitome of Vasubandhu's view of life. To be sure, it is an analysis of consciousness throughout. Traditionally it is interpreted as dealing with the process of the evolution of the world from consciousness.[1] I cannot agree with that interpretation, though. Instead I am suggesting that this text should be understood as an investigation into the origin, contents and operation of an *individual* consciousness. Far from being an analysis of the world process, it is an attempt to explain the experience of an individual in the state of *saṃsāra*, and then to suggest a way out of it. It is an analysis of mind, not of the cosmos; again, it is an analysis of the individual mind, not of any cosmic mind. It is the individual mind that is said to be subject to evolution, not the world. This evolution of mind is said to result in the construction of a world-picture. But that does not imply that there is no real world apart from this mentally constructed (*parikalpita*) world-picture.

The question before the author of *Triṃśatikā*, therefore, is, 'what is consciousness made of?', or 'what are the contents of

1. For example, P. T. Raju says, "The 'Trimsatika' deals with the process of the evolution of the world, the nature of Buddha, and so forth". (*Idealistic Thought of India*, [George Allen and Unwin Ltd., 1953; reprinted with the subtitle "Vedanta and Buddhism in the Light of Western Idealism", New York: Johnson Reprint Corporation, 1973], p. 269). Later, on the same page, apparently referring again to *Triṃśatikā*, he says, "Vasubandhu maintains that the world is due to the *pariṇāma* or transformation of the pure Vijnana".

consciousness ?', or 'what is the consciousness of?', or 'what is it that the consciousness grasps ?' On the contrary, the question, 'what is the world ?', never occurs to him. In other words, the reality of the world *as such* is never the point at issue, but only in so far as it is grasped by consciousness. With this point in mind I shall now make a detailed analysis of the text under reference.

2. Ātman and Dharma as Subjectivity and Objectivity

The text opens with the statement that the various usages (*upacāra*) of the terms *ātman* and *dharma* refer to the transformations (*pariṇāma*) of consciousness (*vijñāna*) :

[Trims. 1] Various indeed are the usages
Of the terms *ātman* and *dharma* :
Thay [all] refer
To the transformations of consciousness;[1]

The first remark to be made about this statement is that the terms *ātman* and *dharma* stand respectively for the categories of subjectivity and objectivity. It has already been made clear that subjectivity and objectivity (*grāhakatva* and *grāhyatva*) are the basic categories of thought recognized by the Yogācārins. All other categories can be classified under them. In other words, all imaginable categories present themselves to the mind either as subjects or as objects.[2] Everything that presents itself as a subject of experience is referred to in the present stanza as *ātman*, and everything that presents itself as an object of experience is referred to as *dharma*. Even a superficial reading of the text will confirm this observation of mine. It is obvious, first of all, that neither *ātman* nor *dharma* is meant in its ordinary sense. Further, commenting on those terms Sthiramati says, "The usages

1. *Ātma-dharma-upacāro hi vividho yaḥ pravartate*
Vijñāna-pariṇāmo'sau...Triṃś. 1

2. Śaṅkara opens his *Brahma-sūtra-bhāṣya* with a similar classification of categories under the terms *yuṣmat* and *asmat* (=thou and I), the former standing for objectivity and the latter for subjectivity (see his introduction to *Brahma-sūtra-bhāṣya*).

of the term *ātman* include *ātman, jiva, jantu, manuja, māṇava* etc., and those of *dharma* include *skandha, dhātu, āyatana, rūpa, vedanā, sañjñā, saṃskāra, vijñāna* etc."[1] This grouping implies that whatever can become the subject of some sort of experience is denoted by *ātman*, and that whatever can become the object of some sort of experience, is denoted by *dharma*. This does not mean that one and the same being cannot become both subject and object of experience. For example, I am obviously the subject of so many experiences. But I am also the object of many experiences of other people. But my subjectivity and objectivity refer to two different aspects of my being : I become the subject of experience only under the aspect of a living (*jiva*), sentient (*jantu*), human (*manuja*) etc. being. On the other hand, to become a subject of experience it is not enough for me to be just a bundle of elements (*skandha* or *dhātu*) or of sense-data (*āyatana* etc.). On the contrary, I become the object of experience only under the aspect of a bundle of elements (*skandha* or *dhātu*) or of sense-data (*āyatana* etc.). That is, although I am a living, sentient, human being, nobody is able to experience me as such. As an object of experience I am only a bundle of elements or sense-data, and as such I become the object of touch, sight, taste and hearing. On the other hand, that I am a living, sentient human being is only inferred by others, it is not experienced by them. Thus, the above quoted classification of categories into *ātman* and *dharma* is evidently based on what is capable of becoming a subject or object of experience : anything that can become a subject of experience is an *ātman*, and anything that can become an object of experience is a *dharma*. Or rather, the terms *ātman* and *dharma* stand for two aspects, namely subjectivity and objectivity respectively, in which things *appear* in one's experience. Things just appear in those aspects, because the latter are, as it shall be explained later, mere mental constructions (*parikalpa*) or transformations of consciousness (*vijñāna pariṇāma*).

1. *Ātmā jīvo jantur-manujo māṇava iti-evam-ādika ātma-upacāraḥ. Skandha dhātava āyatanāni rūpam vedanā sañjñā saṃskāra vijñānam-iti-evam-ādiko dharma-upacāraḥ*. Triṃś. Bh. 1.

There is still another reason why I feel that the terms *ātman* and *dharma* should be understood as standing for subjectivity and objectivity. It is undeniable that Vasubandhu has really meant to bring all imaginable concepts under the two terms : *ātman* and *dharma*. It should be particularly noted that he mentions these two, and only these two, terms. They have, however, various usages, as he says. What are those usages ? Ordinarily 'various usages of a term' means that it is employed in different *senses*. But that is not what Vasubandhu means by 'various usages'. For him different usages of *ātman* and *dharma* mean different *terms* standing for what is meant by *ātman* and *dharma*. What are these terms ? I have quoted above a list of some of them enumerated by Sthiramati.[1] In fact Vasubandhu himself has made a long list of such terms in the subsequent stanzas. His list covers all imaginable terms, and refers to all imaginable concepts. All of them, he says, are just transformations (*pariṇāma*) of consciousness (*vijñāna*), and in the final analysis come under the two categories: *ātman* and *dharma*. I will return to this point later while analysing some of the next stanzas. The question in which I am interested at the moment is what made Vasubandhu choose *ātman* and *dharma* to represent all the terms / concepts referring to experience. The only possible answer I can imagine is that according to Vasubandhu *ātman* and *dharma* stand for two concepts which adequately explain *all* kinds of experience. And from the previous chapters of this study it is more than clear that the two concepts with which Vasubandhu explains *all* kinds of experience are those of *grāhya* and *grāhaka* (the graspable and grasper). Therefore it can be reasonably concluded that in the present context Vasubandhu is replacing *grāhya* and *grāhaka* with *dharma* and *ātman*. It may be noted that even in ordinary langauge *ātman* is generally associated with the idea of an enjoyer, experiencer or grasper. It is also interesting to note that even before Vasubandhu on certain occasions the term *dharma* has been used to mean 'object' of experience. Classical examples of such usages occur in phrases like *dhammāyatana*, meaning the *object* perceived by *manāyatana*, and *dhammadhātu*, meaning the *object* perceived by *manodhātu*. Hence using the terms *ātman* and *dharma*

1. See above note 1 on page 129.

to mean *subject* and *object* of experience respectively, Vasubandhu is not really deviating from tradition.

Again, that Vasubandhu is purposefully referring to the subjectivity and objectivity of experience is clear also from the fact that he mentions both *ātman* and *dharma*, and not just one of them, for example, *dharma*. On the contrary, had he wanted to refer just to *all* concepts standing for the transformations of consciousness, without bringing in their distinction between subjectivity and objectivity, he could very well have done so by mentioning just one term, namely *dharma*. For, as Stcherbatsky's analysis testifies,[1] *dharma* is a term that can be used for each and every concept / element in Buddhism. Therefore, if Vasubandhu is particular to mention *both ātman* and *dharma*, and not just the latter, it means that he is referring not only to all concepts, but also to their distinction as subjective and objective with reference to experience. Hence my conclusion : the terms *ātman* and *dharma* in the first stanza of *Triṃśatikā* stands respectively for subjectivity (*grāhakatva*) and objectivity (*grāhyatva*).

Another point I want to emphasize is that what Vasubandhu refers to as 'transformations' (*pariṇāma*), are not any *thing* (*padārtha*), but only the *usages* (*upacāra*) of the terms *ātman* and *dharma*, or rather the concepts expressed by such usages. The term *upacāra*, which I have translated as 'usage', is never used in Sanskrit or other Indian languages with reference to things (*padārtha*) or substances (*dravya*). Etymologically this term means 'conventional behaviour' (*upacāra*), and is very often used with reference to social and linguistic behavioural patterns. For example, *upacāra* is very commonly used to mean 'good manners', and the phrase *ācāra-upacāra* is still more commonly used to mean 'the respect and manners' proper for guests, teachers, etc. Similarly, in linguistic contexts, *upacāra* means 'behaviour of words' or 'usage' of words, or 'employment' of words;[2] and more generally it means secondary or figurative or

1. He has made an analysis of the term *dharma* in his *The Central Conception of Buddhism and the Meaning of the Word 'Dharma'*, 2nd ed., (Calcutta: Susil Gupta (India) Ltd., 1956).

2. For example, V. S. Apte, *The Practical Sanskrit English Dictionary*, 3rd rev. enl. ed., (Delhi, Varanasi, Patna: Motilal Banarsidass, 1965), p. 283 quotes from *Rāmāyaṇa*: *vākyopacāre kuśala*, and translates it as 'skilled in the employment of words'.

metaphorical use or application of words as opposed to their primary or literal (*mukhya*) use or application.[1] F. Edgerton in his *Buddhist Hybrid Sanskrit Dictionary* has pointed out two unusual meanings of *upacāra* rarely occurring in Buddhist writings. They are (1) environs, neighbourhood; and (2) access. Now, from the above discussion one arrives at four meanings for the term *upacāra* : (i) social manners, (ii) (secondary) use of terms, (iii) environs, and (iv) access.[2] Of them the last two —environs and access—may be said to be referring to 'things' (*padārtha*) or 'substances' (*dravya*). But they would make no sense when associated with the terms *ātman* and *dharma*, and, therefore, do not fit into the context of *Triṃśatikā*.[3] The first meaning, i.e., social manners, too, has nothing to do with the context, and, therefore, can be left out of consideration. Thus, in the end there is only one meaning of the term *upacāra* that is relevant to the context, and that is '(secondary) use of terms'. Hence my translation of *upacāra* as 'usage'. Thus '*ātma-dharma-upacāra*' in the text means 'the usage of the terms *ātman* and *dharma*'.

What, therefore, could be the implication that Vasubandhu had in mind when he said that 'the various usages of the terms *ātman* and *dharma* are all transformations (*pariṇāma*) of *vijñāna* (consciousness)' ? As such his words sound meaningless. For, neither words nor their usages could possibly be transformations of consciousness. The only way, therefore, to make sense of his statement is to say that for him 'the various usages of the term *ātman* and *dharma*' means 'the various concepts implying *ātman* and *dharma*'.[4] Therefore, in the final analysis of Vasubandhu *upacāra* means "concepts"[5] and the final meaning of the opening statement

1. For examples, see Ibid.

2. F. Edgerton, *Buddhist Hybrid Sanskrit Dictionary*, Vol. II, (New Haven: Yale University Press, 1953, reprint ed., Delhi, Varanasi, Patna : Motilal Banarsidass 1972), p. 134.

3. Or, perhaps, 'environs of *ātman* and *dharma*' would mean secondary uses of those terms, which then would not be different from meaning (ii).

4. To put it clearly, they are concepts all of which imply what *ātman* and *dharma* stand for, namely subjectivity and objectivity, and, therefore, are not just concepts of *ātman* and *dharma*.

5. In fact Wei Tat has translated '*ātma-dharma-upacāra*' as "Concepts of Atman and dharmas". (See Hsüan-tsang, *The Doctrine of Mere-Consciousness*, trans. Wei Tat [Hong Kong: 1973] p. LVII)

of *Triṃśatikā* turns out to be : "The various concepts implying *ātman* and *dharma* are all transformations of consciousness". That is, what is said to be the transformation of consciousness is not *things* existing outside consciousness, but *concepts* apart from which there can be no consciousness itself. Such concepts can be grouped under two terms, namely *ātman* and *dharma*, the former standing for subjectivity and the latter for objectivity. A list of such concepts, part of which I have already quoted above from Sthiramati,[1] will eventually emerge in the course of this analysis.

The term *pariṇāma*, which I have translated as 'transformation' too, needs an explanation. It should be remembered that the Indian thinkers do make a distinction between *pariṇāma* and *vivartta*, the latter term meaning 'unfolding'. For example, *brahma-pariṇāma-vāda* means the theory which says that Brahma transforms *itself* into the world of multiplicity, so that the latter (i.e. the transformations) is not essentially different from Brahma itself; on the other hand *brahma-vivartta-vāda* means the theory which says that itself remaining unchanged Brahma just makes the world of multiplicity *appear*, so that what thus appears is mere illusion and, therefore, unreal.[2] Thus *pariṇāma* implies transformation of a substratum into different modes of existence, while *vivartta* implies making some illusions *appear*. Thus by *vijñāna-pariṇāma* Vasubandhu means that *vijñāna* (= consciousness) transforms *itself* into different modes of existence, which are not essentially different from *vijñāna* itself. Such transformations of *vijñāna* are what one calls concepts. In other words, concepts being transformations of *vijñāna*, are not essentially different from it. Therefore in the final analysis, as I have already said, consciousness has no existence apart from its tranformations, namely concepts.

About the term *vijñāna* I need only to recall what has been already said in a previous chapter of this study, namely that it does not denote the absolutely accomplished nature (*pariniṣpanna-*

1. See above note 1 on page 129.

2. For a treatment of this distinction see M. Hiriyanna, *Outlines of Indian Philosophy*, (London: George Allen and Unwin, Ltd., 1932; 1st Indian reprinted., 1973) pp. 62-63.

svabhāva) of an individual,[1] but only the first stage, so to say, of his psychic development.

The discussion so far may be summed up as follows: *Triṃśatikā* is basically an analysis of an individual consciousness. The saṃsāric experience of an individual starts with the emergence of consciousness which bifurcates itself into subjectivity and objectivity. All transformations of consciousness can be grouped under those two terms.[2] I may put these ideas in a diagram:

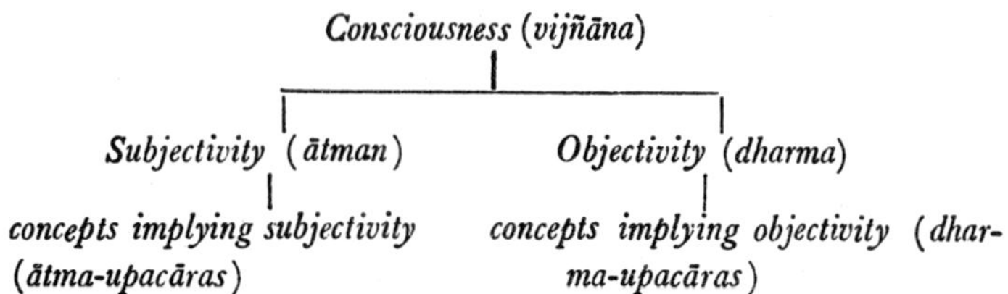

3. The Transformation of Consciousness

Now Vasubandhu proceeds to examine the transformations of consciousness (*vijñāna*). The self-transformation of consciousness results in three different derivatives of the same consciousness. Or rather, transforming itself the consciousness takes on three different modes of existence. They are store-consciousness *ālaya-vijñāna*), thought-consciousness (*mano-vijñāna*) and active consciousness (*pravṛtti-vijñāna*): they respectively represent three stages in the development of consciousness, namely, maturing, thinking, and knowing of objects:

[Triṃś. 1 cont'd.] Threefold is such transformation:

[Triṃś. 2] They are, namely,
Maturing, thinking, and representation of consciousness of object.[3]

1. See, for example, above pages 48-49
2. The same discussion is found in other words also in MVK. I. 4 and Vasubandhu's commentary on it. See my analysis of it above pp. 46ff
3. ... *pariṇāmaḥ sa ca tridhā*
Vipāko mananākhyaśca vijñaptir-viṣayasya ca. Triṃś. 1-2

Vasubandhu now describes each of those derivatives or modes of consciousness.

The store-consciousness

(ālaya-vijñāna)

[Triṃś. 2 cont'd.] There the maturing [consciousness]
Is otherwise called the store-consciousness,
Which carries the seeds of all [past experiences].[1]

[Triṃś. 3] It has [within itself)
The representations of consciousness
Of unknown objects and places;[2]
It is always associated with
Touch, attentiveness, knowledge,
Conception, and volition.[3]

[Triṃś. 4] The feeling therein is that of indifference;
It [i.e. store-consciousness] is unobscured and undefined;[4]
Similarly indifferent are touch etc.,
And it [i.e. the store-consciousness] is like a torrent of water;

[Triṃś. 5] And it ceases to exist at the attainment of *arhattva*.[5]

To paraphrase the above lines, *ālaya-vijñāna* (store-consciousness) is the individual unconscious, which carries within it the seeds of all past experiences. It has within itself the representations of consciousness of unknown objects (*upādi*, literally meaning 'what one grasps', or 'clings to') and places (*sthāna*). It is invariably associated with the experiential categories such as touch (*sparśa*), attentiveness (*manaskāra*), knowledge (*vid*= awareness), conception (*sañjñā*=idea), volition (*cetanā*) and

1. *Tatra-ālayākhya vijñānam vipākaḥ sarvabījakam.* Ibid. 2
2. *Asaṃviditakopādisthāna-vijñaptikam ca tat.* Ibid. 3
3. *Sadā sparśa-manaskāra-vit-sañjñā-cetanā-anvitam.* Ibid. 3
4. *Upekṣā vedanā tatra-anivṛtā-avyākṛtam ca tat.* Ibid. 4
5. *Tathā sparśa-ādayas-tacca vartate srotasaugha-vat*
   Tasya vyāvṛtir-arhattve... Ibid. 4-5

feeling (*vedanā* = sensation). None of those experiences at this stage is particularly pleasant (*sukha*) or *unpleasant* (*duḥkha*). Therefore, they are all equally indifferent (*asukha-aduḥkha* = *upekṣā*). The *ālaya-vijñāna* is not yet obscured by *āvaraṇas*, whether *kleśa-āvaraṇas* or *jñeya-āvaraṇas*, and, therefore, is described as unobscured (*anivṛtam*). Nor can it be defined as either good (*kuśala*) or as bad (*akuśala*), and, therefore, it is described as undefined (*avyākṛtam*). The *ālaya-vijñana*, which is like a torrent of water (*srotasaugha-vat*), ceases to exist only at the attainment of *arhattva*.

The thinking consciousness

(*manana-vijñāna*)

[Triṃś. 5 cont'd.] The consciousness called *manas*
Has the store-consciousness for its support and object.
It is essentially an act of thinking.[1]

[Triṃś. 6] It is always associated with four defilements,
Which are themselves obscured and undefined;
Those four defilements are, namely,
Belief in self, ignorance about self,
Pride in self, and love of self.[2]

[Triṃś. 7] It [i.e. *mano-nāma-vijñāna*] is associated
Also with others like touch etc.,
Which are all of the same nature
As the region in which one is born.[3]
It does not belong to one in the state of arhatship;
Nor does it operate
In the state of suppressed consciousness,
Nor in the supra-mundane path.

1. ... *tad-āśritya pravartate*
Tad-ālambam mano-nāma vijñānam mananātmakam. Triṃś. 5
2. *Kleśais-caturbhiḥ sahitam nivṛta-avyākṛtai sadā*
Ātma-dṛṣṭi-ātma-moha-ātma māna-ātma-sneha-sañjñitai. Ibid. 6
3. *Yatrajas-tanmayair-anyaiḥ sparśa-ādyaiś-ca*. Ibid. 7

[Triṃś. 8] It is the second transformation [of consciousness].[1]

The above lines describe the second mode or derivative of consciousness, which is called *manas*. To be sure, it is not what goes by the name *mano-vijñāna*. The latter is one of the six active consciousnesses, which belongs to the third transformation of consciousness. What is being discussed by the above quoted lines is described as simply the "consciousness called *manas*" (*mano-nāma vijñānam*). Sthiramati in his commentary refers to it as defiled consciousness (*kliṣṭam manaḥ*).[2] He has described it using the same expression, i. e. *kliṣṭam manaḥ*, in his commentry on MVK. I. 4.[3] According to *Triṃśatikā*, which is being examined here, this consciousness called *manas* is an act of thinking or cogitation (*mananātmakam*). Hence I have named it as *manana-vijñānam*, the thinking consciousness. For its origin and operation it depends on the store-consciousness (*tad ālaya-vijñānam āśritya pravartate*). It has the same store-consciousness for its object (*tad-ālambam*), too. For, its thinking activity consists basically in mistaking the store-consciousness for self (*ātma*),[4] and for that reason it is always associated with belief in self (*ātma-dṛṣṭi*), ignorance about self (*ātma-moha*), pride in self (*ātma-māna*), and love of self (*ātma-sneha*). These latter associates are all obscured but undefined. It is also associated with touch (*sparśa*), attentiveness (*manaskāra*), knowledge (*vit*), conceptions (*sañjñā*) and volition (*cetanā*). These associates are of the same nature as the region (*dhātu-bhūmi*) in which one is born (*yatrajas-tan-maya*).[5] The consciousness called *manas* (*mano-nāma vijñāna* or *mananākhya vijñāna*) does not exist for an *arhat* (*arhato na tat*), and does not operate in the state of suppressed consciousness (*nirodha-samā-*

1. ...*arhato na tat*
   Na nirodha-samāpattau mārge lokottare na ca.
   Dvitīyaḥ pariṇāmo'yam... Ibid. 7-8
2. See Sthiramati's commentary on Triṃś. 5
3. *Ātma-pratibhāsam kliṣṭam manaḥ, ātma-mohādi-samprayogāt.* MVKB. I. 4
4. *Ālaya-vijñāna-ālambanam-eva sat-kāya-dṛṣṭi-ādibhiḥ samprayogād-aham-mama-iti-ālayavijñāna-ālambanatvāt.* Triṃś. Eh. 5
5. *Tan-mayair-iti yatra dhātau bhūmau vā jātas-tad-dhātukaiḥ tad- bhūmikair-eva ca samprayujyate, na-anya-dhātukair-anya-bhūmikair-vā.* Ibid. 7

pattau), nor on the supra-mundane path (*mārge lokottare*). Such, indeed is the second transformation of consciousness.

The active consciousness

(*pravṛtti-vijñānam*)

[Triṃś. 8 con'd.] The third transformation of consciousness
Is the same as the perception of the sixfold object;
It could be good or bad or indifferent in character.[1]

[Triṃś. 9] It is associated with three kinds of mental factors :
Universal, specific and good;
It is associated, similarly,
With primary as well as secondary defilements;
It is subject to three kinds of feelings, too.[2]

[Triṃś. 10] Of those associates the first, [namely the universal] ones,
Are touch etc.,
[The second, namely] the specific ones,
Are desire, resolve and memory,
Together with concentration and knowledge;
Faith, sense of shame, fear of censure,

[Triṃś. 11] The triad of non-covetousness etc., courage,
Composure, equanimity along with alertness,
And harmlessness are [the third, namely] the good ones.[3]

1. ...*tritīyaḥ ṣaḍ-vidhasya ya*
Viṣayasya-upalabdhiḥ sa kuśala-akuśala-advaya. Triṃś. 8

2. *Sarvatra-gair-viniyataiḥ kuśalaiś-cetasair-asau*
Samprayuktā tathā kleśair-upakleśais-trivedanā. Ibid. 9

3. *Ādyāḥ sparśādayaś-chanda-adhimokṣa-smṛtayaḥ saha*
Samādhi dhībhyām niyataḥ śraddhā-atha hrīr-apatrapā. Ibid. 10
Alobha-ādi trayam vīryam praśrabdhiḥ sa apramādikā
Ahiṃsā kuṣalāḥ... Ibid. 11

[Triṃś. 11 cont'd.] The defilements are passionate attachment,
Grudge, stupidity,

[Triṃś. 12] Pride, [false] views and doubt.
Aoger, hatred, hypocrisy, envy, jealousy, spite along with deceit,

[Triṃś. 13] Dishonesty, arrogance,
Harmfulness, shamelessness, defiance of censure,
Sluggishness, conceit, unbelief, indolence,

[Triṃś. 14] Carelessness, bad memory,
Distraction of mind,
Thoughtlessness, remorse, sleepiness,
Reasoning and deliberation,
Are the secondary defilements.
The latter two couples, [namely,
Remorse and sleepiness, reasoning and deliberation],
Can be of two kinds, [namely, defiled and undefiled].[1]

[Triṃś. 15] Depending on the conditions available
The five sense-consciousnesses,
Together or separately,
Originate on the root-consciousness,
Just as waves originate on water.[2]

[Triṃś. 16] The thought-consciousness, however,
Manifests itself at all times,
Except for those [i] who are born

1. *...kleśa rāga-pratigha-mūḍhayaḥ*
Māna-dṛk-vicikitsāś-ca krodha-upanahane punaḥ
Mṛkṣaḥ pradāśa īrṣyā-atha mātsaryam saha māyayā
asaṭyam mado'vihiṃsā-hrīr-atrapā styānam-uddhavaḥ
Aśrddhām-atha kausīdyam pramādo muṣitā smṛtiḥ
Vikṣepo'samprajanyam ca kaukṛtyam middhameva ca
Vitarkaś-ca vīcāraś-ca-iti-upakleśa dvaye dvidhā. Ibid. 11-14

2. *Pañcānām mūla-vijñāne yathā-pratyayam-udbhavaḥ*
Vijñānānām saha na vā taraṅgāṇām yathā jale. Ibid. 15

Into the region where the beings are in a
state of unconsciousness,
[ii] who have entered either of the two trances,
In which there is no operation of consciousness,
[iii] who are unconscious by reason
Of sleepiness or faint.[1]

What I make of the above description of the threefold transformation of consciousness, is that all such transformations and their associates refer only to psychological and epistemological categories, not to any ontological categories, and that, therefore, it is not warranted to say that consciousness evolves into the external world of multiplicity. There is no indication at all that the transformations of consciousness include any of the ontological categories (*padārtha*). While describing the third transformation of consciousness, namely, the sixfold active consciousness. Vasubandhu did have real occasion to refer to external *things*, if he wanted to do so. That is, a sense-consciousness involves a sense and its object, the latter being in most cases an external *thing*. Therefore, to be a real idealist Vasubandhu should have said that the sense and its object are both transformations of consciousness. But he makes no such remarks. Instead of saying that the sense and the object involved in a sense-perception are both transformations of consciousness, he says just that 'the representation of consciousness of objects' (*vijñaptir-viṣayasya*)[2] or 'the perception of the sixfold object' (*ṣaḍ-vidhasya yā viṣayasya-upalabdhiḥ*),[3] is the third transformation of consciousness. In other words, it is the representations of consciousness (*vijñapti*) or perception (*upalabdhi*) that Vasubandhu says is one of the transformations of consciousness, not either the sense-organ or the object. And there is nothing idealistic about such a view.

Another point that throws doubt upon the idealistic interpretation of *Triṃśatikā*, is Vasubandhu's statement that 'the five

1. *Mano-vijñāna-sambhūtiḥ sarvadā-asañjñikād-ṛte,*
   Samāpatti-dvayān-mūrchanād-api acittakāt. Ibid. 16
2. Triṃś. 2; see above p. 134, note 3.
3. Triṃś. 8; see above p. 138 note 1.

mūla-vijñāna* or *ālaya-vijñāna

- *cakṣur-vijñāna* (visual consciousness)
- *śrotra-vijñāna* (auditory consciousness)
- *ghrāṇa-vijñāna* (olfactory consciousness)
- *jihvā-vijñāna* (gustatory consciousness)
- *kāya vijñāna* (tactile consciousness)
- *mano-vijñāna* (thought-consciousness)

ṣaḍ-pravṛtti-vijñānāni (six active consciousnesses) — ***caitasāḥ*** **(*mental associates*).**

- *sarvatraga-caitasa* (universal associates): *sparśa* (touch), *manaskāra* (attentiveness), *vid* (knowledge), *sañjñā* (conception), *cetanā* (volition)
- *viniyata-caitasa* (specific associates): *chanda* (desire), *adhimokṣa*, (resolve), *smṛti* (memory), *samādhi* (concentration), *dhi* (knowledge)
- *kuśala-caitasa* (good associates): *śraddhā* (faith), *hri* (sense of shame) *apatrapā* (fear of censure), *alobha* (non-covetousness), *adveṣa* (non-anger), *amoha*, (non-ignorance), *virya* (courage), *praśrabdhi* (composure), *upekṣā* (equanimity), *apramādikā* (alertness), *ahiṃsā* (harmlessness).
- *kleśa-upakleśa* (defilements : primary and secondary): *rāga* (passionate attachment), *pratigha* (grudge) *mūḍhi* (stupidity), *māna* (pride), *dṛk* (false views), *vicikitsā* (doubt), *krodha* (anger), *upanaha* (hatred), *mṛkṣa* (hypocrisy), *pradāśa* (envy), *irṣyā* (jealousy), *mātsarya* (spite), *māyā* (deceit), *asatyam* (dishonesty), *mada* (arrogance), *avihiṃsā* (harmlessness), etc., etc.,

sense-consciousnesses originate *on* the root-consciousness (*mūla-vijñāne*).[1] What he does not want to say is that the five sense-consciousnesses originate *from* the root-consciousness (*mūla vijñānāt*).[2] The latter is the way an idealist would look at sense-consciousness. For him sense-consciousness is not only built *upon* the root-consciousness, but also is built *out of* it. For him, again, the root-consciousness is the only source of sense-consciousness, the sense-organ as well as its object being what the former projects out of itself. But Vasubandhu at least leaves it open that sense-consciousness could arise from some other sources, and then be built onto the root-consciousness. He is probably referring to MV.I.11, where the sensation is described as 'the threefold determination' (*triparicchedа*) of the individual concerned. Here 'the three-fold determination' means, says Vasubandhu, the 'contact' (*sparśa*),[3] which according to Sthiramati's commentary, means the coming together (*sanni-pāta*) of sense-organ (*indriya*), object (*viṣaya*) and consciousness (*vijñāna*) resulting in pleasant or unpleasant or indifferent feeling'.[4] Thus the author of MVK., Vasubandhu and Sthiramati explicitly admit that sense, object and consciousness are all involved in the generation of sense-consciousness. Thus they admit *things* existing outside and independent of consciousness, a position that cannot by any means be reconciled with idealism !

If sense-consciousness is the result of the co-operation of sense, object and consciousness, how can it still be called a transfor-

1. Triṃś. 15; see above p. 139 note 2.

2. However, one should not make much of Vasubandhu's use of the locative *mūla-vijñāne* rather than the ablative *mūla-vijñānāt*. It may very well be a printing mistake. Moreover, Sthiramati, in his subsequent commentary, uses the ablative *ālaya-vijñānāt* rather than the locative *ālaya-vijñāne* (see below p. 143, note 1). Hence my argument in this paragraph is not a conclusive, but only a tentative, one.

3. *Tri-paricchedāt sparśena*. MVBK. I. 11

4. *Trayāṇām hi-indriya-viṣaya-vijñāna-sannipāte indriyasya sukhādi-vedanā-utpatti-anukūlo yas-triprakāro vikāras-tat-paricchedaḥ sparśaḥ*. MVKBT. I. 11. In literal translation it would mean: "When the three, namely, sense-organ, object and consciousness come together, the sense-organ is subjected to three kinds of change, which will lead to the threefold feeling such as pleasure etc. *Sparśa* means to be determined by those three kinds of change."

mation of consciousness (*vijñāna-pariṇāma*) ? The answer to this question is implied in the analogy of 'the waves on water' (*taraṅgāṇām yathā jale*). Waves arise on water *only* under certain atmospheric conditions. In other words, the arising of waves depends not only on water but also on the atmospheric conditions. But, that the waves arise depending on the atmospheric conditions, does not make it impossible to say that those waves are just modifications (*pariṇāma*) of water on which they arise. Similarly, consciousness depending on certain factors such as sense-organ and object, transforms itself into sense-consciousness. However, that the sense-organ and object co-operate with the consciousness in producing the sense-consciousness, does not in any way contradict the fact that the latter is a transformation of consciousness.

Sthiramati, too, finds it necessary to refer to objects (*ālambana*) for adequately explaining the emergence of sense-consciousness. According to him the point of comparison between 'five sense-consciousnesses on *mūla-vijñāna*' and' 'waves on water' is that just as waves can *together or separately* arise on the *same* water, so the five sense-consciousnesses can arise *together or separately* on/from the *same mūla-vijñāna*.[1] There are two kinds of causes at work in both cases: antecedent causes (*samanantara-pratyaya*) and objective causes (*ālambana-pratyaya*). The former of these, for example, *water* or *mūla-vijñāna*, remaining always the same, the latter keep changing. It is according to the number and nature of the [objective] causes available (*yathā-pratyayam*),[2] that waves or sense-consciousnesses arise together or separately. By the objective cause (*ālambana-pratyaya*) of any consciousness is meant the object of that consciousness. But in the case of sense-consciousness it has got to be *external* objects, not the so-called *internal* objects such as seeds (*bīja*) left behind in the *ālaya-vijñāna* by past experiences, *saṃskāras* and *vāsanās*. For, while those internal objects remain always the same, the external objects can keep

1. *Taraṅgāṇām yathā jale iti. Ālaya-vijñānāt-pravṛtti-vijñānam yugapad-ayugapac-ca-utpattau dṛṣṭāntaḥ.* Triṃś. Bh. 15 (see above p. 142 note 2).

2. *Yathā-pratyayam-udbhavaḥ.* Triṃś. 15
Yathā-pratyayam-udbhavaḥ iti yasya yasya yaḥ pratyayaḥ sannihitas-tasya tasya niyamena-udbhavaḥ ātma-lābhaḥ. Triṃś. Bh. 15

changing from time to time, and from place to place, and thus can provide for different and multiple sense-consciousnesses. My conclusion that the object (*viṣaya* or *ālambana*) of sense-consciousness is an external object, is sufficiently justified by the way Vasubandhu and Sthiramati introduce this point. In the case of *ālaya-vijñāna* and *manana-vijñāna* they specified the respective objects: *ālaya-vijñāna* has for its object what it carries within itself, and the place where it is located,[1] while *manana-vijñāna* has *ālaya-vijñāna* itself for its object.[2] But they do not at all specify the object of sense-consciousnesses. Instead, they use the general term such as '*viṣaya*' and '*ālambana*',[3] thereby implying that the reader should understand those terms in their usual, ordinary, sense as when a layman says, 'object (*viṣaya*) of eye.'[4] Having said that, I must recall what was said under MV.I. 4 : namely, that what the consciousness apparently grasps are the forms constructed and imposed by it on the things concerned. In other words, although there are external things, the consciousness never succeeds in reaching and grasping them as they are in themselves, but only as they appear (*pratibhāsa*). Being conditioned by innate *bījas*, *vāsanās* and *saṃskāras*, the consciousness can make only approximations of things, and that too under the aspects of subjectivity and objectivity.

I have mentioned above that all transformations of consciousness refer either to psychological or to epistemological categories. They are *citta* and *caittas*, not *bhūta* and *bhautikas*. To substantiate this I shall now produce a list of the transformations and their associates mentioned in the text. It is only a list of all the terms involved in their English alphabetical, not any conceptual, order :

1. *Upādi-sthāna--vijñaptikam*. Triṃś. 3

2. Tad (=*ālaya-vijñāna*)-*ālambam mano-nāma vijñānam*. Ibid. 5

3. *vijñaptir-viṣayasya ca*. Ibid. 2; *ṣaḍ-vidhasya yā viṣayasya-upalabdhiḥ*. Ibid. 8; *ālambana-sadbhāve pañcānām-api ca-utpattir-iti abhyupeyam*. Triṃś. Bh. 15

4. Hsuan Tsang, the great Chinese interpreter of *Triṃśatikā* commenting on stanza 15 says, "This means that the five consciousnesses are dependent internally upon the mūla-vijñāna (Ālaya), and that, externally, they can only manifest themselves by conforming to a concatenation of conditions, such as the act of attention (*manaskāsa*), the five sense-organs (*indriyas*), the

adhimokṣa
adveṣa
ahiṃsā
ālaya-vijñāna (=*vipāka*)
alobha
amoha
apatrapā
apramādikā
asamprajanya
avihiṃsā
aśraddhā
ātma-dṛṣṭi
ātma-māna
ātma-sneha
ātma-moha
atrapā
cetanā
chanda
dhī
dṛk
hrī
īrṣyā
kaukṛtya
kausīdya
krodha
mada
māna
manana-ākhyam-vijñāna (=*mano-nāma-vijñāna*)
mano-nāma-vijñāna (=*manana-ākhyam-vijñāna*)
manaskāra
mātsarya
māyā
middha
mṛkṣa
mūḍhi
muṣitā
pradāśa
pramāda
praśrabdhi
pratigha
pravṛtti-vijñāna (=*vijñaptir-viṣayasya*) (=*viṣayasya upalabdhiḥ*)
rāga
samādhi
sañjñā
śāṭhya
sparśa
smṛti
śraddhā
styāna
uddhava
upahana
upekṣā
vedanā
vicāra
vicikitsā
vid
vijñaptir-viṣayasya (=*pravṛtti-vijñāna*) (=*viṣayasya upalabdhiḥ*)
ikṣepa
vipāka (=*ālaya-vijñāna*)
vīrya
viṣayasya upalabdhiḥ (=*vijñāptir-viṣayasya*) (=*pravṛtti-vijñāna*)
vitarka

4. All is Mere Representation of Consciousness

That all *citta* and *caittas* are transformations of consciousness has been said. Now the text proceeds to say that all *citta* and *caittas* invariably involve the distinction (*vikalpa*) between subject

external objects (italics mine) sensed by these organs (*viṣaya*), etc." (Hsuan-tsang, *The Doctrine of Mere Consciousness*, trans. Wei Tai [Hong Kong, 1973], p. 479)

and object, but that this distinction having no extra-mental basis is a mere representation of consciousness. The next stanza, therefore, is a re-affirmation of what the first one stated, namely that all *upacāras* (usages / concepts) of *ātma* and *dharma* (subjectivity and objectivity) are transformations of consciousness.

[Triṃś. 17] This [threefold] transformation of consciousness
Is [just] the distinction [between subject and object];
What is thus distinguished,
Does not exist as [subject and object]
Therefore this is all mere representation of consciousness.[1]

Introducing this stanza Sthiramati says : what has been said above, namely that all *upacāras* of *ātma* and *dharma* being just transformations of consciousness, have no independent existence, is further clarified here.[2] This is what he means : the *upacāras* of *ātma* and *dharma*, namely, *citta* and *caittas*, are transformations of consciousness, and, therefore, do not have extra-mental existence. In any case, what the stanza describes as representations of consciousness cannot include anything more than (i) subjectivity and objectivity (*ātma* and *dharma*), (ii) the distinction (*vikalpa*) between them, and (iii) *citta* and *caittas*. It does not include any of the *bhūtas* and *bhautikas*. However, *citta* and *caittas* may belong to any of the three worlds depending on where the individual concerned happens to be : "The above mentioned threefold transformation of consciousness is just the distinction [between subject and object]. They [subjects and objects] are *citta* and *caitta* belonging to three worlds, and have for their objects mentally constructed forms", says Sthiramati.[3]

1. *Vijñāna-pariṇāmo'yam vikalpo yad-vikalpyate*
Tena tan-nāsti tena-idam sarvam vijñapti-mātrakam. Triṃś. 17

2. *Idānīm ātma-dharma-upacāro yaḥ prajñāpyate sa vijñāna-pariṇāma eva na vijñāna-pariṇāmāt-sa pṛthag-asti-ātma dharma vā-iti yat-pratijñātam tat-prasādhanār-tham-āha*. Triṃś. Bh. 17

3. *Yo'yam vijñāna-pariṇāmas-tri-vidho'nantaram-abhihitaḥ so'yam vikalpaḥ. Adhyāropita-artha-ākāraḥ trai-dhātukas-citta-caitta vikalpa ucyate. Yathoktam—Abhūta-parikalpastu citta-caittās-tridhātukāḥ* (MVK I. 9). Triṃś. Bh. 17

Again, the emphasis is on the subject-object dualism, as Hsuan Tsang observes :

> We have examined the three categories of consciousness that are capable of evolution and manifestation, namely, the Alayavijnana, Manas, and the first six consciousnesses, and explained that each of these eight consciousnesses is the basis or infra-structure for a twofold manifestation, the perceived division and the perceiving division (*nimittabhaga* and *darsanabhaga*). We have said that Atman and dharmas are merely conventional designations of this double manifestation of consciousness, of its Nimittabhaga and Darsanabhaga; that they are not real entities apart from these two Bhagas; and that, in consequence, 'all is mere consciousness' or nothing exists but consciousness.[1]

5. The Origin of Vikalpa and Ālayavijñāna

The self-transformation of consciousness starts with *ālaya-vijñāna*, and results in *vikalpa*, so to say. However, nothing has been so far said about the origin of those two terms of evolution. As for the other two forms of transformation, namely *mano-nāma-vijñāna* and *pravṛtti-vijñāna*, Vasubandhu did mention how they come into being. But while introducing *ālaya-vijñāna* he made no mention of how it originates Similarly, how *vikalpa*, the bifurcation of consciousness into subjectivity and objectivity, which is the end-result of *vijñāna-pariṇāma*, takes place, has not been touched upon. Hence the next two stanzas, of which the first one deals with the origin of *vikalpa*.

[Triṃś. 18] The consciousness contains all seeds;
Its such and such transformations
Proceed by mutual influence,
On account of which such and such [subject-object] discriminations arise.[2]

1. Hsuan-tsang, op. cit., p. 503. Hsuan Tsang's version of Triṃś. 17 is equally interesting:
   The various consciousnesses manifest themselves in what seem to be two divisions:
   Perception (*Darsanabhaga*) and the object of perception (*nimittabhaga*).
   Because of this, Atman and dharma do not exist.
   For this reason, all is mere consciousness. (Ibid., pp. CXXXI-III)
2. *Sarva-bījam hi vijñānam pariṇāmas-tathā tathā*
   Yāti-anyonya-vaśād yena vikalpaḥ sa sa jāyate. Trimś. 18

According to Sthiramati this stanza says how the various kinds of subject-object distinctions in the absence of any extra-mental means come to actuality from *ālaya-vijñāna*, which is itself without a basis.[1] The stanza does so by referring to the context in which the subject-object distinctions arise, namely the inter-action between *ālaya-vijñāna* and *pravṛtti-vijñāna*. "The consciousness that contains all seeds" is obviously *ālaya-vijñāna*;[2] and "its such and such transformations" refer to *pravṛtti-vijñāna*.[3] The latter keep arising by the mutual influence of itself and ālaya-vijñāna. This statement might sound a vicious circle. But the point is that the actual origination of *pravṛtti-vijñāna* is occasioned by the coming-together (*sannipāta* = *sparśa*) of *indriya*, *viṣaya* and *vijñāna*, as explained above.[4] The *pravṛtti-vijñāna* thus originated will subsequently strengthen the *ālaya-vijñana* so that the latter can again co-operate in the production of further *pravṛtti-vijñānas*.[5] Thus the continuous production (implied by the verb *yāti*) of *pravṛtti-vijñāna* has to be attributed to the mutual influence of itself and *ālaya-vijñāna*. Now, the 'such and such subject-object distinctions arise on account of the mutually influencing *ālaya-vijñāna* and *pravṛtti-vijñāna*.' This means : the inter-action between *ālaya-vijñāna* and *pravṛtti-vijñāna* leads to the production of a new *pravṛtti-vijñāna*, which being 'knowledge of something' should necessarily involve the distinction between subject and object. This distinction, although arising in the context of the inter-action between *ālaya-vijñāna* and *pravṛtti-vijñāna*, derives solely from the former, which in this respect is supported by nothing else : "Thus on account of the mutual influence of *ālaya-vijñāna* and *pravṛtti-vijñāna*. . .the various kinds of [subject-object] distinctions

1. *Katham mūla (-ālaya)-vijñānād anadhiṣṭhitād asati kāraṇe vikalpāḥ pravartante iti-āha*. Trimś. Bh. 18

2. *Tatra sarva-dharma-utpādana-śakti-anugamāt sarva-bījam vijñānam-iti-ālaya-vijñānam*. Ibid.

3. It is clear from Sthiramati's statement quoted below under note 5.

4. See above pp. 140-142

5. *Anyonya-vaśād-iti tathā hi cakṣurādi-vijñānam sva-śaktiparipoṣe vartamāne śakti-viśiṣṭasya-ālays-vijñāna-pariṇāmasya nimittam so'api ālaya-vijñāna-pariṇāmaḥ cakṣurādi-vijñānasya nimittam bhavati*. Triṃś. Bh. 18

arise from *ālaya-vijñāna,* which is supported by nothing else."[1] Thus, to conclude, the subject-object distinction (*vikalpa*) is essentially associated with *pravṛtti-vijñāna*, but is supplied solely from within by *ālaya-vijñāna*, and, therefore, does not at all belong to the extramental things in themselves.

Incidentally, let me say a word about the multiplicity or variety of subject-object distinctions. Both Vasubandhu and Sthiramati have suggested that the subject-object distinction may take on more than one form. For example, the former speaks of 'such and such *vikalpa*',[2] and the latter of 'various kinds of *vikalpas*'.[3] How could there be a multiplicity or variety of subject-object distinctions ? It is possible, because the subject-object distinction can appear in various forms such as the distinction between 'knower and knowable', (*jñātṛ* and *jñeya*), grasper and graspable (*grāhaka* and *grāhya*), enjoyer and enjoyable (*bhoktṛ* and *bhojya*), etc., etc.

The next stanza deals with the origin of *ālaya-vijñāna*. More precisely, it says how *ālaya-vijñāna* continues from birth to birth. The *ālaya-vijñāna*, as already indicated, is the individual unconscious in which seeds (*bījas*) of all past experiences are stored up. But once those seeds develop and express themselves in various deeds, there can no longer be the *ālaya-vijñāna*. The extermination or exhaustion of *ālaya-vijñāna* means the end of the present life. But it can result either in *nirvāṇa* or in another birth in *saṃsāra*, depending on how the *ālaya-vijñāna* has been exhausted. Exhaustion of *ālaya-vijñāna* by yogic practices, which would make the seeds therein *defunct*, will lead to *nirvāṇa*. On the contrary, if its exhaustion takes place by the natural development of seeds into deeds engendering new experiences, it will inevitably lead to another birth in *saṃsāra*. For, those deeds contain fresh seeds of experiences, which will collect to build up a new *ālaya-vijñāna* ensuring another saṃsāric existence for the individual concerned. This is what the stanza says :

1. *Evam-anyonya-vaśād-yasmād-ubhayam pravarttate tasmād-ālayavijñānād anyena-anadhiṣṭhitād aneka-prakāro vikalpaḥ sa sa jāyate.* Ibid.
2. *Vikalpaḥ sa sa jāyate.* Triṃś. 18
3. . . . *aneka-prakāro vikalpaḥ sa sa jāyate.* Triṃś. Bh. 18

Triṃś. 19 Once the previous stage of maturation
Has been exhausted,
The impressions of deeds
Along with those of the twofold grasping
Engender the next stage of maturation.[1]

The *vipāka*, here translated as 'the stage of maturation' evidently refers to *ālaya-vijñāna*, as already mentioned above in the second stanza.[2] It gets exhausted (*kṣīṇa*) in the course of time. But it continues to exist, so to say, through the *vāsanās* (habit-energies) left behind by the deeds (*karma*) it promoted, and by the *grāha-dvaya* (the twofold grasping) it exercised. *Vāsanās* are the impressions or habits, or characters, or traces, or habit-energies, left behind by past experiences. They are also capable (*samartha*) of producing future experiences. They are like seeds (*bījas*) which are produced by trees, and are also capable of producing future trees. For Sthiramati *vāsanā* means ability (*sāmarthyam*).[3]

There are two factors that produce *vāsanā*, namely *karma* (deed) and *grāha-dvaya* (the twofold grasping). Of them *grāha-dvaya* means the idiosyncrasy for subjectivity and objectivity. "The two graspings are (i) the grasping of graspable, and (ii) the grasping of grasper. Among them the grasping of the graspable is the belief that there are graspables independent of consciousness, although in fact they are what the stream of consciousness projects itself. The belief that such graspables are apprehended or known or grasped by the consciousness is the grasping of the grasper. And the habit-energies of the twofold grasping are the seeds, which being produced by the earlier graspings of graspable and grasper, are now capable the engendering fresh graspings of graspable and grasper of the same kind."[4] All that is being said in this

1. *Karmaṇo vāsanā grāha-dvaya-vāsanayā saha*
Kṣīṇe pūrva-vipāke 'nyad vipākam janayanti tat. Triṃś. 19
2. *Tatra-ālaya-ākhyam vijñānam vipākaḥ sarva-bījakam.* Triṃś. 2
3. *Tena karmaṇa yad-anāgata-ātmabhāva-abhinivṛttaye ālaya-vijñāne sāmarthyam-āhitam sā karma-vāsanā.* Triṃś. Bh. 19
4. *Grāha-dvayam. Grāhya-grāho grāhaka-grāhaś-ca. Tatra vijñānāt-pṛthag-eva sva-santāna-adhyāsitam grāhyam-asti-iti-adhyavasāyo grāhya-grāhaḥ. Tac-ca vijñānena pratīyate vijñāyate gṛhyate iti yo'yam niścayaḥ sa grāhaka-grāhaḥ. Purvotpanna grāhya-grāhaka-grāha-ākṣiptam-anāgata-taj-jātīya-grāhya-grāhaka-grāha-utpatti-bījam grāha-dvaya-vāsanā.* Ibid.

passage is that subject-object idiosyncrasy belonging to one birth leaves its impressions behind, which getting itself attached to the next *ālaya-vijñāna* will eventually develop into the same sort of idiosyncrasy.

What particularly interests me at this point is Vasubandhu's suggestion that the habit-energies of *karma* can produce the next *ālaya-vijñāna* only in collaboration (*saha*) with the habit-energies of the twofold grasping. "The habit-energies of deeds *along with* those of the twofold grasping engender the next stage of maturation",[1] says the text. Commenting on it Sthiramati says, "So, too, the habit-energies of deeds alone, without the help of the habit-energies of the twofold grasping, do not engender the next stage of maturation. Hence the text specifies, 'along with the habit-energies of the twofold grasping.' "[2] This implies that the continuity of *ālaya-vijñāna* and of the consequent saṃsāric existence depends decisively on the subject-object idiosyncrasy. Therefore no wonder that Vasubandhu is advocating its eradication as the means of attaining *nirvāṇa*.

6. The Triple Nature of Reality

The imagined nature

Having discussed the process of *vijñāna-pariṇāma* (transformation of consciousness), Vasubandhu is now making an evaluation of experience. This he does by bringing in the theory of the triple nature of reality (*tri-svabhāva-vāda*). It is the theory which says that reality can take on three different natures : *parikalpita-svabhāva* (the imagined nature), and *para-tantra-svabhāva* (the other-dependent nature), and *pariniṣpanna-svabhāva* (the absolutely accomplished nature). The following stanza deals with the *parikalpita-svabhāva* :

[Triṃś. 20] The subject-matter that is liable
To [subject-object] distinction
By whatsoever sort of [Subject-object] discrimination,

1. See above, p. 150 note 1 for the text.
2. *grāha-dvaya-vāsanayā saha*. Triṃś. 19

Is all just imagined nature;
It does not exist.[1]

The term *vastu*, here translated as 'subject-matter' is often used to mean something abstract as distinguished from concrete things. For example, the phrase '*kathā-vastu*' means the theme (*vastu*) of a story (*kathā*). To use it to mean a concrete thing is not uncommon, though. However, in the present context it cannot mean anything concrete or existential. For, here Vasubandhu is evidently dealing with mentally constructed (*parikalpita*) nature.

The *vastu* that are distinguished into subject and object, are the subjective forms of living and non-living beings, self and representations of consciousness all of which are referred to in MVK. I.4, and have been discussed above.[2] These forms may refer to anything external or internal, falling within the sphere of experience, including even *buddha-dharma*, as Sthiramati observes.[3] But the point is that they are not the things themselves, but the forms (*ākāra* or *prakāra*) that one mentally constructs and projects on to those things. Again, while those things in themselves are neither subjects nor objects, the subjective forms of them can be, and are, categorized into various kinds of subjects and objects, such as graspable and grasper, enjoyable and enjoyer etc. These forms are just mentally constructed nature, having no extra-mental existence. "The *vastu* that is liable to subject-object distinction, as it has no existence [*sattā*] is imagined nature, and not a nature that is subject to external causes and conditions", says Sthiramati.[4] He then illustrates his point as follows : One and the same thing is often subjected to different kinds of subject-object distinctions by different people. For example, a man with bad eyes and another with normal eyesight will see the same thing differently. Or, something may be

1. *Yena yena vikalpena yad yad vastu vikalpyate*
Parikalpita-eva asau svabhāvo na sa vidyate. Triṃś. 20

2. See above, pp. 46ff.

3. *Yad yad vastu vikalpyate—adhyātmikam bāhyam vā antaśo buddha-dharma api.* Triṃś. Bh. 20

4. *Yad vastu vikalpa-viṣayas-tad yasmāt sattā-abhāvān-na vidyate tasmāt tad-vastu parikalpita-svabhāvam-eva, na hetu-pratyaya pratipadya-svabhāvaḥ.* Ibid.

seen by some people as an object of knowledge, while by others as an object of enjoyment, etc. This difference of form under which something is seen or perceived or experienced cannot come from the extra-mental thing, which remains always the same. It must, therefore, come from the mind, which differs from individual to individual. Thus it is the forms of experience that are described as imagined nature, and as having no extra-mental existence.

The other-dependent nature

[Triṃś. 21] The other-dependent nature, however,
Is the [act of graspable-grasper] discrimination;
It depends for its origin on conditions.[1]

The other-dependent nature is the very source of the saṃsāric existence of an individual. In Western terminology it may be called the mind. But, for the school of Vasubandhu it is just the aggregate—may be a purposeful aggregate—of *citta* and *caittas*,[2] all of which have already been described as transformations of consciousness. They are essentially the act of graspable-grasper discrimination (*vikalpa*), and depend for their continued operation on various conditions, as explained above.[3] By reason of their dependence on conditions it is described as the other-dependent nature. Sthiramati summarizes all these points as follows : "There the [graspable-grasper] discrimination is the own-form [= the very essence] of the other-dependent nature. It is named the 'other-dependent', because it comes into being depending upon conditions. There the imagination [of the graspable-grasper discrimination] is the same as the *citta* and *caittas*, good as well as bad, belonging to all three worlds. It has been said : the imagination of the unreal [graspable-grasper discrimination], however, is *citta* and *caittas* belonging to three worlds [MVK.I.9.]."[4] More details about the nature and reality of the

1. *Para-tantra-svabhāvas-tu vikalpaḥ pratyaya-udbhavaḥ.* Triṃś. 21
2. See below, note 4
3. See above pages 145ff
4. *Atra vikalpa-iti para-tantra-svarūpam āha. Pratyaya-udbhava-iti-anena-api para-*

other-dependent nature, which is variously called *vikalpa* or *parikalpa* or *abhūta-parikalpa*, are given elsewhere.[1]

The absolutely accomplished nature

[Triṃś. 21 cont'd] The [absolutely] accomplished [nature]
Is the latter's [i.e. the other-dependent nature's
Perpetual devoidness
Of the former [i.e. the imagined nature].[2]

In plain language it means : if one can neutralize/stop the graspable-grasper-discriminating activity of the mind, there one has the absolutely accomplished nature. It should no more be called mind, though. On the contrary, it is then just the thing-in-itself, the suchness (*tathatā*), the devoidness of graspability and grasperhood (*grāhya-grāhaka-bhāvena virahitatā*).[3] As all this has been said before,[4] here I need only to reproduce Sthiramati's commentary to the above lines: "This nature is called the absolutely accomplished, because it is unchangeably accomplished. 'The former' means the imagined nature and 'the latter' means the other-dependent nature. Where there is the [graspable-grasper] discrimination, there the graspability and grasperhood are imagined. It is said to be imagined because the graspability and grasperhood, which in fact are non-existent, are simply imagined to exist where there is the [graspable-grasper] discrimination. The absolutely accomplished nature is the other-dependent nature's eternal and absolute devoidness of graspability and grasperhood".[5]

tantra-abhidhāna-pravṛtti-nimittam-āha. Tatra parikalpaḥ kuśala-akuśala-avyākṛta-bheda-bhinnaḥ trai-dhātukaś-citta-caittāh yathā-uktam : Abhūta-parikalpas-tu citta-caittās trai-dhātukāḥ. (MV.I.9)

1. See, for example, above pp. 90ff; 94ff

2. *Niṣpannas-tasya pūrveṇa sadā rahitatā tu yā.* Triṃś. 21

3. *Śūnyatā tasya-abhūtaparikalpasya grāhya-grāhaka-bhāvena virahitatā.* MVKB. 1. 2.

4. See above note 1.

5. *Avikāra-pariniṣpattyā sa pariniṣpannaḥ. Tasya-iti paratantrasya pūrveṇa-iti parikalpitena. Tasmin vikalpe grāhya-grāhakabhāvaḥ parikalpitaḥ. Tathā hi tasmin vikalpe grāhya-grāhakatvam avidyamānam-eva parikalpyate iti parikalpitam ucyate. Tena grāhya-grāhakena paratantrasya sadā sarvakālam atyanta-rahitatā yā sa pariniṣpanna-svabhāvaḥ.* Triṃś. Bh.21

At this point Vasubandhu considers also the relationship between the *paratantra* and *pariniṣpanna*. He says that they are not really two different beings, but only two phases of the same being: as *paratantra-svabhāva* it is infatuated by the subject-object idiosyncrasy, while as *pariniṣpanna-svabhāva* it is free of it.

[Triṃś. 22] For that reason, indeed,
It is said to be neither different,
Nor non-different
From the other-dependent nature.
It is like impermanence etc.[1]

This last line adequately explains the relation between *pariniṣpanna* and *para-tantra* as that between an abstract concept (e.g. impermanence)and an existing individual (e.g. an impermanent thing). In concrete experience one cannot have 'impermanence' as separate from 'impermanent things', although in fact they are different from each other. Similarly, the *pariniṣpanna-svabhāva* is not entirely different from the *para-tantra-svabhāva*, but is not quite non-different either. The simile of 'impermanence etc.' should not, however, be stretched too far to say that one can never have *pariniṣpanna-svabhāva* as such. For, the realization of *pariniṣpanna-svabhāva* is the ultimate aim of the Yogācārin. Therefore, the comparison applies only to the 'neither different nor non-different' aspect in both cases.

I may now summarize, as follows, what Sthiramati has to say by way of commentary on the above lines. *Pariniṣpanna* is *paratantra's* eternal devoidness of *parikalpita*. Devoidness (*rahitatā*) is an abstraction (*dharmatā*), which can be neither different (*na-anya*) nor non-different (*na-ananya*) from the individual *dharma* from which it is abstracted. Similarly, *pariniṣpanna*, too, is an abstraction of/from *para-tantra-dharma*, and, therefore, cannot be either different or non-different from the latter. If *pariniṣpanna* were different from *para-tantra*, it would make no sense to say that it is the same *para-tantra* devoid of *parikalpita*. Again, if it were non-different, it would be intrinsically defiled, just as the

1. *Ataḥ eva sa na-eva-anyo na-ananyaḥ paratantrataḥ*
Anityatā-ādi-vad vācyo...Triṃś.22

para-tantra is, and, therefore, could never to purified. Conversely, the *para-tantra*, being non-different from *parinispanna*, would never be intrinsically impure, either. It is, therefore, like *anityatā*, *duḥkhatā* and *anātmatā*, which are neither different nor non-different from the corresponding *saṃskāras*. If *anityatā* were different from *saṃskāras*, it would mean that the latter are *nitya*, which is not the case. On the contrary, if *anityatā* were non-different from *saṃskāras*, it would mean that the latter, too, just as *anityatā*, have lost their own-nature, which is not, again, the case.[1]

Another consideration that is brought in here is how *para-tantra* divested of subject-object forms can ever be known, and if it is not ever known at all, how can one know that there is such a state of reality at all.[2] The answer is :

[Triṃś. 22 cont'd.] As long as this [absolutely accomplished nature]
Is not seen,
That [other-dependent nature], too,
Is not seen.[3]

The message of this statement is that to be able to see that *para-tantra svabhāva* in its absolute nature is neither an object nor a subject, one has got first to see(=realize)the *pariniṣpanna-svabhāva*.[4] And the realization of the *pariniṣpanna-svabhāva* is possible, as Sthiramati observes, only through intuititve and supramundance knowledge.[5]

7. The Threefold Naturelessness

Having explained the three natures of reality, the author is now turning to the negative aspects of the same natures. According to Sthiramati, he is thereby trying to reconcile the theory of three natures with the view that every *dharma* is without own-nature, origin and destruction.[6]

1. See Triṃś.Bh.22
2. *Yadi grāhya-grāhaka-bhāva-rahitaḥ para-tantraḥ katham-asau gṛhyate, agrāhyamāṇo vā katham-asti-iti vijñāyate?* Triṃś.Bh.22
3. *Na-adṛṣṭe asmin sa dṛśyate.* Triṃś.22
4. *Na-adṛṣṭe asmin-iti. Pariniṣpanna-svabhāve sa dṛśyate iti para-tantra svabhāvaḥ.* Triṃś. Bh. 22
5. *Nirvikalpa-lokottara-jñāna-dṛśye pariniṣpanne svabhāve..* Ibid.
6. *Yadi dravyam eva para-tantraḥ katham sūtre sarva-dharma niḥsvabhāva anutpannā aniruddhā iti nirdiśyate. Nāsti virodhaḥ yasmāt* Triṃś. Bh.23

[Triṃś. 23] Corresponding to the threefold nature
There is also a threefold naturelessness;
Referring to this fact it has been said
That there is the naturelessness of all elements.[1]

[Triṃś. 24] The first nature is natureless by its very definition;
The second nature, again, does not come into being by itself,
And this constitutes the second kind of naturelessness.

[Triṃś. 25] That from which all elements have their ultimate reality,
[Is the third naturelessness,]
It is also called suchness,
Because it remains always as such;
That is itself the state [in which one realizes the meaning]
Of mere representation of consciousness, too.[2]

Following the commentary of Sthiramati, I may summarize the theory of threefold naturelessness as follows. Naturelessness (*niḥsvabhāvatā*) means that something lacks certain defining marks, although it may appear to have them.[3] There are three such cases of naturelessness: naturelessness by definition (*lakṣaṇa-niḥsvabhāvatā*), naturelessness with reference to origin (*utpatti-niḥsvabhāvatā*), and the naturelessness of elements in their absolute state of existence (*paramārtha-niḥsvabhāvatā*). The first one, namely, *lakṣaṇa-niḥsvabhāvatā*, applies to *parikalpita-svabhāva*, because the latter lacks a definition (*lakṣaṇa*) by its own characteristics (*sva-rūpa*); whatever characteristics it is believed to

1. *Tri-vidhasya svabhāvasya tri-vidhām niḥsvabhāvatām*
Sandhāya sarvadharmāṇām deśitā niḥsvabhāvatā. Triṃś.23

2. *Prathamo lakṣaṇena-eva niḥsvabhāvo'paraḥ punaḥ*
Na-svayam-bhāva etasya iti-apara niḥsvabhāvatā. Triṃś. 24
Dharmāṇām paramārthaś-ca sa yatas-tathatā-api saḥ
Sarva-kālam tathā-bhāvāt sa eva vijñapti-mātratā. Triṃś.25

3. *Svena svena lakṣaṇena vidyamānavad bhavati.* Triṃś.Bh.23

have, are all imaginary ones (*utprekṣita*), and it has no defining characteristics (*svarūpa-abhāva*) of its own; it is as natureless as an imaginary flower in the sky.[1] The second kind of naturelessness applies to *para-tantra-svabhāva*, which lacks the power of self-origin and self-existence (*svayam-bhāvaḥ*); for its origin as well as existence it depends on other conditions (*pratyaya*), and, is, therefore, like the illusion created, for example, by a magician.[2] The third kind of naturelessness is the very essence of the absolutely accomplished nature, namely that it is absolutely devoid of all subject-object characterization.[3] It always remains as such, and never either as subject or as object.[4] What is ultimately meant by the theory of mere representation of consciousness is that subject-object designations are merely representations of consciousness, and that they do not at all belong to the absolutely accomplished nature.[5]

8. The Realization of Mere Representation of Consciousness

It has been thus established that all subject-object designations are mere representations of consciousness. Therefore, the next consideration is how to realize that they are mere representations of consciousness, and how one can be sure to have realized it.

[Triṃś. 26] As long as consciousness does not abide
In the realization [that the subject-object designations]
Are mere representations of consciousness,
The attachment to the twofold grasping
Will not cease to operate.

1. *Tri-vidhā niḥsvabhāvatā lakṣaṇa-niḥsvabhāvatā utpattiniḥsvabhāvatā paramārtha-niḥsvabhāvatā ca.* Triṃś.Bh.23

Prathamaḥ parikalpitaḥ svabhāvaḥ ayam ca lakṣaṇena-eva niḥsvabhāvaḥ tal-lakṣaṇasya-utprekṣitatvāt rūpa-lakṣaṇā rūpam...iti-ādi. Ataś-ca svarūpa-abhāvāt kha-puṣpavat svarūpeṇa-eva niḥsvabhāvaḥ. Ibid.24

2. *Aparaḥ punar-iti para-tantra-svabhāvaḥ. Na-svayam-bhāvaḥ etasya māyā-vat para-pratyayena-utpatteḥ. Ataś-ca-yathā prakhyāti tathā-asya-utpattir-nāsti-iti ato'sya utpatti-niḥsvabhāvatā-iti-ucyate.* Ibid.

3. *Tasmāt pariniṣpanna eva svabhāvaḥ paramārtha-niḥsvabhāvatā pariniṣpannasya-abhāva-svabhāvatvāt.* Ibid.25

4. *Sarva-kālam tathā-bhāvāt.* Triṃś.25

Sarva-kālam tathā-eva bhavati na-anyathā-iti tathatā-iti-ucyate. Triṃś.Bh. 25

5. *Sa eva vijñapti-mātratā.* Triṃś.25

[Triṃś. 27] One does not abide in the realization
Of mere representation of consciousness
Just on account of the [theoretical] perception
That all this is mere representation of consciousness,
If one places [= sees] something before oneself.[1]

What the above stanzas insist is that (i) only the eradication of subject-object idiosyncrasy (*grāha-dvaya-anuśaya*) can effect the realization of the fact that all forms of subjectivity and objectivity are merely mental representations and (ii) that it can be eradicated not by merely fancying (*upalambhataḥ* = *grahaṇataḥ* = *citrīkaraṇataḥ*)[2] that the objects, as they are perceived, are only mental representations. When can, then, one be assured of the realization that all subject-object designations are mental representations ?

[Triṃś. 28] One does abide in the realization
Of mere [representation of] consciousness
When one does not perceive also a supporting consciousness,
For, the graspable objects being absent,
There cannot either be the grasping of that,
[Namely, the grasping of the supporting consciousness].[3]

Here the realization of mere representation of consciousness is equated with 'seeing the thing as such' (*yathā-bhūta-darśana*),[4] not under the forms of subjectivity and objectivity. The process leading to such realization is : first there is the realization that the form of objectivity (*grāhyatva*), which was believed to be the

1. *Yāvad vijñapti-mātratve vijñānam na-avatiṣṭhati*
Grāha-dvayasya-anuśayas-tāvan-na vinivartate. Triṃś.26
Vijñapti-mātram-eva-idam-iti-api hi-upalambhataḥ
Sthāpayan-agrataḥ kiṃ-cit tanmātre na-avatiṣṭhate. Ibid.27
2. See Triṃś.Bh.27
3. *Yadā tu-ālambanam jñānam na-eva-upalabhate tadā*
Sthito vijñāna-mātratve grāhya-abhāve tad-agrahāt. Triṃś.28
4. See below p. 160 note 1

basis (*ālambana*) of knowledge, is merely a mental construction;[1] then, the belief in objectivity being thus falsified, the belief in subjectivity, too, becomes non-sensical;[2] finally, having thus abandoned the idiosyncrasy for objectivity and subjectivity (*grāha-dvayasya-anuśaya*), one attains the intuitive (*nirvikalpa*) and supramundane (*lokottara*) knowledge, whereby one sees things as such (*yathā-bhūta-darśana*).[3]

The next two stanzas further describe the state of realization :

[Triṃś. 29] That indeed is the supramundane knowledge
When one has no mind that knows,
And no object for its support ;
It follows the revulsion of basis
Through the twofold removal of wickedness;

[Triṃś. 30] That itself is the pure source-reality,
Incomprehensible, auspicious and unchange-
able;
Being delightful, it is the emancipated body,
Which is also called the truth [-body] of the
great sage.[4]

The first characteristic of enlightenment is the supra-mundane knowledge, which operates without depending on the subject-object distinction.[5] Such knowledge is beyond the reach of ordinary man, and intuitive in character. Hence the name

1. *Yasmin kāle..ālambanam jñānam bahiś-cittāt na-upalabhate na paśyati na gṛhṇāti na-abhiniviśate, yathā bhūta-artha-darśanāt na tu jātyā-andhavat, tasmin kāle vijñāna-grāhasya prahāṇam sva-citta-dharmatāyām ca pratiṣṭhito bhavati.* Triṃś. Bh.28

2. *Grāhye sati grāhako bhavati na tu grāhya-abhāva iti. Grāhya-abhāve grāhaka-abhāvam-api pratipadyate na kevalam grāhya-abhāvam.* Triṃś.28

3. *Evam hi samam-anālambya-ālambakam nirvikalpakam lokottaram jñānam-utpadyate, grāhya-grāhaka-abhiniveśa-anuśaya prahīyante sva-citta-dharmatāyām cittam-eva sthitam bhavati.* Ibid.

4. *Acitto'nupalambho'sau jñānam lokottaram ca tat*
Āśrayasya parāvṛttir-dvidhā dauṣṭulya-hānitaḥ; Triṃś.29
Sa eva-anāśravo dhātur-acintyaḥ kuśalo dhruvaḥ
Sukho vimukti-kāyo'sau dharma- ākhyo-'yam mahā-muneh. Triṃś.30

5. *Tatra grāhaka-citta-abhāvāt grāhya-artha-anupalambhāc-ca acitto'nupalambho'sau.* Triṃś.Bh.29

'supra-mundane'.[1] It follows the revulsion of the basis, namely the store-consciousness.[2] The revulsion of the basis ultimately means that the seeds of experience that were implanted in the store-consciousness, have been exterminated by yogic practices.[3] The revulsion of the basis takes place through the twofold removal of wickedness, namely the *jñeya-āvaraṇa* and *kleśa-āvaraṇa*.[4] How *jñeya-āvaraṇa* and *kleśa-āvaraṇa* correspond respectively to one's attachment to objectivity and subjectivity has been elsewhere explained.[5]

The final stanza is describing the reality of an individual in his absolutely accomplished nature. It is source-reality (*dhātu*) in the sense that it is the source of all noble qualities.[6] It is the emancipated body (*vimukti-kāya*), also called the truth-body (*dharmakāya*), of the great sage (*mahā-muni*). Interpreting the term *mahāmuni* Sthiramati says that it refers to Bhagavān Buddha (= the enlightened lord).[7] What I want to point out here is that the 'enlightened lord' (*bhagavān buddha*) need not necessarily be Gautama Buddha, the founder of Buddhism. He can be any individual who attains enlightenment. Therefore, reference to *mahā-muni* or *bhagavān buddha* at this point should not be interpreted as supporting some kind of monism.

9. Conclusion

I may conclude this analysis of *Triṃśatikā* by referring to the introductory remarks of Sthiramati. Explaining the purpose of the entire text he said : This text is intended to explain the meaning of *pudgala-nairātmya* and *dharma-nairātmya*.[8] How has the

1. *Aparicitatvāt (akliṣṭatvāt) loke samudācāra-abhāvāt nirvikalpakatvāt-ca lokād-uttīrṇam-iti jñāpanārtham lokottaram ca tad-iti.* Ibid.
2. *Āśrayo atra sarva-bījakam-ālaya-vijñānam.* Ibid.
3. See above page 149
4. *Dvidhā-iti kleśa-āvaraṇa-dauṣṭulyam jñeya-āvaraṇa-dauṣṭulyam ca.* Ibid.
5. See above pp. 14 ff.
6. *Ārya-dharma-hetutvād dhātuḥ. Hetu-artho hi-atra dhātu-śabdaḥ.* Triṃś. Bh.30
7. *Mahā-muner-iti parama-mauneya-yogāt buddho bhagavān maha-munir-iti.* Ibid.
8. *Pudgala - dharma- nairātmyayor-apratipanna-vipratipannānām-aviparīta-pudgala-dharma-nairātmya-pratipādanārtham triṃśatikā-vijñaptipti-prakaraṇa-ārambhaḥ.* Triṃś Bh. Introduction.

text achieved that purpose? Referring to a passage in *Viṃśatikā-vṛtti* I have elsewhere said that "the old theory of *nairātmya* is thus explained as meaning the non-substantiality of the imagined nature, not of the ineffable nature".[1] Then, what *Triṃśatikā* has done is just to explain that meaning of *nairātmya* further. According to this text *pudgala-nairātmya* and *dharma-nairātmya* would mean respectively the non-substantiality of subjectivity (*ātman*) and objectivity (*dharma*) in their various usages (*upacāras*).[2] All the usages of *ātman* (subjectivity) and *dharma* (objectivity) are transformations of consciousness,[3] and, therefore, non-substantial.

Sthiramati continues : the correct understanding of *pudgala-nairātmya* and *dharma-nairātmya* will help one to destroy the *kleśa-āvaraṇa* and *jñeya-āvaraṇa*, and thus will lead one to liberation (*mokṣa*) and omniscience (*sarvajñatva*) ; the knowledge of *pudgala-nairātmya* counter-acts *satkāya-dṛṣṭi*, and thereby destroys the *kleśas*, while the knowledge of *dharma-nairātmya* counter-acting the *jñeya-āvaraṇa* destroys it; the destruction of *kleśa-āvaraṇa* and *jñeya-āvaraṇa* respectively results in the attainment of *mokṣa* and *sarvajñatva*.[4] When read in the light of *Triṃśatikā*, what Sthiramati says should make the following equations : belief in *pudgala* = *sat-kāya-dṛṣṭi* = *kleśas* = bondage of *saṃsāra* = belief in *ātman* (subjectivity). Therefore, belief in *pudgala-nairātmya* = removal of *sat-kāya-dṛṣṭi* = destruction of *kleśa-āvarāṇa* = attainment of *mokṣa* (liberation) = the belief that *ātman* (subjectivity) is but transformation of consciousness, and, therefore, non-substantial. Similarly, belief in *dharma* (objectivity) = belief in *jñeya* = *akliṣṭam-ajñānam*.[5] Therefore, belief in *dharma-nairātmya* = removal of

1. See above p.23
2. See above pp. 94ff. for my explanation of *ātma-dharma-upacāras*.
3. *Ātma-dharma-upacāro hi vividho yaḥ pravartate*
   Vijñāna-pariṇāmo'sau. Triṃś.1
4. *Pudgala-dharma-nairātmya-pratipādanam punaḥ kleśa-jñeya-āvaraṇa-prahāṇa-artham. Tathā hi-ātma-dṛṣṭi-prabhavā rāga-ādayaḥ kleśāḥ. Pudgala-nairātmya-avabodhaś-ca satkāya-dṛṣṭeḥ pratipakṣatvāt tat-prahāṇāya pravarttamānaḥ sarva-kleśān prajahāti. Dharma-nairātmya-jñānād-api-jñeya āvaraṇa-pratipakṣatvāt jñeya-āvaraṇam prahīyate. Kleśa-jñeya-āvaraṇa-prahāṇam-api mokṣa-sarvajñatva-adhigamārtham* Triṃś. Bh. Introduction.
5. *Jñeya-āvaraṇam-api sarvasmin jñeye jñāna-pravṛtti-pratibandha-bhūtam-akliṣṭam-ajñānam.* Ibid.

jñeya-āvaraṇa = omniscience (*sarvajñatva*). The removal of *kleśa-āvaraṇa* and *jñeya-āvaraṇa*, which leads to liberation and omniscience is definitely referred to in stanza 29,[1] and, therefore, Sthiramati's contention is certainly borne out by the text.

Another objective, says Sthiramati, that Vasubandhu could have in composing *Triṃśatikā*, is to repudiate the two exclusive claims : one, that *vijñeya* (knowable = object) is as much a substance (*dravyataḥ*) as *vijñāna* (knowledge = consciousness = subject) ; two, that *vijñāna* is as much a convention (*saṃvṛtitaḥ*) as *vijñeya*.[2] The text has disproved both of these claims by establishing that both *vijñana* and *vijñeya* are neither substance (*dravyataḥ*) nor convention (*saṃvṛtitaḥ*), but transformations of consciousness (*vijñāna-pariṇāma*).

1. For this text and explanation see above pp. 160-161

2. *Vijñānavad-vijñeyam-api dravyata eva-iti kecin-manyante, vijñeyavad vijñānam-api saṃvṛtita eva na paramārthata iti-asya dviprakārasya-api-ekānta-vādasya pratiṣedhārthaḥ prakaraṇārambhaḥ.* Triṃś. Bh. Introduction.

Chapter Five

A TREATISE IN TWENTY STANZAS (*VIMŚATIKĀ*)[1]

1. Introduction

Viṃśatikā, a treatise in twenty stanzas, is a thorough defence of Vasubandhu's own theory of knowledge against the correspondence theory of knowledge. By this latter theory I mean "the thesis that everything that we perceive is part of the surface of a material object—a thesis that is too naive even to warrant consideration".[2] *Viṃśatikā* is often interpreted as providing 'answers to realism' and thus as showing 'that the universe as representation-only is still a serious and tenable conception'.[3] But I am suggesting that far from providing 'answers to realism' it provides answers to the 'realistic theory of knowledge', which says that there is one-to-one correspondence between concepts and extra-mental obiects. What Vasubandhu is trying to show is not that the universe is 'representation-only' but that what are taken to be the objects of experience are 'representation-only'. In short, *Viṃśatikā* is polemics not against realism, but against the realistic theory of knowledge.

1. This chapter includes translation of *Viṃśatikā-kārikā*, and my interpretation of it based on Vasubandhu's own *Vṛtti* (commentary) on the same text. A full translation of the *Vṛtti* is given in the appendix.

2. D. W. Hamlyn, *The Theory of Knowledge*, (London and Basingstoke: The Macmillan Press Ltd., 1970; reprint ed., 1974), p. 147.

3. Cf. C. H. Hamilton, *Wei Shih Er Shih Lun Or The Treatise in Twenty Stanzas on Representation-only*, (New Haven; American Oriental Society, 1938), p. 6.

For other similar interpretations see: S. D. Sharma, *A Critical Survey of Indian Philosophy*, (Delhi, Varanasi, Patna: Motilal Banarsidass, 1964), pp. 114-116; and P. T. Raju, *Idealistic Thought of India*, (George Allen & Unwin Ltd., 1953; reprint ed. with the subtitle 'Vedanta and Buddhism in the Light of Western Idealism', New York: Johnson Reprint Corporation, 1973)p. 269.

Vasubandhu's theory of knowledge may be named as the 'transformation-theory of knowledge' in so far as t holds that knowledge results from the self-transformation of consciousness which carries within it the seeds of subjectivity and objectivity. He establishes his theory :

(i) by showing the unwelcome consequences of the correspondence theory of knowledge, namely that it cannot explain illusory experiences such as dreams and hallucinations;

(ii) by providing a new interpretation to the theory of *ātma-dharma-nairātmya*;

(iii) by arguing that no possible conception of extra-mental objects will justify the correspondence theory of knowledge; and

(iv) by answering the objections to his transformation-theory of knowledge, namely : How can it explain the difference between waking consciousness and dream-consciousness? How can it explain the inter-action and inter-relation between individuals ? How can it explain moral retribution, and how can it explain the knowledge of other minds ?

2. Vasubandhu's Thesis

Vasubandhu opens his *Vṛtti* by stating that "in the Mahāyāna system it has been established that those belonging to the three worlds are mere representations of consciousness".[1] What are 'those'? From the analysis of *Triṃśatikā*, which I did in the previous chapter, it is clear that 'those' are *citta* and *caittas*, and not *bhūta* and *bhautikas*.[2] MVK, too, confirmed that view, when its author declared that "the imagination of the unreal is *citta* as well as *caittas*, belonging to all three worlds".[3] Hence what Vasubandhu describes as "mere representations of consciousness" are not the three worlds or things therein, but only *citta* and *caittas*. Hence I refuse to accept such translations of the above quoted statement of Vasubandhu as "In the Mahāyāna it is

1. *Mahāyāne traidhātukam vijñapti-mātram vyavasthāpyate.* Viṃś.Vṛ.1
2. See above pp. 140ff
3. *Abhūta-parikalpaś-ca citta-caittas-tridhātukāḥ.* MVK.I.9

established that the three worlds are representation-only".[1] This latter translation ignores the fact that the term '*traidhātuka*' is an adjective meaning belonging to the three worlds', and that it is not a substantive meaning 'the three worlds'. Thus, being an adjective the term '*traidhātuka*' should qualify a noun or nouns, which the reader has to supply; and from the context of *Triṃśatikā* and MV it is clear that the noun under reference is *citta-caittas*. Hence I understand the above statement as meaning that the *citta* and *caittas* belonging to the three worlds are all mere representations of consciousness. Hence the thesis of Vasubandhu :

[Viṃś. 1] It is all mere representation of consciousness,
Because there is the appearance of non-existent objects;[2]

What the above lines imply mav be expressed in other words: Whatever are taken to be the objects of various experiences are all mere appearances, and, therefore, mere representations of consciousness, too It means, things-in-themselves being neither objects nor subjects, the forms of subjectivity and objectivity can come only from consciousness—these forms are stored up in the unconscious, and present themselves at appropriate times.

3. Argument from Illusory Experience

To substantiate his position Vasubandhu points to the experience of a man with bad eyes :

[Viṃś. 1 cont'd.] Just as a man with a cataract
Sees hairs, moons etc.,
Which do not exist in reality.[3]

That is, the objects experienced by a man with a cataract, do not correspond to extra-mental realities. His experience, thus, suggests that there could be experiences having no one-to-one correspondence with extra-mental objects, which thus makes a case for Vasubandhu's position.

1. C. H. Hamilton, op.cit., p.19
2. *Vijñapti-mātram-etad-asadartha-avabhāsanāt.* Viṃś.1
3. *Yathā taimirakasya-asatkeśa-candra-ādi darśanam.* Ibid.1

An objection

The proponents of the correspondence-theory immediately raise the following objection :

[Viṃś. 2] If the representations of consciousness
Are without [extra-mental] objects,
Then there would be no determination of experience with regard to space and time,
Nor would there be indeterminacy of it with regard to streams [i.e. individuals][1]
Nor would there be determination of actions prompted [by a particular experience].[2]

Normally an experience is determined by the place where, and the time when, its object is given; it is not, however, determined with regard to the individuals enjoying it, in the sense that anybody present at that place and time inevitably has that experience; finally, it is also observed that a particular experience always prompts the same sort of actions. All this is so, it is argued, because the experience corresponds to extra-mental objects. On the contrary, if such correspondence between the experience and objects, is denied, then an experience might nappen at any place and time, but not necessarily to everybody present; again, an experience invariably leads to an action in accordance with the nature of its object, which would not happen if the experience did not have to correspond with the object.

Vasubandhu's reply

[Viṃś. 3] Determination of space etc., is obtained
Just as [in] the case of a dream;
Again, indeterminacy [of experience] with regard to streams [i. e. individuals] is obtained
Just as [in] the case [of the experience] of ghosts :
All of them have the same vision of pus-river etc.[3]

1. The term *santāna*, literally meaning 'a stream', for all practical purposes stands for an individual.

2. *Yadi vijñaptir-anarthā niyamo deśa-kālayoḥ*
Santānasya aniyamaś-ca yuktā kṛtya-kriyā na ca. Viṃś.2

3. *Deśa-ādi-niyamaḥ siddhaḥ svapnavat pretavat-punaḥ*
Santāna-aniyamaḥ sarvaiḥ pūya-nadī-ādi-darśane. Viṃś.3

The dream of certain objects occurs only at certain places, and that too, only at certain times. Thus, dream-experience, too, even though it does not correspond to extra-mental objects, is determined by space and time. Again, all ghosts are believed to have the same experience of pus-river (*pūya-nadī*) etc., although the latter are not extra-mental objects. So experience shared by all individuals present does not necessarily guarantee reference to extra-mental objects.

[Viṃś. 4] Determined actions [resulting from experience]
Are obtained as those [obtained] by a dreamer.[1]

That certain fixed actions result from an experience is no guarantee that there is an extra-mental object corresponding to that experience. This view is proved by the fact that even dream experiences produce fixed action. For example, says Vasubandhu, sexual dreams can lead to the discharge of semen.

[Viṃś. 4 cont'd.] Again, all those four factors are obtained
As in the case of hells;
There all [its inhabitants without exception]
Behold the infernal guards etc.,
And experience the torments by them.[2]

It implies that : (i) the infernal guards are only imaginary beings; however, (ii) experience of them by the inhabitants of hell is spatially and temporally restricted to hell, (iii) this experience is shared by all the inhabitants, and, therefore, is not determined with regard to individuals, (iv) this experience also produces fixed results, namely, torments. Thus the experience in hell refutes all the objections raised by the proponents of the correspondence theory of knowledge.

According to Vasubandhu the infernal guards cannot be real beings born in hell. For, if they were, they also should be undergoing the torments and sufferings of hell. In that case they cannot be themselves tormentors as well. On the contrary, if they do not deserve the punishments of hell, i.e. if they are

1. *Svapna-upaghātavat kṛtya-kriyā.* Ibid.4
2. *..narakavat punaḥ,*
Sarvam naraka-pālādi-darśane taiś-ca-bādhane. Ibid.4

not sinners condemned to hell, there is no reason why they should be there at all. In the face of these difficulties Vasubandhu argues that the so called infernal guards are just psychological projections of those condemned to hell. This is the message conveyed by the next stanza :

[Viṃś. 5] Animals are born in heaven,
However, they are not similarly born in hell,
Nor are the infernal guards[1] born in hell,
For, they do not experience the sufferings of hell.[2]

Animals could be born in heaven provided they deserve it by their good deeds. However, the infernal guards cannot deserve hell, through their deeds, for in that case they would be all in the same boat as those condemned to hell, and, therefore, would not be tormentors. Now the opponent, admitting that the infernal guards are not real beings, wants to suggest that they are what the hell-inhabitants by virtue of their deeds project. This suggestion, too, does not satisfy Vasubandhu. Instead of saying that the infernal guards are what the hell-inhabitants by virtue of their deeds project, Vasubandhu holds that they are transformations of the consciousness of the hell-inhabitants :

[Viṃś. 6] If the birth of [special] beings[3] in hell
Can be traced to the deeds of the hell-inhabitants,
Why not say that they are transformations of the latter's consciousness.[4]

1. Here the term translated as infernal guards is *preta*. The usual translation of this term is 'ghost', which can mean one condemned to hell and therefore undergoing the sufferings of hell. However, in the present context this term refers to the tormentors of hell as is clear from *Vṛtti*, and hence my translations of it as 'infernal guards'.

2. *Tiraścām sambhavaḥ svarge yathā na narake tathā*
Na pretānām yatas-tajjam duḥkham na-anubhavanti te. Viṃś.5

3. *Bhūta*, usually meaning 'being', is often used to mean evil spirit, infernal guards, satan, etc.

4. *Yadi tat-karmabhis-tatra bhūtānām sambhavas-tathā*
Iṣyate pariṇāmaś-ca kim vijñānasya na iṣyate. Viṃś.6

Vasubandhu further finds an additional difficulty in accepting that the infernal guards could be projections of one's own deeds : namely, that such a view implies that the deeds do not produce their fruits in the same place as where they were done :

[Viṃś. 7] The impression of deed is imagined to be in one place,
And its fruit in another place :
Why not instead recognize the fruit
In the same place as the impression ?[1]

By implication Vasubandhu is saying that it is not the impressions of deeds that are ultimately responsible for the projection of the so called objects of experience, but the consciousness which carries within it the seeds of subjectivity and objectivity. Vasubandhu has made the same point in *Triṃśatikā*, too, when he said :

The impressions of deeds
Along with those of the twofold grasping
Engender the next stage of maturation.[2]

All that Vasubandhu has been saying so far (Stanzas 1-7) could be summarized as follows: Experience does not guarantee one-to-one correspondence between concepts and extra-mental objects. Dream-experience disproves the correspondence theory of knowledge. Experience starts not with extra-mental objects, but with consciousness, which alone can supply the forms of subjectivity and objectivity, which are necessary presuppositions of any experience in the state of *saṃsāra*.

4. Non-substantiality of Ātman and Dharma

In the next two stanzas Vasubandhu is interpreting the old theory of *āyatanas* (= bases of knowledge) in his own way. The Buddha is reported to have said that there *are* twelve bases of knowledge, namely the sense-organs and their objects. This, the

1. *Karmaṇo vāsanā-anyatra phalam-anyatra kalpyate*
Tatra-eva na-iṣyate yatra vāsanā kim nu kāraṇam. Viṃś.7
2. Triṃś.19. See above p. 150

opponents argue, is an indication that, according to the Buddha, knowledge arises from extra-mental objects (*rūpa-ādi-āyatana*). Vasubandhu's answer to them is that the Buddha's statement that there *are* twelve *āyatanas*, has to be understood in such a way that as knowable objects (*spṛṣṭavya* etc.) and knowing senses (cakṣus etc.) they are transformations or representations of consciousness. That is, the *āyatanas* are the externalization of the seeds of subjectivity (represented by sense-organs) and of objectivity (represented by the so called objects). Indeed, Vasubandhu is not saying that there are no extra-mental things at all. Instead, speaking in the context of knowledge, he is saying that what is taken to be subjects and objects of knowledge are only transformations or representations of consciousness. And according to him, by *āyatanas* the Buddha meant such transformations of consciousness :

[Viṃś. 8] It was with a hidden meaning
That he [the Buddha] spoke to his disciples,
About the existence of the bases like colour etc.,
Just as he spoke about things that are [apparently] born by metamorphosis.[1]

The Buddha spoke of beings that are apparently born by metamorphosis (*upapāduka-sattva*), thereby meaning that there is continuity of the stream of consciousness.[2] Similarly his statement that there are bases of knowledge, too, has to be understood in its hidden meaning. What is that hidden meaning ?

[Viṃś. 9] What the sage spoke of as the two bases [of knowledge]
Are (i) the own-seed
From which a representation of consciousness [develops],

1. *Rūpādi-āyatana-astitvam tad-vineya-janam prati*
Abhiprāya-vaśād-uktam-upapāduka-sattvavat. Viṃś.8
Here *upapāduka-sattva* is a technical term referring to beings born by metamorphosis, or sudden change of organism.

2. *Yathā-asti sattva upapāduka iti-uktam bhagavatā, abhiprāya-vaśāc-citta-santati-anucchedam-āyatyām-abhipretya.* Viṃś. Vr.8

And (ii) the form in which [that representation] appears.[1]

Vasubandhu explains it further as follows : There is, for example, a representation of consciousness (*vijñaptiḥ*) which appears in the form of colour (*rūpa-pratibhāsa*). It develops from its own seed (*svabijāt. . .utpadyate*), which was there in the unconscious, namely *ālaya-vijñāna*. Then at the proper times it externalizes itself in the form of colour. The seed in this case functions as the sense-organ, namely, the sense of vision, and the form that has been projected functions as a perceivable object (*draṣṭavya*).[2]

The above interpretation of the theory of the bases of knowledge leads to a new look at the theory of the non-substantiality of *ātman* and *dharma* (*ātma-dharma-nairātmya*). It has been elsewhere[3] observed that for Vasubandhu *ātman* and *dharma* stand respectively for subjectivity and objectivity. It becomes still clearer in the present context. For, after having established in the previous two stanzas that subjectivity and objectivity, represented by *āyatanas*, are forms of consciousness, now he is going to say that the non-substantiality of the same subjectivity and objectivity is what is meant by the non-substantiality of *ātman* and *dharma*. Thus the next stanza :

[Viṃś. 10] By this one is definitely initiated
Into the theory of the non-substantiality of self [*pudgala*]
Again, on the other hand,
By this instruction one is initiated
Into the non-substantiality of objects [*dharma*]:

1. *Yataḥ sva-bījād-vijñaptir-yadābhāsa pravartate*
Dvi-vidha-āyatanatvena te tasya munir-abravīt Viṃś.8

2. *Rūpa-pratibhāsa-vijñaptir-yataḥ svabījāt-pariṇāma-viśeṣaprāptād-utpadyate tac-ca bījam yat-pratibhāsa ca sa te tasya vijñapteścakṣu-rūpa-āyatanatvena yathā-kramam bhagavān-abravīt.* Viṃś.Vr.9

3. See above pp. 94ff

[The self and the objects are non-substantial]
With regards to their imagined nature.[1]

It means, the doctrine (*deśanā* = instruction) that the *āyatanas*, representing subjectivity and objectivity, are projections of consciousness, explains the non-substantiality of *ātman* and *dharma*. The *indriya-āyatanas* (sense-organs) make up what is called self (*pudgala*), and is a collective name for subjectivity; and they being mere representations of consciousness, *pudgala*, too, turns out to be non-substantial (*nairātmya*). Similarly, the *viṣaya-āyatanas* (knowable forms) being mere representations of consciousness, the objectivity which they represent, too, is non-substantial, this being the meaning of *dharma-nairātmya*.

The last part of the above stanza, which says that the non-substantiality (*nairātmya*) of self (*pudgala*) and object (*dharma*) applies only to their imagined nature (*kalpita-ātma*), is very significant in understanding Vasubandhu's view of reality. Read along with Vasubandhu's subsequent commentary, it points right at the heart of his philosophy, and puts the whole of it in the right perspective. As I have already explained the passage concerned in one of the previous chapters,[2] here I may just summarize it as follows: Vasubandhu makes a clear distinction between the imagined (*kalpita*) and ineffable (*anabhilāpya*) aspects of reality. It is the imagined aspect of reality that becomes either subject or object of on ordinary man's experience, while its ineffable aspect is far beyond the range of his experience. Consequently, it is the forms of subjectivity and objectivity that are traced to imagination (*parikalpa* or *vikalpa*), and, therefore, called the transformation of consciousness (*vijñāna-pariṇāma*), and characterized as non-substantial (*nairātmya*). On the contrary, the ineffable aspect of reality, which becomes neither subject nor object of experience, is the suchness (*tathatā*), the thing as it is (*yathā-bhūta-vastu*), and therefore, substantial (*dravyataḥ*). Only the enlightened ones can know the ineffable aspect of reality as such (*anabhilāpyena ātmanā yo buddhānām viṣayaḥ*).

1. *Tathā pudgala-nairātmya-praveśo hi anyathā punaḥ*
Deśanā-dharma-nairātmya-praveśaḥ kalpita-ātmanā. Viṃś.10
2. See above pp. 23ff

Now, the distinction between the imagined and ineffable aspects of reality has decisive application to Vasubandhu's theory of knowledge, too. For, it explains his contention that there is no one-to-one correspondence between the objects known and the extra-mental realities. The objects known refer to the imagined aspect of reality, which is subject to graspable-grasper distinction, while the extra-mental realities refer to the ineffable aspect of reality. Hence there is no chance of having correspondence between the objects known and the extra-mental realities.

5. Vasubandhu's Criticism of Realism

A realist as he is, Vasubandhu criticises that sort of realism, which does not distinguish between the imagined and ineffable aspects of reality. Stanzas 11-15 contain such a criticism of realism. One can very easily be tempted to interpret these stanzas as a blanket refutation of realism.[1] Read out of context they do yield such an interpretation. But if one takes into account what Vasubandhu says immediately before and after those stanzas, one will find it impossible to interpret them as unqualified refutation of realism. For, his criticism of realism follows the distinction between the imagined and the ineffable aspects of reality, and the clear admission that beings in their ineffable nature are beyond the experience of ordinary men.[2] In other words, before starting his criticism of realism, he made it clear that there is a plurality of beings, each of them having an ineffable nature. Therefore, his criticism of realism cannot by any means imply a denial of extra-mental reality. On the contrary,

28. Referring to those stanzas Hamilton (op.cit., p. 10), for one, says: "Vasubandhu's reply, extending through several stanzas, is a powerful destructive dialectic against the concept of an exte rnal world".

29. Even Hamilton, who described Vasubandhu's position as "a powerful destructive dialectic against the concept of an external world" (op.cit., p.10), has observed that according to Vasubandhu, "The nature of elements within the domain of Buddha's insight is indeed beyond words, but it is not inexistent. What the "realization of the substantiality of elements" actually denies is any and every form of elemen t falsely conceived by the common, unenlightened consciousness". (Ibid. p. 10). However, he does not seem to take seriously the consequence of admitting 'the nature of elements which is beyond words', namely, that it endorses realism.

all it can mean is that : things-in-themselves being ineffable are not experienced by ordinary men; what are being experienced are one's own mental constructions; hence no possible conceptualization of reality can correspond to the extra-mental world.

The stanzas following the criticism of realism, too, are such that they cannot be understood without presupposing a plurality of real beings, who influence, and interact on, each other. I shall return to this point later.[1]

Let me now examine Vasubandhu's criticism of realism. For the most part it is directed against the atomic realism of the Vaiśeṣika system. However, Vasubandhu's aim seems to be to point out that no possible conceptualization of reality can adequately represent the extra-mental world. In most cases, he shows, such conceptualizations are self-contradictory. According to his description, the reality could be conceived either as (i) a single being endowed with qualities, or (ii) as a multiplicity of atoms, or as an aggregate of atoms. Each of these conceptions Vasubandhu finds contradictory, and, therefore, unacceptable :

[Viṃś. 11] The object is [experienced]
Neither as a single entity,
Nor as many discrete atoms,
Nor as an aggregate of them,
Because not a single atom is obtained [in experience at all].[2]

Here, in the first place, Vasubandhu is not speaking about things-in-themselves, but about objects (*viṣaya*) of experience. In one of the previous stanzas it was said that the Buddha's statement that there are twelve bases of knowledge, has to be understood in such a way that, as knowable objects and knowing senses, those bases are only transformations of consciousness. The present stanza, says Vasubandhu, further explains, how one can conclude that according to the Buddha the objective bases

1. See below pp. 188 ff.
2. *Na tad-ekam na ca-anekam viṣayaḥ paramāṇuśaḥ*
Na ca te saṃhatā yasmāt paramāṇur-na sidhyati. Viṃś. 11

(*rūpa-ādi-āyatanas*) of knowledge are not things existing by themselves.[1] Hence the discussion is definitely about things inasmuch as they become objects of knowledge. In what mode are they known or experienced : as a single entity, or as many discrete atoms, or an aggregate of atoms ? Vasubandhu finds that neither of those modes is part of one's experience. Commenting on the above stanza he says :

> 'The objective bases, namely *rūpa* etc., supposedly become the objects (*viṣaya*) of the concept of colour etc., respectively. Is each of them [namely, the objective bases of colour etc.] experienced as a single whole, just as the Vaiśeṣikas speak of the colour-whole etc. ? Or are they experienced as many discrete atoms ? or as an aggregate of atoms ? One cannot speak of a single whole-object, because there is never the experience of the whole-colour as distinct from parts. Nor are the objects experienced as many discrete atoms, because there is never the experience of single atoms. Nor are they experienced as aggregates of atoms, because not a single atom is obtained [in experience].[2]

All that Vasubandhu is saying here is that the objects as they are experienced cannot be described as a single entity, nor as a plurality of discrete atoms, nor as an aggregate of atoms. He then proceeds to say that an atom cannot possibly be obtained in experience because the concept of atom involves so many contradictions, such as:

[Viṃś. 12] One atom joined at once to six other atoms
Must have six parts.
On the other hand, if they are said

1. *Katham punar-idam pratyetavyam-anena-abhiprāyeṇa bhagavatā rūpa-ādi-āyatana-astitvam-uktam na punaḥ santi-eva tāni yāni rūpādivijñaptīnām pratyekam viṣayībhavanti-iti. Yasmāt*— [now follows stanza 11.] Viṃś.Vr.11

2. *Yad-rūpādikam-āyatanam rūpādi-vijñaptīnām pratyekam viṣayaḥ syāt-tad-ekam vā syād-yathā avayavī rūpam kalpyate vaiśeṣikaiḥ. Anekam vā paramāṇuśaḥ saṃhatā vā ta-eva paramāṇavaḥ. Na tāvad-ekam viṣayo bhavati-avayavebhyo 'nyasya-avayavī-rūpasya kvacid-api-agrahaṇāt. Na-api-anekam paramāṇūnām pratyekam agrahaṇāt. Na-api te saṃhatā viṣayībhavanti. Yasmāt paramānur-ekam dravyam na sidhyati.* Viṃś.Vr.11

To occupy the same place,
Then their aggregate would mean
Nothing more than a single atom.[1]

This stanza is suggesting two alternatives, which would make aggregates of atoms possible : either atoms join to each other and thus form an extended body, or they join to each other in such a way that even their aggregates remain atomic, needing no more space than a single atom. Both of these alternatives are contradictory : the first one is contradictory because it implies that an atom has parts, which no atom has by definition; the second one is contradictory, because it does not explain the distinction between a single atom and a collection of them. Hence the concept of aggregates of atoms does not make sense.

Now the Kāśmīra-Vaibhāṣikas argue that, though the atoms cannot join to each other, their aggregates can join, and that, thus, there is no problem involved in having aggregates of atoms. Vasubandhu's reply to them is simply that, if the atoms cannot join, neither can they make aggregates, which would subsequently join to each other.[2]

[Viṃś. 13] As there is no joining of atoms,
Whose joining can be attributed on their aggregates.[3]

In other words, when the aggregates are said to join to one another, they should do so by the joining of their component atoms. But as atoms do not ever join together, it is non-sensical to say that their aggregates join to each other.

Further,

[Viṃś. 13 There can be no joining of atoms,
cont'd.] Not because they have no parts.[4]

1. *Ṣaṭkena yugapad-yogāt-paramāṇoḥ ṣaḍaṃśatā*
Ṣaṇṇām samāna-deśatvāt-piṇḍaḥ syād-aṇumātrakaḥ. Viṃś.12

2. *Mā bhūd-eṣa doṣa-prasaṅgaḥ saṃhatas-tu parasparam saṃyujyanta iti kāśmīra-vaibhāṣikās-ta idam pṛṣṭavyāḥ. Yaḥ paramāṇūnām saṅghāto na sa tebhyo' rtha-antaram-iti.* Viṃś.Vṛ.13

3. *Paramāṇor-asaṃyoge tat-saṅghāte'sti-kasya saḥ.* Viṃś.13

4. *Na ca anavayavatvena tat-saṃyogo na sidhyati.* Viṃś.13

Vasubandhu illustrates his point as follows : The aggregates of atoms cannot join to one another, not just because they do not have parts, but because there cannot be aggregates of atoms at all. Similarly, the atoms do not join to each other, not just because they do not have parts, (but because the very concept of atom is contradictory).[1]

What ultimately Vasubandhu means may be expressed as follows. That the world is composed of atoms is only a conceptual image of the world. Such a conceptual image does not guarantee that the world in reality is composed of atoms. Moreover, one cannot consistently argue that the world is composed of (unextended) atoms, because this position involves self-contradictions such as have been explained above. This does not, however, in any case mean that the world is non-existent or illusory. It means only that ordinary human conception is inadequate to reach the world as it is, which is known only to the enlightened ones.

Now Vasubandhu proceeds to point out some more inconsistencies presented by the atomic conception of the world: atoms are either with or without extension, both cases, however, having practical difficulties, such as,

[Viṃś. 14] That which has different parts
Cannot make a unity,
[On the contrary, if it has no parts,]
How come it is subject to shadow and concealment ?
It cannot be argued that they [i.e. shadow and concealment]
Belong to the aggregate of atoms,
Unless the aggregate is admitted to be
Different from atoms.[2]

An atom by definition is an indivisible unit, and therefore cannot have parts or extensions. If, however, the world is composed

1. *Na tarhi paramāṇūnām niravayavatvāt saṃyogo na sidhyati-iti vaktavyam. Sāvayavasya-api hi saṅghātasya saṃyoga-anabhyupagamāt.* Viṃś.Vṛ.13

2. *Dig-bhāga-bhedo yasya-asti tasya-ekatvam na yujyate*
Chāyā-āvṛti katham vā anyo na piṇḍaś-cet-na-tasya te. Viṃś.14

of such indivisible, partless and extensionless units, then, at sunrise, for example, it would not have one side with shadow and another without shadow. Similarly, atoms having no parts, there could be no case of one atom being obscured by another, for no atom has an "other" side which would be obscured by the arrival of another atom. Nor can it be said that aggregates of atoms are responsible for the phenomena of shadow and obscuration, for it is meaningless to say that extensionless atoms can form extended aggregates.[1]

The next consideration is what would happen if the whole world were conceived as a single, indivisible, extensionless unit. Vasubandhu finds that such a position will leave a number of questions unanswered:

[Viṃś. 15] [If it is assumed that the earth is] a single unit
Then there would be no progressive movement,
Nor simultaneous grasping and non-grasping,
Nor would there be discrete states of many [beings],
Nor would there be subtle and invisible [beings].[2]

If the earth were a single unit, there would be no progressive movement, because just one step would cover the entire earth; there would be no simultaneous grasping and non-grasping, because if anything is grasped at all, it would amount to grasping the entire world; there would be no discrete states of many beings, because all of them would be occupying the only single unit of space available; there would be no subtle and invisible beings, because all beings being of equal size, there would be no point in distinguishing between gross and subtle beings, and between visible and invisible beings.[3]

Vasubandhu's criticism of realism ends here. Nowhere during the discussion does he say that there is no extra-mental world.

1. See Viṃś. Vṛ.14
2. *Ekatve na krameṇa-etir-yugapan-na grāha-agrāhau*
Vicchinna-aneka-vṛttiś-ca sūkṣma-anikṣā ca no bhavet. Viṃś.15
3. See Viṃś.Vr.15

Instead he has thrice said that "an atom is not obtained".[1] The term translated here as 'is obtained' is *sidhyati*. To be sure, this term does not mean 'to exist' (*asti*). Therefore, to translate the above sentence as "an atom does not exist" would be a gross mistake. The usual meanings of the term *sidhyati* are 'to be obtained (in experience),' 'to be given (in experience)' or 'to be proved to be true' etc.[2] So Vasubandhu's main criticism against the atomic realism is that the atoms are neither given in experience nor proved. Therefore he does not really say that there are no atoms at all, although he is not prepared to admit that things-in-themselves which are ineffable, could be conceived in terms of atoms.

Let me once again recall that the entire discussion takes place in the context of knowledge. What Vasubandhu is primarily concerned about is to show that no mode of existence suggested by atomic realism can stand the test of experience. The objects experienced are never in the mode of a single atom, nor of many discrete atoms, nor of aggregates of atoms. So atomic realism cannot be defended on the basis of experience.

Further, even if atomic realism were the correct way of conceiving the extra-mental world, it does not justify the correspondence theory of knowledge. For, the objects attained in knowledge do not correspond to any of the modes suggested by atomic realism: that is, the objects are never experienced either as a single atom or as many discrete atoms or as aggregates of atoms. So no matter whether atomic realism is correct or not, Vasubandhu's thesis that the objects insofar as they are experienced, are subjective forms of consciousness, and therefore comparable to objects experienced in dreams, stands.

Vasubandhu has also brought out the practical difficulties involved in conceiving the world as composed of indivisible atoms. The Vaiśeṣikas, who hold such an atomic realism, also claim that an ordinary man's experience of the world, too, is realistic. It would mean that an ordinary man's experiences of

1. *Paramāṇur-na sidhyati.* Viṃś.11
Paramāṇur-ekam dravyam na sidhyati. Viṃś.Vr.11 and 13

2. See V. S. Apte, *The Student's Sanskrit-English Dictionary*, Delhi, Patna, Varanasi: Motilal Banarsidass, (1965), p. 603. Hamilton (op. cit., p. 43, 45 & 49) has translated *sidhyati* as "is proved".

extension, movement, partial knowledge, shadow and concealment, quantity, difference, relation etc. , etc. , have all to be real, and corresponding to the extra-mental world. But, as Vasubandhu has shown, atomic realism cannot in any way explain, or account for, such experiences. Thus atomic realism suffers seriously from internal inconsistencies, and therefore cannot be accepted as a valid explanation of the extra-mental world.

Finally, Vasubandhu's criticism of atomic realism does not amount to the denial of an extra-mental world. Instead, it means only that he refuses to conceive the extra-mental world in terms of atomic realism. And in fact, he refuses to accept any sort of theoretical formulation about the extra-mental world, because for him the extra-mental world, which consists of things-in-themselves, is ineffable (*anabhilāpya*), and therefore beyond all human formulations. What one can think of and speak of is one's own mental construction (*parikalpita*=*kalpita-ātma*), which has little correspondence with the extra-mental world.

Again, that Vasubandhu believes in an extra-mental world is beyond doubt. For, just before starting the criticism of realism, he made it absolutely clear that there is an extra-mental world of beings, whose ineffable nature is perceived only by the enlightened ones.[1] Therefore it would be unreasonable to think that Vasubandhu's criticism of realism is meant to deny the existence of an extra-mental world.

6. Refutation of the Correspondence Theory of Knowledge

Now Vasubandhu squarely faces the supporters of the correspondence theory of knowledge. The latter, as already mentioned, maintain that every piece of knowledge corresponds to an extra-mental reality. From this they argue that the fact that one has knowledge of something can be taken as a proof for the extra-mental existence of that thing. And conversely, too, according to them there would be no knowledge, especially sense-perception, if there were no extra-mental realities. Vasubandhu formulates

1. See above pp. 23ff

their arguments as follows: "Existence or non-existence [of something] is proved using the means of knowledge. Of all the means of knowledge sense-perception is the strongest one. If so, there being no object, how does one get the awareness such as 'this thing is being perceived by me?'"[1] I may reformulate this argument as follows. Existence or non-existence of something is established on the basis of the evidence of knowledge. And the most valid form of knowledge is sense-perception. So whenever there is a sense-perception, it is most certain that there is an extra-mental reality corresponding to that sense-perception. And, again, that there are sense-perceptions, is a fact. Thereore, that there are extra-mental realities corresponding to those sense-perceptions, too, is a fact.

Interestingly enough, Vasubandhu's reply to the above argument does not at all attempt to deny the existence of extra-mental realities. On the contrary, what he does is to falsify the premise that every piece of knowledge testifies the existence of an extra-mental reality, and thus to show that existence of an extra-mental reality cannot be established on the basis of the evidence of knowledge. In other words, what he is interested in is to refute the correspondence theory of knowledge. Here, again, his argument against the correspondence theory of knowledge is drawn from illusory experiences. It just says that dream-experience is a case against the claim that every perception necessarily refers to an extra-mental reality:

> [Viṃś. 16] Perception [can occur without extra-mental objects],
> Just at it happens in a dream etc.[2]

The rest of the above stanza makes an analysis of perception and concludes that even in waking experience perception does not get at extra-mental objects. He says that at the time of perception there is no longer the presence of extra-mental object, which would be the object of that perception:

1. *Pramāṇa-vaśād-astitvam nāstitvam vā nirdhāryate. Sarveṣām ca pramāṇānām pratyakṣam pramāṇam gariṣṭham-iti-asati-arthe katham-idam buddhir-bhavati pratyakṣam iti.* Viṃś.Vṛ. 16

2. *Pratyakṣa-buddhiḥ svapnādau yathā.* Viṃś.16. Commenting on it Vasubandhu says : *vinā-api-arthena-iti pūrvam-eva jñāpitam.* Viṃś.Vṛ.16

[Viṃś. 16 cont'd.] At the time when that [perception occurs],
The [corresponding external] object is not found;
How can then one speak of its perception?[1]

In other words, by the time perception arises, the perceptive faculty will have already lost touch with the object in question, so that the perception cannot be of that object. Vasubandhu gives two arguments to this effect. (i) He distinguishes two moments in the process of perception: one, the moment of contact between the sense and the object; two, the moment of reflection whereby one realizes that one has the preception of something. For Vasubandhu perception occurs at this second moment of reflection, when the sense no longer has to be in contact with its object. For example, in the first moment there is contact between the sense of vision and its object. In the second moment one can close one's eyes, and still reflect to realize that one perceives such and such an object. This reflective awareness is what is called perception. Hence, it is evident that at the moment when perception takes place, there is no contact between the sense and the object. If so, of what is the perception? Or, what is the object of perception? It is nothing other than the image constructed by the mind. Vasubandhu's own words in this context may be paraphrased as follows: Perception is the reflective awareness that 'I have perception of such and such an object'. However, when it occurs, the object is not seen at all. For, the eye-consciousness is obstructed at that time. Hence the perception is determined only by thought-consciousness. So how can it be said that an external object is perceived?[2]

(ii) The second argument is based on the theory of momentariness, which says that everything is momentary.[3] The objects

1...*sa ca yadā tadā*
Na so'rtho dṛśyate tasya pratyakṣatvam katham matam, Viṃś.16

2. *Yadā ca sā pratykṣa-buddhir-bhavati-idam me pratyakṣam iti-tadā na so'rtho dṛśyate mano-vijñānena-eva paricchedāc-cakṣurvijñānasya ca tadā niruddhatvād-iti katham tasya pratyakṣatvam iṣṭam.* Viṃś.Vṛ.16

3. *Sarvam kṣaṇikam*

as well as senses being momentary, they may still come into contact with each other for a single moment. But in the second moment of reflective awareness, when perception takes place, there will be neither the same object nor the same sense-organ (=subject). Therefore, perception cannot have for its object an extra-mental reality.[1] Instead, what is being perceived is just an image constructed by the mind.

Thus the question that interests Vasubandhu is not whether there are external objects or not. He almost takes it for granted that there are such objects. Then the question before him is whether they are as such obtained in perception. He answers this question negatively; namely, that the object arrived at in perception is never the thing-in-itself, but only the image constructed by the mind. It is interesting to note how the later logicians, Diṅnāga and Dharmakīrti, took over this idea and made it the central thesis of their epistemology. They distinguished between the moment of pure sensation and of conceptualization. A perception is complete only when the moment of sensation is followed by an act of conceptualization.[2] The moment of pure sensation is marked by a momentary contact between the object and the sense-faculty, which creates just a sense-impression. This sensation is momentry,[3] and, therefore, not subject to mental construction.[4] Being a moment of experience it is neither conceivable nor communicable, it is not even worth the name of knowledge. It becomes knowledge or perception only when it is associated with certain conceptual forms (*kalpanā*) supplied by the mind. Such conceptual forms are defined as a distinct cognition of what appears, which (=cognition) is capable of being

1. *Viśeṣeṇa tu kṣaṇikasya viṣayasya tadānīm niruddham-eva tadrūpam rasādikam vā.* Viṃś.Vṛ 16

2. *Pratyakṣasya sākṣāt-kāritva-vyāpāro vikalpena-anugamyate.* (*Nyāya-bindu-ṭīka.* 3.12)

3. *Pyatyakṣasya hi kṣaṇa eko grāhyaḥ.* (Ibid. 1.12)

4. *Kalpanā-apoḍham-abhrāntam pratyakṣam.* This is the definition given by Dharmakīrti in his *Nyāya-bindu*, 1.4. In Diṅnāga's definition the term *abhrāntam* does not appear. However, for various reasons Dharmakīrti and his commentators thought this term to be essential to the definition of *pratyakṣa*. For details see my "A Study of the Buddhist Epistemology according to Dharmakīrti's *Nyāya-bindu*", (M.A. dissertation, University of Poona, 1974), pp. 30ff.

expressed in words.[1] So it is the conceptual forms (*kalpanā*) that make a sense-experience a piece of knowledge, which is conceivable and expressible in words. Thus knowledge in the empirical sense of the term must involve mental construction, and therefore, cannot guarantee an accurate representation of things-in-themselves. And this is all that Vasubandhu, too, says.

The defenders of the correspondence theory of knowledge still insist that there has to be an invariable connection between knowledge and external realities. They are now prepared to concede that knowledge in its final form is far removed from, and out of touch with, extra-mental realities. But they argue that every knowledge presupposes a 'first moment' of real contact with extra-mental realities. They cite particularly the instance of memory: at the time when memory takes place, mind is not at all in touch with the external object concerned. But it was once in the past in direct touch with that object, which experience alone makes the present memory possiple.[2] So, they conclude, even those experiences which have no apparent contact with external realities, are ultimately based on some extra-mental reality.

Vasubandhu's answer is the same as ever: What appear to be objects of knowledge are no more than representations of consciousness. Memory is possible because such representations of consciousness occurring at one time may be later recalled. Therefore, memory is not based on external objects any more than knowledge or perception itself is:

[Viṃś. 17] It has [already] been said
That there is a representation of consciousness,
Which appears as that, [namely the respective object];
From it [i.e. from a representation of consciousness]
Does the memory arise.[3]

1. *Abhilāpa-saṃsarga-yogya-pratītiḥ kalpanā.* (*Nyāya-bindu*, 1.5).
2. *Na-ananubhūtam-mano-vijñānena smaryata iti-avaśyam artha-anubhavena bhavitavyaṁ tac-ca darśanam-iti-evam tad-viṣayasya rūpadeḥ pratyakṣatvam matam.* Viṃś.Vṛ.17
3. *Uktam yathā tad-ābhāsa vijñaptiḥ smaraṇam tataḥ.* Viṃś.17

Commenting on those lines Vasubandhu says: It has already been said that even in the absence of extra-mental objects there arise representations of consciousness, which appear as objects of visual consciousness etc. From those representations there can arise thought-representations, which associated with memory-power will appear as the same objects, namely colour etc., hence the fact of memory does not prove the experience of [extra-mental] objects.[1]

The next objection raised by the opponents gives Vasubandhu an opportuntiy to make an important point. Their objection is as follows. Everybody knows that his dream experiences do not have extra-mental realities for their objects. Similarly, if the waking experiences, too, did not have extra-mental realities for their objects, then everybody would naturally know that their experiences did not correspond to any extra-mental realities. But it is not the case. Therefore, on the basis of dream-experience one cannot argue that waking experiences, too, do not correspond to extra-mental realities.[2] Vasubandhu's answer is:

> [Viṃś 17 cont'd.] Those who are not awake
> Do not realize that the objects they see in a dream
> Do not exist.[3]

What Vasubandhu suggests here is that the dream-experience is to be taken only as a model towards understanding the entire saṃsāric experience. It is true that everybody knows that the objects experienced in dreams are not real, but only mental images. But one comes to realize it only once one wakes up from sleep. Similarly, as long as one is in the state of *saṃsāra*, one is in a transcendental sleep, under the influence of which one

1. *Vinā-api-arthena yathā-artha-ābhāsa cakṣur-vijñana-ādika vijñaptir-utpadyate tathā-uktam. Tato hi vijñapteḥ smṛti-saṃprayuktā tat-pratibhāsa-eva rūpādi-vikalpika mano-vijñaptir-utpadyāt iti na smṛtyutpādād-artha-anubhavaḥ sidhyati.* Viṃś.Vr.17

2. *Yadi yathā svapne vijñaptir-abhūta-artha-viṣaya tathā jāgrato'pi syāt-tathā-eva tad-abhāvam lokaiḥ svayam-avagacchet. Na ca-evam bhavati. Tasmān-na svapna iva-artha-upalabdhiḥ sarvā nirarthikā.* Viṃś.Vr.17

3. *Svapne dṛg-viṣaya-abhāvam na-aprabuddho'vagacchati.* Viṃś.17

dreams of so many objects, which are mistaken for real, extra-mental, realities. One will not realize that those objects are only his own mental images, as long as one is in that transcendental sleep, namely, *saṃsāra*. But the moment one attains enlightenment, one will spontaneously realize that what one so far took for realities, were only imaginary dream-objects, and that things-in-themselves are nothing like those images. Commenting on the obove lines Vasubandhu says: The world is fast asleep. It is a sleep characterized by the habit of vainly distinguishing between subject and object. The world so asleep sees unreal objects, just as in a dream. As long as it is not awoken it cannot properly realize the unreality of those objects. The supra-mundane-intuitive knowledge will act as a remedy to this sleepiness. When through such knowledge one is awakened, the previously attained impure, mundane, knowledge will vanish, and consequently one will properly realize the unreality of the mistaken objects. Thus, the dream-experience and the waking experience are similar to each other.[1]

Here all of a sudden it becomes clear that the example of dream-experience for Vasubandhu means much more than an argument against the correspondence theory of knowledge. It is now a model explaining the saṃsāra-experience itself. Thus, what he ultimately says is that the individuals in the state of *saṃsāra* are in a cosmic slumber, which makes them dream so many objects. Mental images as they are, those dream-objects are mistaken for things-in-themselves by the unenlightened. This does not mean that there are no things-in-themselves at all, only they are not as such perceived by the unenlightened people. Once the latter are enlightened by the supra-mundane-intuitive knowledge, they will come out of their slumber, and will on the one hand realize the unreality of those dream-objects, and, on the other, see things-in-themselves as they are.

1. *Evam vitatha-vikalpa-vāsanā-nidrayā prasupto lokaḥ svapna iva abhūtam artham paśyan-na prabuddhas-tadabhāvam yathāvan-na-avagacchati. Yadā tu tat-prati-pakṣa-lokottara-nirvikalpa-jñāna-lābhāt-prabuddho bhavati tadā tad-praṣṭa-labdha-aśuddha-laukika-jñāna-samukhībhāvāt-viṣaya-abhāvam yathāvad-avagacchati-iti samā-nam-etat.* Viṃś.Vṛ.17

7. Inter-action and Inter-relation Between Individuals

Now it comes about that all experiences and happenings in this saṃsāric realm are only phenomenal and, therefore, affect nobody in a substantial manner. Consequently, it would appear that people, as long as they live in this realm, never get to know each other, nor can influence each other, nor can help each other, nor can even injure each other. Thus Vasubandhu's philosophy seems to call into question the meaning of social life. It also seemingly fails to explain the moral merits and demerits of actions, these actions being no better than those done by a dreamer. Vasubandhu's answer to these difficulties is given in the remaining stanzas of the treatise.

Before starting to analyse the text, let me recall what I already mentioned in the introductory chapter.[1] That is, this final section of the treatise cannot be understood without presupposing a plurality of individuals. If Vasubandhu did not believe in a plurality of individuals, he could very easily dismiss the above difficulties, saying that there being only one being the questions about social relations are irrelevant. Therefore, the very fact that he takes those questions seriously, and that he tries to solve them satisfactorily, is clear evidence that he admits a plurality of beings. One might argue that Vasubandhu's admission of a plurality of beings applies only to the phenomenal realm of existence, just as the non-dualist Śaṅkara's admission of a plurality of beings does. But I should say that there is a great difference between the ways these two authors speak. First of all Vasubandhu never even once positively says that there is only one being, and that plurality is only apparent; while the basic thesis of Śaṅkara is that "being is only one, without a second".[2] Secondly, Vasubandhu more than once refers to a plurality of enlightened beings (*buddhas*), who evidently belong to the noumenal realm of existence, and who alone know the ineffable nature (*anabhilāpya-ātma*) of each other and of other beings;[3] while Śaṅkara all through his writings is positively fighting against the possibility of having a plurality of liberated (*mukta*)

1. See above.
2. *Ekam-eva advitīyam*
3. For example, see *Viṃś.*10 and 21 along with *Vṛtti.*

beings. Thirdly, assumption of a plurality of beings makes no part of Vasubandhu's writings meaningless, but, on the contrary, makes many passages much more meaningful than they would be from a monistic point of view; while assumption of a plurality of beings (in the noumenal level) would contradict the very basic thesis of Śaṅkara, and would make most of his writings absolutely meaningless. Therefore it is no use comparing the systems of Śaṅkara and Vasubandhu in establishing that the latter is a monist. On the contrary, taking the whole context into account, I feel that the admission of a plurality of beings, even in the noumenal level of existence, is Vasubandhu's basic assumption, and that such an assumption has one of its clear applications in interpreting the following stanzas.

The objector says: It has been said that the objects experienced by sentient beings are representations of consciousness which appear as objects. These representations, again, are said to arise from transformations of the stream-consciousness of the respective individuals, not from particular, external, objects. (It implies that nothing external can influence or determine those representations of consciousness). If so, how come that sentient beings have their representations of consciousness determined by acquaintance with good or bad friends, or by listening to good or bad discourses. In fact there could be neither contact with good or bad friends, nor such discourses.[1]

Vasubandhu replies:

[Viṃś. 18] The representations of consciousness
Are determined by mutual influence
Of one [individual] on another.[2]

Vasubandhu explains it: The representations of consciousness of all sentient beings are determined by mutual influence of one [individual] on another, according as it is fitting. Thus, a particular representation arises on a certain stream-consciousness

1. *Yadi sva-santāna-pariṇāma-viśeṣād-eva sattvānām arthapratibhāsa vijñaptaya utpadyante na-artha-viśeṣāt, tadā ya pāpa-kalyāṇa-mitra-samparkāt sad-asad-dharma-śravaṇāc-ca vijñapti-niyamaḥ sattvānām sa katham sidhyati asati sad-asat-samparke tad-deśanāyām ca.* Viṃś.Vṛ.18

2. *Anyonya-adhipatitvena vijñapti-niyamo mithaḥ.* Viṃś.18

by the influence of a particular representation on another stream-consciousness, not on account of any particular external object.[1]

Here is a point worth mentioning. The discussion so far has been mostly about how people know each other, or experience each other. In that case the reality of the subject who knows or experiences was mostly taken for granted, and then always the question was about the reality of the objects known or experienced. Here, on the other hand, the question is about how people influence each other, and how their character is affected by mutual friendship, conversation etc. This question inevitably presupposes a multiplicity of really existing individuals. The only genuine problem in this regard is how those individuals, whose ultimate natures are ineffable and incommunicable, can reach each other in order to influence each other. About objects of knowledge Vasubandhu said that they are nothing extra-mental, but only mental images. But when he says that two individuals influence each other in one way or another, he must mean that they are really existing beings. For example, to say that I am affected by someone else, I must first believe that there is someone else than myself. Thus, Vasubandhu clearly admits that there are different individuals inter-acting and influencing each other. But since he believes that the real nature of each individual is inaccessible and incommunicable, he must explain how the inter-action and mutual influencing of individuals is possible. This is what he does in the stanzas under discussion. His explanation may be put as follows. The real nature of individuals is ineffable, inaccessible, and incommunicable. But in their phenomenal nature they are, and act, like individual streams of mental energy, which can influence and affect each other. In other words, each individual is somehow determined by other individual streams of mental energy, although the ultimate nature of all of them would always remain untouched.

Another question is about what makes one more responsible for one's actions done while one is awake than for one's actions done in dream. Vasubandhu says that one's experiences in dream-

1. *Sarveṣām hi sattvānām anyonya-vijñapti-adhipatitvena mitho vijñapter-niyamo bhavati yathā-yogam. Mitha iti parasparataḥ. Ataḥ santāna-antara-vijñapti-viśeṣāt-santāna-antare vijñapti-viśeṣa utpadyate na-artha-viśeṣāt.* Viṃś.Vṛ.18

ing and waking states are equally without corresponding objects. If so, one's reactions to such experiences, no matter whether one is dreaming or awake, should all have the same moral worth. But evidently nobody holds himself responsible for what he happens to do in dreams, while everybody readily accepts responsibility for what he does in a waking state. How would Vasubandhu account for these different ways of looking at actions done in a dream on the one hand, and at those done in a waking state, on the other. Vasubandhu replies :

[Viṃś. 18 cont'd.] In a dream mind is overpowered by sleepiness,
And, therefore, fruits [of the actions done in a dream]
Are not on a par with [the fruits of the actions done in a waking state].[1]

For Vasubandhu, an ordinary dream happens within the transcendental dream, namely the state of *saṃsāra*; or sleep in the ordinary sense of the term takes place within the transcendental sleep, namely the very state of *saṃsāra*. One is more responsible for what he does in the transcendental dream or sleep, than for what he does while dreaming or sleeping in the ordinary sense of those terms. For in the former cases one is capable of having more control over one's actions than in the latter cases. In fact Vasubandhu would not say that man is ever fully responsible for what he does while in the state of *saṃsāra*, because, for him, the state of *saṃsāra* is characterized by ignorance, which makes man unable to evaluate his actions properly. However, Vasubandhu admits that through yogic practices man can get rid of this ignorance, and thus can come out of his transcendental sleepiness a fully enlightened man.

The next question is how one can possibly bring about a biological change in another being. For example, how can one kill another being? The being that is killed, in so far as it is experienced by the killer, is only a mental representation, not a real being with a real body. If so, how can a butcher, for

1. *Middhena-upahatam cittam svapne tena-asamam phalam.* Viṃś.18

example, be accused of killing animals, while all that he is dealing with is his own mental representation ?[1]

If Vasubandhu were an idealist or a monist or both, he should not have taken this objection seriously. Instead he could very easily dismiss it saying that nobody kills anybody in the real sense of the term. But that is not the way Vasubandhu faces this question. On the contrary, tacitly admitting that there are real beings who can kill each other, he is now trying to give a new explanation to the phenomenon of death—an explanation that will fit in well with his philosophical system. It runs through the next two stanzas :

[Viṃś. 19] Death is a change of course caused by
A particular mental representation of another being,
Just as the loss of memory etc. of other beings
Are caused by the thought-power of demons etc.[2]

[Viṃś 20] Otherwise how can it be said that
The Daṇḍaka-forest was destroyed by the anger of the sages ?
Or, how could mental torture be considered
To be a great punishment ?[3]

In these and the previous stanza Vasubandhu considers mind, designated variously as *manas* or *citta* or *vijñapti*, as a real power, which can influence or even alter minds, and on whose controlling power depends the moral worth of an action. Of course, minds for him are not real things-in-themselves, but only phenomenal streams of energy, so to speak. But every mind points to a real being behind it. Again Vasubandhu seems to believe that the phenomenal world is an interplay of such minds,

1. *Yadi-vijñapti-mātram-eva-idam na kasya-cit kāyo-asti na vāk. Katham.. aurabhrikādibhir-urabbrādīnām maraṇam bhavati ? Atatkṛte vā tan-maraṇe katham-aurabhrikādīnām prāṇātipatavadyena yogo bhavati ?* Viṃś. Vṛ.19

2. *Maraṇam para-vijñapti-viśeṣād-vikriyā yathā*
Smṛti-lopādikā-anyeṣām piśācādi-manovaśāt. Viṃś.19

3. *Katham vā daṇḍakāraṇya-śūnyatvam-ṛṣikopataḥ ?*
Mano-daṇḍo mahāvadyaḥ katham vā tena sidhyati ? Viṃś.20

and that representations issuing from one mind can act on those issuing from other minds, the real nature of the individuals still remaining unaffected.

Even the phenomenon of death is explained along the same line of thought. Vasubandhu describes death as the disruption of the individual stream-consciousness, which would otherwise keep flowing homogeneously (*sabhāga-santati-viccheda-ākhyam maraṇam*). Such a disruption of the stream-consciousness is caused by a fatal alteration of the vital organ (*jīvita-indriya-virodhinī kācid-vikriyā*). Such a fatal alteration of the vital organ, again, says Vasubandhu, can be effected by the mental representations issuing from other individuals (*para-vijñapti-viśeṣa-ādhipatyāt*).[1] Thus, Vasubandhu maintains that death as well as the fact that it can be caused by others, is real experience of the phenomenal level of existence, namely *saṃsāra*. An individual stream of consciousness, if left to itself, will keep flowing homogeneously. But it can be interrupted, and its momentum disturbed, by external forces. Yogic practices can stop it altogether, which will mean liberation and enlightenment of the individual concerned. Or, some inimical force, issuing from other individual streams, can interfere and break it off abruptly, which will mean death resulting in another birth on the phenomenal level itself.

To show that mental power is something really effective on the phenomenal level, Vasubandhu cites various scriptural stories : stories of demons causing loss of memory, dream-visions etc., the story of a certain magician who worked wonders by his thought-power, the story of a certain king, who under the mental influence of a sage had dream-visions, the story of another king put to flight by the mental power of some sages, the story of the evacuation of Daṇḍaka forest attributed to the mental rage of the sages therein, and, finally the belief that mental torture is the greatest of punishments.[2] It may be further noted that in the yogic tradition of India, mental power is the greatest force that can be used for the advantage or disadvantage of others. So it is quite natural for Vasubandhu to make so much of it.

1. *Para-vijñapti-viśeṣa-ādhipatyāt pareṣām jīvita-indriya-virodhinī kācid-vikriyā-utpadyate yayā sabhāga-santati-viccheda-ākhyam maraṇam bhavati.* Viṃś. Vṛ.19

2. Cf. Viṃś. and Viṃś. Vṛ. 19-20.

A final question discussed by Vasubandhu is about the knowledge of other minds. In a way it is a very fitting conclusion to the whole treatise, which started off with the question of knowledge, but towards the end was slightly diverted to some other related questions. Now, once again Vasubandhu's attention is called directly to the question of knowledge which gives him one more opportunity to make his position absolutey clear. The question, when plainly expressed, is if people can know each other's mind. Or, can they know what is going on in each other's mind? It may be recalled that Vasubandhu positively defended the idea that minds can influence each other, that the freedom of mind determines the moral worth of actions, and that minds can cause harm to each other. But now, when it comes again to the question of knowledge, his enthusiasm suddenly drops, and he re-assumes the rather negative view that knowledge of ordinary men cannot ever reach the extra-mental realities as they are.

The objector puts his question about the knowledge of other minds as follows : People claim to know other minds. But if what they come to know are only their own mental representations, how can their claim be true?[1] Vasubandhu's answer is that no such claim can be true :

[Viṃś. 21] Knowledge of those,
[Who claim] to know other minds,
Is unreal,
Just as one's knowledge of one's own mind
[Is unreal].
For, in the manner in which [the mind] is known
To the enlightened ones,
It is unknown [to ordinary men].[2]

Vasubandhu then explains it further : the ineffable nature of minds is known to the enlightened ones (*buddhānām gocaraḥ*),

1. *Yadi vijñapti-mātram-eva-idam paracitta-vidāḥ kim paracittam jānanti-atha na. Kim-ca-ataḥ. Yadi na jānanti katham paracitta-vido bhavanti? Atha jānanti.* Viṃś.Vṛ.21

2. *Para-citta-vidām jñānam-ayathārtham katham yathā*
Svacitta-jñānam ajñānād-yathā buddhasya gocaraḥ. Viṃś.21

while the ordinary people are ignorant of it. Therefore, the ordinary people's knowledge of minds has got to be unreal. They can only fancy unreal appearances (*vitatha-pratibhāsatayā*), because their idiosyncrasy for subject-object distinction has not yet been destroyed.[1] In these few lines Vasubandhu seems to have summarized the whole system of his thought : that every being has an ineffable and a phenomenal aspect of existence; that there are a multiplicity of enlightened beings, who alone can know things in their ineffable aspect of existence; that the saṃsāric existence is characterized by the idiosyncrasy for subject-object distinction, due to which one in the state of *saṃsāra* can perceive only the unreal forms (*vitatha-pratibhāsa*) of one's own consciousness.

8. Conclusion

Vasubandhu concludes the treatise with a note of warning that the theory of representations-only is so incomprehensible that it can be properly understood only by the enlightened ones, and that, therefore, his own presentation of it is subject to limitations :

[Viṃś. 22] This treatise on the theory
Of mere representation of consciousness
Has been composed by me
According to my ability;
It is not possible, however, to discuss
This [theory] in all its aspects;
It is known [only] to an enlightened one.[2]

Vasubandhu then adds : People like me cannot work out this doctrine in all its implications because it is beyond the limits of logical thinking. Who could then possibly comprehend it in its

1. *Yathā tan-nirabhilāpyena-ātmanā buddhānām gocaraḥ. Tathā tad-ajñānāt-tad-ubhayam na yathārtham vitatha-pratibhāsatayā grāhya-grāhaka-vikalpasya-aprahīṇatvāt.* Viṃś.Vṛ.21

2. *Vijñapti-mātratā-siddhiḥ sva-śakti-sadṛśī mayā*
Kṛtā-iyam sarvathā sā tu na cintyā buddha-gocarā. Viṃś.22

totality? Indeed the enlightened lords can comprehend it in all its aspects, for they have no more any impediment to the real knowledge of all knowable objects.[1]

In this last stanza and the subsequent explanation is Vasubandhu asking to be excused for any inconsistencies that might have crept into his treatise?

1. *Sarva-prakārā tu sā mādṛśaiś-cintayitum na śakyate. Tarka-aviṣayatvāt. Kasya punaḥ sā sarvathā gocarā?..Buddhānām hi sā bhagavatām sarva-prakāram gocarā sarva-ākāra-sarva-jñeya-jñāna-avighātād-iti.* Viṃś.Vṛ.22

Chapter Six

IDEALISM OR REALISM?

1. Introduction

Now that I have finished analysing some of the basic texts of the Yogācāra school, it is time I checked on my initial statement that "the Yogācāra-writings, especially those under discussion, are open to interpretation in terms of realistic pluralism".[1] I feel that my analysis of the text has undeniably proved the validity of this statement. However, I do not mean to censure outright other possible ways of looking at the same texts. All that I positively claim is that the four texts I have chosen for my study are *open* to interpretation in terms of realistic pluralism, and this I have shown in the previous four chapters by giving an analysis of those texts. To say the least, to make sense of those texts one does not have to assume that consciousness or idea is the final mode of existence, nor that ultimately there is only one being. On the contrary, it is quite possible, and at some points even easier, for one to make sense of them assuming that consciousness or idea is not the final mode of existence, and that there is a plurality of beings, even in the state of *nirvāṇa*. This is what I have been trying to establish in the previous four chapters, and I hope to have achieved my goal.

To make my own position clearer it may be useful at this stage if I consider the points on which I disagree with other interpreters of Vasubandhu. All through this work I have been rather diffident in saying that the many interpreters of Vasubandhu in the past have all gone wrong, however explicit might be the difference between my findings and theirs. Even now I do not mean to say that their interpretations are totally unacceptable. Instead, I am only interested to find out how my

1. See above, p. 6, note 1

conclusions happen to be different from theirs, and vice versa. It may be a question of difference in approach, or a question of difference in terminology. At least in some cases, however, there have been misinterpretations of the texts, either by way of reading them out of context, or by way of reading unwarranted meanings into them.

2. The Meaning of Vijñapti-mātra

The Yogācāra system has always been interpreted, invariably by all commentators and historians, as idealism of one kind or another. And this is the most basic point on which I explicitly disagree with the past interpreters. I do not see any reason whatsoever why the Yogācāra system, especially as it is found in Vasubandhu's writings, should be described as idealism. Vasubandhu spares no effort in making it clear that reality as such (*yathā-bhūta*) cannot be described at all in terms of consciousness (*vijñāna*).[1] Then how is it that the Yogācāra system came to be regarded as an idealism? The basic reason for this seems to be a gross misunderstanding, and the consequent misinterpretation, of the phrases *vijñapti-mātra*, *prajñapti-mātra* and *citta-mātra*. By the way, as I have already pointed out, for Vasubandhu, these three phrases are synonymous with each other, and therefore, interchangeable.[2] They are commonly translated as follows:

vijñapti-mātra/prajñapti-mātra = mere-consciousness/ representation-only

citta-mātra = mind-only

Linguistically these renderings are sufficiently justified indeed. But, as to what is described as *vijñapti-mātra/prajñapti-mātra/citta-mātra*, most of the interpreters seem to have been misled. They have mistaken these phrases for descriptions of the final mode of existence. The following are some instances of this mistake:

A. K. Chatterjee, in the introduction to his *Readings on Yogācāra Buddhism* says,

1. See, for example, my analysis of MVK.I.4 above, pp. 45ff and of MVK.I.15-16, above pp. 75ff
2. See above, P. 6, note 1

> Parinispanna is the Absolute, the undefiled, undifferentiated, non-dual consciousness (vijñaptimātratā).[1]

Again in his *The Yogācāra Idealism* he says,

> Once this idea of objectivity is eradicated, all the three Vijñānas revert to the pristine purity of Vijñaptimātratā.[2]

Th. Stcherbatsky in his *Madhyānta-vibhāga: Discourse on Discrimination between Middle and Extremes*, which is a translation of the first chapter of *Madhyānta-vibhāga*, says,

> There is a transcendent Absolute Reality of the Pure Spirit (*vijñaptimātratā*), Hegel's Absolute Idea.[3]

Dr. C. D. Sharma in his *A Critical Survey of Indian Philosophy* says,

> Reality, says the Triṃśatikā, is pure Consciousness. This Reality (Vijñaptimātra) on account of its inherent power (shakti) suffers threefold modification . . . Behind these three modifications is the permanent background of eternal and unchanging Pure Consciousness (Vijñāna or Vijñaptimātra).[4]

P. T. Raju in his *Idealistic Thought of India* says,

> This Vijñaptimātra is some supra-mundane consciousness beyond mind and picturing thought. It is the pure element called *Dharma*, that is Dharmadhātu, of Buddha and is the same as his Dharmakāya.[5]

S. N. Dasgupta in his *Buddhist Idealism* says,

> As a ground of this ālayavijñāna we have the pure consciousness called the *vijñaptimātra*, which is beyond all experiences,

1. A. K. Chatterjee, *Readings on Yogācāra Buddhism*, (Banaras Hindu University, 1970), p. 31

2. A. K. Chatterjee, *The Yogācāra Idealism*, 2nd rev. ed., (Delhi, Varanasi, Patna: Motilal Banarsidass, 1975), p. 87

3. Th. Stcherbatsky, *Madhyānta-vibhāga: Discourse on Discrimination between Middle and Extremes*, (Bibliotheca Buddhica, Vol. XXX, 1936, reprint. ed., Calcutta: Indian Studies, Past and Present, 1971) p. 8

4. C. D. Sharma, *A Critical Survey of Indian Philosophy*, (Delhi: Varanasi, Patna: Motilal Banarsidass, 1964), P. 117

5. P. T. Raju, *Idealistic Thought of India*, (George Allen & Unwin Ltd., 1953; reprint ed. with the subtitle 'Vedānta and Buddhism in the Light of Western Idealism', New York: Johnson Reprint Corporation, 1973) p. 269

transcendent and pure consciousness, pure bliss, eternal, unchangeable and unthinkable. It is this one pure being as pure consciousness and pure bliss, eternal and unchangeable like the Brahman of the Vedānta, that forms the ultimate ground and ultimate essence of all appearances; . . .[1]

All the above quoted passages clearly show that their authors almost unanimously accept *vijñapti-mātratā* or *prajñapti-mātratā* or *citta-mātratā* as the Yogācārin's description of the absolute, undefiled, undifferentiated, non-dual, transcendent, pure, ultimate, permanent, unchanging, eternal, supra-mundane, unthinkable, Reality, which, according to them, is the same as *Pariniṣpanna-svabhāva*, or *Nirvāṇa*, or Pure Consciousness, or *Dharma-dhātu* or *Dharma-kāya*, or the Absolute Idea of Hegel, or the Brahman of Vedānta. This is a totally misinformed interpretation of what the Yogācārins, particularly Vasubandhu, meant by *vijñapti-mātratā/prajñapti-mātratā/citta-mātratā*, and consequently it cannot pass the test of textual analysis. To support the view that these phrases describe the absolute state of existence, one may quote such passages as:

It is all mere representation of consciousness,
Because there is the appearance of non-existent objects.[2]

In the Mahāyāna system it has been established that those belonging to the three worlds are mere representations of consciousness.[3]

Depending upon the perception that there are only representations of consciousness, there arises the non-perception of knowable things.[4]

Through the perception
That there is only thought
There arises the non-perception of knowable objects.[5]

1. S. N. Dasgupta, *Indian Idealism*, (Cambridge, The Syndics of the University Press, 1962), pp.119-120
2. *Vijñapti-mātram-eva-etad-asad-artha-avabhāsanāt.* Viṃś.7
3. *Mahāyāne traidhātukam vijñapti-mātram vyavasthāpyate.* Viṃś.Vṛ.1
4. *Vijñapti-mātropalabdhim niśritya-artha-anupalabdhir-jāyate.* MVK.I.7
5. *Citta-mātra-upalambhena jñeya-artha-anupalambhatā.* TSN.30

These quotations from Vasubandhu, if they are read out of context, would easily give the impression that 'mere representation of consciousness' (*vijñapti-mātra*) or 'thought-only' (*citta-mātra*) is the absolute reality for Vasubandhu. But the fact is that when one carefully analyses these texts within the context of their occurrence, one will realize that the phrases *vijñapti-mātra* and *citta-mātra* in them do not at all refer to the absolute reality, or to the final mode of existence. What is more, nowhere does Vasubandhu use these phrases to describe the absolute state of existence. Instead, whenever he uses these phrases, he means that whatever falls within the reach of one's saṃsāric experience, is mere representation of consciousness or thought-only or mind-only. In other words, far from being a description of the absolute state of existence, *vijñapti-mātra/prajñapti-mātra/citta-mātra* is an evaluative description of the objects of one's experiences in the state of *saṃsāra*. This is clear from the textual analyses in the previous four chapters. However, to illustrate my point still more clearly, I shall once again recall the instances in Vasubandhu's writings where the phrase *vijñapti-mātra/prajñapti-mātra/citta-mātra* occurs.

(i) The first obvious instance of *vijñapti-mātra* is MVK. I.7, and its commentary by Vasubandhu:

> Depending upon perception
> There arises non-perception,
> And depending upon non-perception
> There arises non-perception.[1]

[Vasubandhu's commentary]:

> Depending upon the perception that there are mere-representations of consciousness [*vijñapti-mātra*] there arises the non-perception of knowable things. Depending upon the non-perception of knowable things there arises the non-perception of the mere representation of consciousness [*vijñapti-mātrasya*].

1. *Upalabdhim samāśritya nopalabdhiḥ prajāyate*
Nopalabdhim samāśritya nopalabdhiḥ prjāyate. MVK.I.7

Thus one understands the negative definition of graspable and grasper.[1]

Here, obviously, the phrase *vijñapti-mātra* does not at all refer to anything absolute or ultimate. On the contrary, the perception of *vijñapti-mātra* is presented only as the first step towards the realization of the unreality of graspable-grasper duality. Thus the reality of *vijñapti-mātra* is introduced in the first half of the stanza only then to be denied in the second half. I shall explain it further.

Vasubandhu understands this stanza as a further illustration of the negative definition of the *abhūta-parikalpa*, namely that it is lacking in graspable-grasper duality (*abhūta-parikalpasya grāhya-grāhakabhāvena virahitatā* MVKB.I.2; *grāhya-grāhakayor-asattvam-eva asal-lakṣaṇam* MVKBT.I.7).[2] So, what this stanza wants to get across ultimately is the unreality of the graspable-grasper duality.[3] As it is, the unreality of such duality is a fact that has already been established in the previous stanza; and the present stanza is only suggesting a technique (*upāya*) of realizing the same (... *asal-lakṣaṇa-anupraveśa-upāya-lakṣaṇam paridīpayati* MVKB. I.7). What is that technique ?

First of all one must realize the fact that whatever is experienced as an object, is mere representation of consciousness (*vijñapti-mātra*). This is, indeed, a fact that has already been indirectly established by stanza I.4, which says that all objective categories are just appearances of consciousness.[4] The same stanza clearly says also that there are no perceivable objects.[5] If there are no perceivable objects (*upalabhya-artha-abhāve* MVKB. I. 7), what else, then, is experienced by the ordinary people as objects (*bālānām asatyarthe' rtha-upalambhaḥ* MVKBT.I.8) ? They are all, as stanza I.5 says, 'imagination of the unreal'[6] or, as stanza I.8 says, 'appearance of unreal objects' (*abhūta-artha-*

1. *Vijñapti-mātra-upalabdhim niśritya-artha-anupalabdhir-jāyate. Artha-anupalabdhim niśritya vijñapti-mātrasya-api-anupalabdhir-jāyate. Evam asal- lakṣaṇam grāhya-grāhakayoḥ praviśati.* MVKB.I.7

2. ..*tasmin-eva-abhūta-parikalpe' sal-lakṣaṇa-anupraveśa-upāyalakṣaṇam paridīpayati.* MVKB.I.7

3. *Evam-asal-lakṣaṇam grāhya-grāhakayoḥ praviśati.* MVKB.I.7

4. *Artha-sattva-ātma-vijñapti-pratibhāsam prajāyate vijñānam,.* Ibid.

5. *Nāsti-ca-asya vijñānasya arthaḥ.* Ibid.

6. *Abhūta-parikalpatvam siddham-asya..* MVK.I.5
*Abhūta-parikalpatvam-ca teṣām caturṇām vijñānānām siddham*MVKBT. I.5

pratibhāsa). This 'imagination of the unreal' or the 'appearance of the unreal object', the present stanza calls *vijñapti*, the representation of consciousness, and starting with this idea it recounts the whole process of realization once again.

Thus the first step towards the realization of the unreality of the graspable-grasper duality is the perception that there are only representations of consciousness (*vijñapti-mātra-upalabdhi*). This perception, or rather the conviction, that there are only representations of consciousness for the objects of one's experience, will at once lead to the second step, namely that there are no objects falling within the reach of one's experience. This is the non-perception of objects (*artha-anupalabdhi*), as Vasubandhu says, which arises depending upon the first perception of *vijñapti-mātra* : "Depending upon perception, there arises non-perception", as the first half of the stanza has put it.

Now comes the third, and, as far as the present discussion is concerned, the decisive step in the process of the realization of the unreality of the subject-object duality. This is the non-perception of even the mere representation of consciousness (*vijñapti-mātrasya-api-anupalabdhiḥ*). In other words, as the third step one realizes that there is not even the mere representation of consciousness. How ? The representations of consciousness (*vijñaptayaḥ*) are after all forms of consciousness itself, and, therefore, are forms of subjectivity as well. But, the term consciousness will not make sense unless it is consciousness of some object,[1] nor will the term subjectivity make sense unless it is contrasted with objectivity.[2] That there are no perceivable objects, and that, therefore, the name 'objectivity' is a misnomer, was the point made by the second step of one's realization of the unreality of the subject-object duality. This second step (i.e. *artha-anupalabdhi*) then naturally leads one to the third, namely 'the non-perception of even the mere representation of consciousness (*vijñapti-mātrasya api-anupalabdhiḥ*)'. Or, in Vasubandhu's own words, "Depending on the non-perception of objects there arises

1. *Vijānāti-iti vijñānam grāhya-abhāve vijānana-api ayuktam. Tasmāt artha-abhāvāt-vijñātṛtvena vijñānam-asad.* MVKBT.I.4

2. *Grāhya-grāhakayoḥ parasparā-nirapekṣatvāt.* MVKBT.I.7

the non-perception of even the mere representation of consciousness".[1] Thus, he concludes, "one comprehends the negative definition of the graspable and grasper".[2] That is, through the non-perception of the objects (*artha-anupalabdhi*) one comprehends the unreality of the graspable, and through the non-perception of even the mere representation of consciousness (*vijñapti-mātrasya-api-anupalabdhiḥ*) one comprehends the unreality of the grasper. Thus finally one attains to the realization of the unreality of the graspable-grasper duality.

The above analysis makes the following points undeniably clear. (i) *Vijñapti-mātra* does not stand for the absolute state of reality / existence / realization. On the contrary, (ii) it means only that what one in the state of *saṃsāra* experiences as objects are mere representations of consciousness, (iii) The realization of *vijñapti-mātra*, far from being itself an absolute state, is only an intermediary step towards final enlightenment, and, therefore, should eventually be transcended. In other words, the belief in *vijñapti-mātra* is the same as the belief in subjectivity, which is as much a hindrance to enlightenment as the belief in objectivity.

Therefore, there is no justification in this context for interpreting *vijñapti-mātra* as a description of the absolute state of reality / existence / realization. A similar analysis can be carried out also with TSN. 36, which is an instance of *citta-mātra* :

Through the perception
That there is only thought
There arises the non-perception of knowable things;
Through the non-perception of knowable things,
There arises the non- perception of thought, too.[3]

As I mentioned in my analysis of this stanza above,[4] here, too, one is led to the same conclusions as the ones from MV.I.7, only the term *Vijñapti-mātra* in this latter case is replaced by the term *citta-mātra* (thought-only).

1. *Artha-anupalabdhim niśritya vijñapti-mātrasya-api-anupalabdhir-jāyate.* MVKB.I.7
2. *Evam-asal-lakṣaṇam grāhya-grāhakayoḥ praviśati.* Ibid.
3. *Citta-mātra-upalambhena jñeya-artha-upalambhatā*
Jñeya-arthānupalambhena syāc-citta-anupalambhatā.
4. See above, pp. 124-125.

(ii) In *Triṃśatikā* one comes across a more comprehensive use of the term *vijñapti-mātra*. In the two instances quoted above (MV.I.7 and TSN. 36) *vijñapti* meant the subjective forms of consciousness which the ordinary people mistake for objects, and thus it ultimately meant forms of subjectivity. But in *Triṃśatikā* it includes not only forms of subjectivity but also forms of objectivity, although in the final analysis all of them will turn out to be just appearances / transformations of consciousness. In other words, in *Triṃśatikā*, *vijñapti* is the general term for graspable-grasper distinction. Hence here *vijñapti-mātra* means that the forms of graspability and grasperhood on the one hand, and the distinction (*vikalpa*) between them on the other, are all mere representations of consciousness. Let me illustrate this usage with the following passage from *Triṃśatikā* :

> This [threefold] transformation of consciousness
> Is [just] the distinction [between subject and object];
> What are thus distinguished,
> Does not exist [as subject and object]
> Therefore they are all mere representation of consciousness.[1]

I have already given a detailed analysis of this stanza above.[2] Here I need to give only a summary of my findings there : The transformations of consciousness include the *citta* and *caittas*, and nothing more than them. These *citta* and *caittas* invariably involve the distinction (*vikalpa*) between the subject and object. This distinction, however, having no extra-mental basis is but mere representation of consciousness (*tena idam sarvam vijñapti-mātrakam*). Further, as Sthiramati suggests,[3] all *citta* and *caittas*, and the forms of subjectivity and objectivity in which they appear, too, are here referred to as mere representation of consciousness. "In any case, what the stanza describes as mere representation of consciousness cannot include anything more than (i) subjectivity and objectivity (*ātman* and *dharma*),[4] (ii) the distinction

1. *Vijñāna-pariṇāmo'yam vikalpo yad-vikalpyate*
Tena tan-nāsti tena-idam sarvam vijñapti-mātrakam. Triṃś.17
2. See above, pp. 145-147
3. See above, p. 146, and p. 144 note 4 in the same chapter.
4. See above, pp. 128ff for the explanation of *ātman* and *dharma* as forms of subjectivity and objectivity respectively.

between them (*vikalpa*), and (iii) *citta* and *caittas*. It does not include any of the *bhūtas* and *bhautikās*."[1] In short, what is described as *vijñapti-mātra* in this context are the contents of one's epistemological / empirical / psychological experience, and not anything supra-mundane or transcendental or absolute or ultimate.

(iii) However, *vijñapti-mātratā* as against *vijñapti-mātra*, can also mean the state in which one realizes that the entire contents of one's saṃsāric experience are mere representation of consciousness. Here I am obviously making a distinction between *vijñapti-mātra* and *vijñapti-mātratā*. Whenever Vasubandhu uses the term *vijñapti-mātra* he means to say that the contents of saṃsāric experience, (such as the subject-object distinction, the forms of subjectivity and objectivity), are all merely representations of consciousness. But whenever he uses the term *vijñapti-mātratā* he refers to the state in which one realizes (*sākṣāt-karoti*) the fact that the contents of one's saṃsāric experience are, or rather were, mere representations of consciousness. *Vijñapti-mātratā-siddhiḥ*, which happens to be the general title for Vasubandhu's two treatises, *Triṃśatikā* and *Viṃśatikā*, thus would mean 'the attainment (*siddhi*) of the state in which one realizes that whatever is experienced in the state of *saṃsāra* is mere representation of consciousness'. The point I am trying to make may be expressed differently: *vijñapti-mātra* refers to the fact that the contents of one's experience are mere representation of consciousness, while *vijñapti-mātratā* refers to the state of *nirvāṇa* in which one *realizes* the same fact. This does not mean that the state of *nirvāṇa* is itself mere representation of consciousness. To take an example from ordinary life, one wakes up from sleep to realize that what one was experiencing in sleep was all mere dream. This does not mean that the wakefulness in which alone one has this realization, is itself mere dream.[2]

A few instances of *vijñapti-mātratā* meaning the state in which one realizes that the contents of saṃsāric experience are mere representation of consciousness, may be cited from *Triṃśatikā*:

1. See above, p. 146
2. See Viṃś.17

That from which all elements have their ultimate reality
[Is the third naturelessness],
It is also called suchness,
Because it remains always as such,
That is itself the state [in which one realizes
That what one experienced in the state of *saṃsāra*
Was] mere representation of consciousness.[1]

Literally understood this stanza would mean just that the ultimate reality (*dharmāṇām paramārthaḥ*), which is otherwise called suchness (*tathatā*), is itself the state of mere representation of consciousness (*sa-eva vijñapti-mātratā*). Then one might easily argue that here *vijñapti-mātratā* is obviously a description of the ultimate state of reality, which is called suchness, a view undoubtedly worth the name idealism. However, one cannot subscribe to this interpretation without accusing Vasubandhu of being inconsistent, for to describe suchness as a state of mere representation of consciousness is just the opposite to what he said a few stanzas above in the same treatise, namely that what is described as mere representation of consciousness, is only the contents of saṃsāric experience, including the threefold transformation of consciousness, *citta* and *caittas*, and the subject-object distinction (*vikalapa*) (Cf. Triṃś. 17).[2] It will also contradict many other texts including MVK. 1. 7, and TSN. 36, both of which I have shown above as using the term *vijñapti* to mean the subjective forms of consciousness which ordinary people mistake for objects (*arthāḥ*).[3] On the contrary, if *vijñapti-mātratā* is understood to mean the state (of *nirvāṇa*) which is the same as suchness, and in which one realizes that what one experiences in the state of *saṃsāra* is mere representation of consciousness, it will not, on the one hand, contradict any texts, and, on the other, it will positively make the above quoted stanza (Triṃś. 25) intelligible. The same interpretation of *vijñapti-mātratā* applies also to *Triṃśatikā* 26, 27, and 28:

1. *Dharmāṇām paramārthaś-ca sa yatas-tathatā-api-ca*
   Sarva-kālam tathā-bhāvāt sa-ev vijñapti-mātratā. Triṃś.25
2. See above pp. 205ff
3. See above pp. 201ff

As long as consciousness does not abide
In *vijñapti-mātratā*,
The attachment to the twofold grasping
Will not cease to operate.[1]

One does not abide in it [i.e. *vijñaptimātratā*]
Just on account of the [theoretical] perception
That all this is *vijñapti-mātra*,
If one places [= sees] something before oneself.[2]

One does abide in *vijñapti-mātratā*[3]
When one does not perceive also a supporting consciousness,
For, the graspable objects being absent,
There cannot either be the grasping of that,
[Namely, the grasping of the supporting consciousness].[4]

In these stanzas *vijñapti-mātratā* (or *vijñāna-mātratā*, in stanza 28)[5] stands for the state (of *nirvāṇa*) in which one realizes the fact that the contents of the saṃsāric experience are *vijñapti-mātra*. This realization alone will stop one's passion/attachment (*anuśaya*) for the two-fold grasping (*grāha-dvaya*), namely the passion for subjectivity and objectivity, which is characteristic of any saṃsāric experience. How to attain this realization ? Stanzas 27 and 28 answer this question, by expressing differently what was said in MVK.I. 7 and TSN. 36. These latter two stanzas explained the process leading to the realization of the unreality of graspable-grasper duality as follows: the perception of *vijñapti-mātra* leads to the non-perception of objects, then this latter non-perception leads to the non-perception of even *vijñapti-mātra*. This same process is recommended by Triṃś. 27-28, too. Stanza 27 says that for the attainment of the state of *vijñapti-mātratā* mere perception of *vijñapti-mātra* is not enough, but that one must also stop placing

1. *Yāvad-vijñapti-mātratve vijñānam na-avatiṣṭhati*
Grāhya-dvayasya-anuśayas-tāvan-na vinivartate. Triṃś.26
2. *Vijñapti-mātram-eva-idam-ityapi-hi-upalabhataḥ.*
3. Note that here the phrase is *vijñāna-mātratā*, rather than *vijñapti-mātratā* or *citta-mātratā*. It may be a misprint for *vijñapti-mātratā*. In any case, that it means the same as *vijñapti-mātratā* is obvious from the comparison of this stanza with MVK.I.7 and TSN.36, which is brought out below.
4. *Yada-ālambanam vijñānam na-upalabhate tadā*
Sthitam vijñāna-mātratve grāhya-abhāve tad-agrahāt. Triṃś.28
5. See above note 3.

before oneself something (*kiñcit*) as an object (*artha*). That is, in terms of MVK. I.7 and TSN. 36, besides the perception of *vijñapti-mātra* one should also come to the non-perception of objects (*artha-anupalabdhiḥ*). Then stanza 28 says that one should stop perceiving the supporting-consciousness (*ālambanam vijñānam*). Here, the supporting consciousness (*ālambanam vijñānam*),when it is seen in the light of MVK. I.7 and TSN. 36, should be understood as standing for *vijñapti-mātra*, and, therefore, non-perception of the supporting consciousness turns out to be the same as the non-perception of *vijñapti-mātra* (*vijñapti-mātrasya-api anupalabdhiḥ* MVKB. I.7). Thus there, too, one finds the same process as in MVK. I.7 and TSN. 36: perception of *vijñāpti-mātra* followed by the non-perception of *kiñcid-artha*(something as an object), which again is followed by the non-perception of the supporting consciousness(*ālambanam-vijñānam*, which is the *vijñapti-mātra* of MVKB. I.7 and the *citta-mātra* of TSN. 36). The result of this process, too, is the same as that envisaged in MVK. I.7 and TSN. 36: in these latter cases it was said to be the realization of the unreality of the graspable-grasper duality (*asal-lakṣaṇam grāhya-grāhakayoḥ praviśati* MVKB. I.7), and in the present case it is said to be the realization of the state of *vijñapti-mātratā* (*vijñapti-mātratve. . . avatiṣṭhati* Triṃś. 26) which stops one's passion for graspable-grasper duality (*grāha-dvayasya-anuśayo vinivartate* Triṃś. 26).

Thus, once again it becomes clear that neither *vijñapti-mātra* nor *vijñapti-mātratā* can be cosntrued as being a description of the absolute state of reality/existence.

(iv) I shall now examine the occurrences of the term *vijñapti* on its own, without being in combination with *mātra* or *mātratā*. In such occurrences its application seems to be much restricted. A typical case is found in MVK. I.4 where *vijñapti* stands for one of the four appearances(*pratibhāsa*)of consciousness (*vijñāna*), the other three being *artha*, *sattva* and *ātman*.[1] Normally one would expect the Yogācārin to say that all appearances of consciousness are *vijñaptis*. However, according to the present stanza, *vijñapti* does not include all appearances of consciousness, but only a particular one of them. Which is that particular

1. *Artha-sattva-ātma-vijñapti-pratibhāsam prajāyate vijñānam.* MVK.I.4

one? Vasubandhu's answer is that "the appearance of consciousness as *vijñaptis* is the sixfold consciousness (*ṣaḍ vijñānāni*)",[1] that is the five sense-consciousness plus the mind-consciousness. In this context, it may be said that only these six kinds of consciousness are properly called the representations of consciousness (*vijñaptayaḥ*), while the other three categories (i.e. *artha, sattva* and *ātman*) may be so called only in an indirect sense insofar as they are equally appearances (*pratibhāsa*) of consciousness. Consequently the doctrine of *vijñapti-mātratā* would imply only that the six kinds of consciousness are only different representations of consciousness, which does not sound anything extraordinary, still less idealistic. Here the Yogācāra system may be better called a system of *vijñāna-mātratā*, not, however, meaning that it [is idealism, but that it] reduces all categories of experience[2] to appearances of *vijñāna*. This may be an explanation, too, for Vasubandhu's use of the term *vijñāna-mātratā* in *Triṃśatikā* 28.[3]

Sthiramati in his MVKBT uses the term *vijñapti* to define *śāstra*, (this latter term usually meaning a 'sacred science'). He says: "*Śāstra* is the *vijñaptis* expressed in a body of nouns (*nāma-pada*) and symbols (*vyañcana*). Or, *śāstra* is the *vijñaptis* expressed in words conducive to the supra-mundane knowledge".[4] Here *vijñaptis* may mean *ideas* or concepts which the sages expressed in words and symbols with a view to leading their disciples to the supra-mundane knowledge. This meaning of vijñapti does not seem to have anything to do with the doctrine of *vijñapti-mātratā*. Or else it may imply that the Yogācāra system consists solely of the respresentations of the consciousness of the sages, which, too, does not have anything idealistic about it.

Triṃśatikā 2 uses the phrase *viṣayasya vijñaptiḥ* to mean one of the three transformations of consciousness (*vijñāna-pariṇāma*).[5] Later in stanza 8 Vasubandhu further explains that *viṣayasya*

1. *Vijñapti-pratibhāsam ṣaḍ-vijñānāni.* MVKB.I.4
2. See above, my analysis of *Madhyānta-vibhāga*, pp. 45ff
3. See above note 3 on page 208
4. *Nāma-pada-vyañcana-kāya-prabhāsā vijñaptayaḥ śāstram. Athavā lokottara-jñāna-prāpaka-śabda-viśeṣa-prabhāsā vijñaptayaḥ śāstram.* MVKBT. Introduction
5. *Vijñānapariṇāmo'sau pariṇāmaḥ sa ca tridhā*
   Vipāko-manana-ākhyaś-ca vijñaptir-viṣayasya ca. Triṃś.1-2

vijñaptiḥ means *ṣaḍ-vidhasya viṣayasya-upalabdhiḥ*.[1] This implies that here *vijñaptiḥ* is synonymous with *upalabdhiḥ*, the latter meaning 'perception'. In other words, in this context, *vijñaptir* (*viṣayasya*) means the perception (of objects). To call the perceptions of the six kinds of objects (*ṣaḍ-vidhasya viṣayasya upalabdhiḥ*) representations of consciousness (*vijñaptayaḥ*) is in line with MVK. I.4, which called the sixfold consciousness *vijñapti*. Again, it is quite understandable that the perceptions of objects are after all mere representations of consciousness, for to perceive an object is to become conscious of it. Therefore, in this context, too, Vasubandhu's use of the term *vijñapti* does not imply anything worth the name idealism.

(v) That the perceptions of objects are all representations of consciousness (*vijñaptayaḥ*) is an appropriate introduction to the treatise called *Viṃśatikā*, and its use of the phrase *vijñapti-mātra*. By saying that the perceptions of the sixfold object (*ṣaḍ-vidhasya viṣayasya upalabdhiḥ*) are all representations of consciousness Vasubandhu is registering his strong objection to the correspondence theory of knowledge, according to which there is invariably a one-to-one correspondence between concepts and extra-mental objects. Against this Vasubandhu argues that the perceptions of objects are representations of consciousness in the sense that they are by and large determined by one's psychological dispositions, especially one's idiosyncrasy for subject-object distinction, the seeds of which are already stored up in the unconscious called *ālaya-vijñāna*. This is in general the thesis of *Viṃśatikā*, and consequently its opening stanza,

> This is mere representation of consciousness,
> Because of the unreal appearance of objects,[2]

means that the perception of the sixfold object (*ṣaḍ-vidhasya viṣayasya upalabdhiḥ*) is mere representation of consciousness. In other words, in perception one's psychological dispositions, especially the idiosyncrasy for subject-object distinction, makes the object (*artha*) appear in a way in which it does not really exist (*asat*). Thus the way an object is perceived is mere

1. ..*tritīyaḥ ṣaḍ-vidhasya yā viṣayasya upalabdhiḥ*..Triṃś.8
2. *Vijñapti-mātram-eva-etad-asad-artha-avabhāsanāt.* Viṃś.1

representation of consciousness (*vijñapti*). This applies to all epistemological experiences. For example, Vasubandhu later in the same treatise explains 'memory' in terms of *vijñapti*:

It has [already] been said
That there is a representation of consciousness,
Which appears as that, [namely the respective object] ;[1]
From it [i.e. from a representation of consciousness]
Does the memory arise.[2]

Here Vasubandhu is saying that memory is not necessarily to recall a past experience of a real object, but is to recall one of the past representations of consciousness.[3]

Vasubandhu then says that the fact that all experiences are basically representations of consciousness does not imply that communication between individuals is impossible, for he says that the individuals can influence each other through the representations of consciousness :

The representations of consciousness
Are determined by mutual influence of one [individual] on another.[4]

That is, the individuals in the society can influence each other's thinking, inspite of the fact that all experiences are mere representation of consciousness.[5] This may sound a dogmatic assertion, but it indicates that Vasubandhu is not subscribing to the idealistic position that would lead to solipsism. Sthiramati, too, has touched on this problem of social communication. Defining *śāstra* in terms of *vijñapti*,[6] he emphasised that the fact that the contents of *śāstra* are representations of consciousness, does not prevent its being *effectively* expressed in written as well as spoken words.[7] Sthiramati seems to imply that the representations

1. *Yathā tad-ābhāsa=yathā-artha-ābhāsa.* See Viṃś. Vṛ. 17
2. *Uktam tathā tad-ābhāsa vijñaptiḥ smaraṇam tataḥ.* Viṃś.17
3. See Viṃś. Vṛ.17, see also my analysis of it, pp. 186-187
4. *Anyonya-adhipatitvena vijñapti-niyamo mithaḥ.* Viṃś.18
5. For details see my analysis of *Viṃśatikā*, pp. 190ff
6. See above, pp. 209-210
7. *Katham vijñaptayaḥ praṇīyanta ucyate vā? Praṇetṛ-vaktṛ-vijñapti-prabhavatvāt prajñaptīnām na-atra doṣaḥ.* .MVKBT. Introduction

of consciousness are somehow under the control of the individual to whom they belong, so that they can freely express them in words. Vasubandhu, towards the end of his treatise *Viṃśatikā*, speaks of *vijñaptis*[1] as if they are one's psychic power, which one may use for the advantage or disadvantage of others.[2]

(vi) I have now referred to all the important instances of *vijñapti/vijñapti-mātra/vijñapti-mātratā/citta-mātra/vijñāna-mātra* occurring in the four texts under discussion. What clearly comes out of this survey is that the theory of *vijñapti-mātratā* in Vasubandhu's writings is not an ontological theory worth the name idealism : it does not say that reality in its ultimate form is in the nature of consciousness. On the contrary, for the most part it is an epistemological theory, which says that one's (empirical) experience of objects is determined by one's psychic dispositions, especially the idiosyncrasy for subject-object distinction, and that, therefore, one in the state of *saṃsāra* does not at all come to know the things in their suchness (*tathatā*). Things in their suchness are ineffable, and as such are known only to the enlightened ones (*buddhas*).[3] Even the theory of *vijñapti-mātratā* cannot be adequately known by the unenlightened ones, but only by the enlightened ones :

> It is not possible, however, to discuss
> This [doctrine of *vijñapti-mātratā*] in all its aspects,
> Which can be perceived only by an enlightened one.[4]

Therefore, the state of enlightenment, in which alone one fully realizes this doctrine, can itself be indirectly called *vijñapti-mātratā*, which is not however a description of the own-nature of the enlightened one. To be sure, *vijñapti* is definitely an empirical/phenomenal/saṃsāric factor, which should be given up for one to attain to the state of *nirvāṇa*. One has to come out of the dream to realize that one was dreaming; similarly one has

1. E.g., *Maraṇam para-vijñapti-viśeṣād-vikriyā.* Viṃś.19
2. See Viṃś. 19-21, and my analysis of the same, above pp. 192ff
3. *anabhilāpyena-ātmanā yo buddhānām viṣayaḥ iti.* Viṃś.Vṛ10
   nirabhilāpyena ātmanā buddhānām gocaraḥ. Ibid.21
   See also below note 4.
4. *Vijñapti-mātratā-siddhiḥ..*
   ..sarvathā sā tu na cintyā, buddha-gocarā. Viṃś.22

to get out of *saṃsāra* to realize that what one was experiencing there was all representations of consciousness.

(vii) My point is all the more obvious from *Viṃśatikā-vṛtti* 10,[1] where Vasubandhu equates the theory of *vijñapti-mātratā* with the theory of *nairātmya.* The theory of *nairātmya*, according to this text, means that the *dharmas* and *pudgalas* are non-substantial (*nairātmya*) with respect to their mentally constructed nature (*kalpitena-ātmanā*), not with respect to their ineffable nature (*anaphilāpyena-ātmanā*) : thus through the theory of *vijñapti-mātratā* the non-substantiality of all *dharmas* (and *pudgalas*) is taught, not the denial of their existence.[2] Here, if the theory of *nairātmya* means only a denial of substantiality/existence to the mentally constructed nature (*kalpita-ātmanā*), and if the theory of *vijñapti-mātratā* is the same as the theory of *nairātmya*, then the theory of *vijñapti-mātratā* also can mean only that the mentally constructed nature of *dharmas* and *pudgalas* are mere representations of consciousness, and that the same nature of theirs is unreal. Therefore, the theory of *nairātmya* does not concern the ineffable nature (*anaphilāpya-ātma*) of things, nor does the theory of *vijñapti-mātratā.* It may be expressed in the following equation :

The theory of *nairātmya* = the theory of the non-substantiality/non-existence of the mentally constructed nature (*kalpita-ātma*) of things, not of the ineffable nature (*anaphilāpya-ātma*) = the theory of *vijñapti-mātratā* = the theory that the mentally constructed nature of things, not their ineffable nature, is mere representation of consciousness.

3. The Transformations of Consciousness

Another term that is decisive in interpreting Vasubandhu's writings is certainly *vijñāna,* which I have consistently translated as 'consciousness'. The discussion so far has shown that a 'representation of consciousness' (*vijñapti*) refers to no extra-mental *thing* (*vastu*), but to the contents of one's saṃsāric experience, and that, therefore, the theory of 'mere representation

1. *Tathā pudgala-nairātmya-praveśo hi, anyathā punaḥ*
Deśanā dharma-nairātmya-praveśaḥ kalpita-ātmanā. Viṃś.10

2. ..*vijñapti-mātra-vyavasthāpanayā sarvadharmāṇām nairātmya-praveśo bhavati, na tu tadastitva-apavādāt.* Viṃś. Vṛ. 10

of consciousness' (*vijñapti-mātra*) cannot be interpreted in idealistic terms. Then the natural question is what status does Vasubandhu ascribe to consciousness (*vijñāna*) itself. If he were an idealist, then for him, the term 'consciousness' would be the most adequate description of the thing as such (*tathatā*). And, in fact, that is how many people in the past have understood this term in Vasubandhu's writings.[1] For them, cousequently, the phrase *vijñāna-vāda*, meaning idealism, would adequately describe Vasubandhu's view of reality. The fact, however, is that Vasubandhu himself has never used this phrase to describe his system of thought. The common usage of this phrase to describe Vasubandhu's system may be taken, therefore, as a clear example of the general tendency to read the Western idealism into his writings.

For my part I am convinced that for Vasubandhu the term *vijñāna*, especially as it occurs in the text I have analysed, stands for what 'mind' and 'mental' would mean in the West. Or, to use the traditional Buddhist terms, Vasubandhu's use of the term *vijñāna* covers the entire range of *citta* and *caitta*, and nothing else. Referring to the tranditional analysis of an individual into *nāma* and *rūpa*, standing respectively for the psychic and physical make-up of an individual, the former alone comes under the term *vijñāna*, the latter does not. That is, what Vasubandhu describes as *vijñāna* (=consciousness) or transformations (*pariṇāma*) of it, is not the whole individual, let alone the whole reality, as an idealist would have it, but only his psychic make-up. It is true that at Vasubandhu's hands the term *vijñāna* has received a much wider meaning than it had in the early Buddhism. In the latter case, for example, *vijñāna* was only one of the five aggregates (*skandha*) into which the entire psyco-physical phenomena were analysed, the other four aggregates being *rūpa*, *vedanā*, *saññā* and *saṃskāra*. But according to

1. For example, P. T. Raju, op.cit., p. 270, referring to Vasubandhu's *Vijñapti-mātratā-siddhi*, says, "as everything originates from Vijñāna, the latter must be taken as substantially existing, that is, existing like the Substance of Spinoza"; and Prof. Smart in his *Doctrine and Argument in Indian Philosophy* (London: George Allen and Unwin Ltd., 1969), p. 57, says, "..but the psychological interests of the Yoga-Practitioners [including Vasubandhu] led them to describe the Absolute in terms of consciousness [*vijñāna*]".

Vasubandhu's analysis the name *vijñāna* will go also for *vedanā*, *sañjña* and *saṃskāra*, all of them having a psychic content, but definitely not for *rūpa*, the physical make-up of phenomena. If so, Vasubandhu's use of the term *vijñāna*, far from implying an ontological idealism, is only an explanation of the psyche. My textual analysis in the previous chapters has repeatedly borne this point out. However, to get it in focus I shall once again refer to the relevant texts in which the term *vijñāna* figures.

Perhaps one of the most important texts in this regard is *Triṃśatikā* 1-16. The central point of this text is that whatever comes under the names *ātman* and *dharma* is all transformations (*pariṇāma*) of *vijñāna*.[1] It will not be surprising if a casual reader understands this statement as meaning that *vijñāna* (consciousness) is the underlying substance of all phenomena, psychic (*ātman*) as well as physical (*dharma*). But, in the first place, the terms *ātman* and *dharma* here do not mean 'self' and 'things' respectively, as they might in early Buddhism, but concepts/experiences of subjectivity and objectivity respectively.[2] This interpretation of mine of the terms *ātman* and *dharma* in the present context would not have been conclusive without a reference to an exhaustive list of the transformations of *vijñāna*, enumerated by Vasubandhu himself.[3] I have reproduced this list above on pp. 144f. of the chapter on *Triṃśatikā*. What is enlightening about this list is that all the items on it, without exception, come under psychological and/or epistemological categories, and none of them is in an ontological category. In other words, what Vasubandhu calls the transformations of consciousness (*vijñāna-pariṇāma*) are only what was traditionally called *citta* and *caitta* (= mind and its derivatives). What Vasubandhu holds to be transformations of consciousness (*vijñāna*) is not the entire phenomena, as an idealist would have it, but only the psychic part of it. Thus his theory of the transformations of consciousness, too, does not imply an ontological idealiam, but is only an analysis of the psyche.

1. *Ātma-dharma-upacāro hi vividho yaḥ pravartate.*
   Vijñāna-pariṇāmo'sau. Triṃś.1
2. For details see above pp. 128ff
3. See Triṃś. 1-16, and my analysis of it above pp. 134 ff

Another occurrence of the term *vijñāna*, the examination of which will help one determine the status of consciousness according to Vasubandhu, is MV. I.4,

> Under the appearance of things inanimate,
> Living beings, self and representations of consciousness
> Is born the consciousness,[1]

and its commentary by Vasubandhu,

> In the form of colour etc. the consciousness appears as inanimate things, and in that of five senses it appears as living beings. These five senses refer to one's own as well as other's streams of existence. The appearance of consciousness as self is same as defiled thought, because it is associated with self-delusion etc. The representations of consciousness are otherwise called the sixfold consciousness.[2]

The meaning of these texts, in summary, is that consciousness (*vijñāna*) is born (*prajāyate*) under the appearance (*pratibhāsa*) of animate and inanimate beings, self and representations of consciousness. This statement, too, can very easily be interpreted in idealistic terms to mean that the entire phenomena, including living and non-living beings, self and representations of consciousness, have consciousness for their basic substance. But the fact is that, as I have shown in my analysis,[3] the four categories of living and non-living beings, self and representations of consciousness, as far as the present context is concerned, mean only different forms of objectivity and subjectivity. I need not repeat the whole discussion here. I may, instead, put it in a few words as follows. What is traced to consciousness is not things themselves, but only their appearances (*pratibhāsa*). How do they appear? They appear either as subjects or objects of experience. Therefore, it is the forms of subjectivity and objectivity, in which things appear to the perceiver/experiencer, that are

1. *Artha-sattva-ātma-vijñapti-pratibhāsam prajāyate Vijñānam*.. MVK.I.4

2. *Tatra-artha-pratibhāsam yad rūpādi-bhāvena pratibhāsate. Sattva-pratibhāsam yat pañca-indriyatvena-sva-para-santānayoḥ. Ātma-pratibhāsam kliṣṭam manaḥ, ātma-mohādi-samprayogāt. Vijñapti-pratibhāsam ṣaḍ-vijñānāni.* MVKB.I.4

3. See above, pp. 46ff

traced to consciousness. In other words, things as they are experienced, and only as they are experienced, are products of consciousness, not otherwise.

So much for what *vijñāna* produces. What does the present context say about the status of consciousness itself? The remaining part of the stanza under discussion has the answer to this question :

> There is nothing as its [i.e. consciousness's] object,
> And thus that object being absent
> That [consciousness], too, is non-existent.[1]

This text along with its commentary by Vasubandhu has already been analysed in detail.[2] Its meaning may be summarized as follows. The appearances of living and non-living beings, self and representations of consciousness, which are taken to be the objects (*artha*) of consciousness do not really exist (*nāsti*), for after all they are only different forms of consciousness itself. If, then, there are no objects, there cannot be consciousness, either, for consciousness makes sense only with reference to objects. The same argument was used to show that an aspirant to Buddhahood should eventually give up the belief in mere-representations of consciousness, too.[3] Here the text goes further and says that one must give up one's belief in consciousness itself. I feel, the statement that "that consciousness too is non-existent" (*tadvijñānam api-asat* MV.I.4), alone is enough to prevent one from interpreting the Yogācāra system in terms of idealism, for it unconditionally denies any ontological status to consciousness. If anything, consciousness is only an epistemological/psychological/empirical category accounting for the saṃsāric experience of the subject-object duality. Consequently, far from being the Absolute, consciousness is only part of one's saṃsāric experience, which should eventually be transcended for one to attain to the state of *Nirvāṇa*.

The fact that consciousness (*vijñāna*) is only an empirical factor, forces one to take the statement that 'consciousness *is*

1. *Nāsti-ca-asya* [*vijñānasya*] *arthas-tadabhāvāt tad* [*vijñānam*] *api-asat*. MVK.I.4
2. See above, pp. 50ff
3. See above, pp. 201ff

born (*prajāyate*) under the appearance of objects'[1] rather literally. That is, consciousness is not an eternal reality, but is one that *is born* (*prajāyate*) under certain circumstances. To say the least, it is a valid category only as long as one experiences the subject-object duality. Therefore at the dawn of the final realization, where one will no longer distinguish between subject and object, there will be no more consciousness either.

4. The Psychic Complex

That the representations of consciousness (*vijñapti*), and the consciousness (*vijñāna*) itself, are only empirical factors rather than transcendental, phenomenal rather than noumenal, accidental rather than absolute, saṃsāric rather than nirvāṇic, reminds one of a parallel position of the Sāṅkhya system, which in turn confirms the possibility of my interpretation of Vasubandhu. The point I am referring to is that according to the Sāṅkhya system also, the psychic complex, including intellect (*buddhi*), ego-consciousness (*aham-kāra*), mind (*manas*) and senses (*jñāna-indriyāṇi*), is all exclusively part of the empirical principle called *prakṛti*, and not of the transcendental principle called *puruṣa*. It belongs to the phenomenal *prakṛti*, not to the noumenal *puruṣa*. What is more, according to the Sāṅkhya system, too, the bondage of *saṃsāra* consists basically in the *puruṣa's* accidentally getting himself associated with the psychic complex belonging to *prakṛti* : mistaking the psychic functions of *prakṛti*, he imagines himself to be an enjoyer, an experiencer, a knower or a grasper (*grāhaka*) of the physical world, which he takes to be an enjoyable, experiencable, knowable or graspable (*grāhya*) object. Consequently, final liberation consists in freeing the *puruṣa* from his association with the psychic complex of *prakṛti*, which will happen only when *puruṣa* stops thinking of himself as a grasper (*grāhaka*) and the physical world as a graspable (*grāhya*).

I am inclined to believe that the Yogācāra system is an improvement on the Sāṅkhya one. The former retains the latter's view that the psychic complex, which in the case of the Yogācāra system includes *ālaya-vijñāna*, *manana-vijñāna* and the sixfold *pravṛtti-vijñāna*,[2] is on the empiric side of existence, and that it, being

1. See above, p. 217 note 1
2. See the list above pp. 145-146

the limiting force of *saṃsāra*, disappears at the dawn of the final realization. As I mentioned above, the psychic complex for the Yogācārins includes *ālaya-vijñāna* (store-consciousness), *manana-vijñāna* (thinking consciousness) and the sixfold *pravṛtti-vijñāna* (active consciousness). I am specifying these items primarily with a view to pointing out a common misunderstanding that for the Yogācārins consciousness by itself is a separate item on the list of the psychic factors. The fact is that nowhere in the text has it been said that consciousness (*vijñāna*) by itself is a factor added to the other items on the list. Instead, there are statements to the effect that every single item making up the psychic complex is a transformation of consciousness,[1] and that consciousness appears in the form of various objects,[2] and so on. What one may make out, therefore, is that consciousness is an abstract noun denoting the entire range of the psychic complex. Consciousness as such is nowhere given, while what is given in actuality are the particular expressions of consciousness, just as humanity as such is nowhere given, while what is given in actuality are the particular human individuals. To turn once again to the Sāṅkhyan model, the conception of consciousness in the Yogācāra system may be compared to that of *prakṛti* in the Sāṅkhya system : *prakṛti*, although it is the underlying substance of the entire phenomena, is nowhere found as such, while what is given in actuality are its particular manifestations. An important difference, however, between the Sāṅkhyan *prakṛti* and the Yogācārin's consciousness is that the former is an ontological principle while the latter is a psychic principle.

A comparative presentation of the evolutionary process of the phenomena as seen respectively by Īśvarakṛṣṇa's *Sāṅkhya-kārikā* and Vasubandhu's *Triṃśatikā* may be helpful at this point:

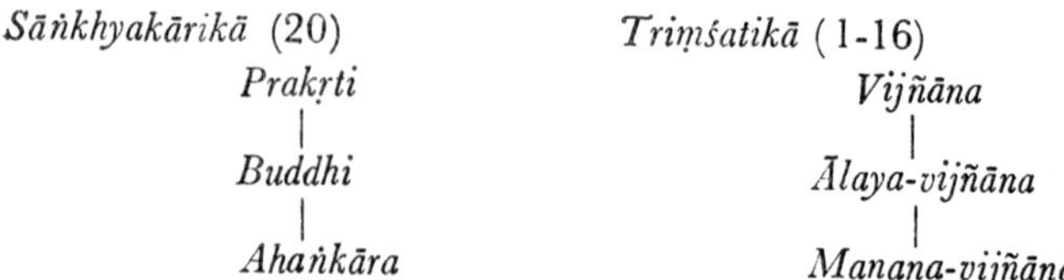

1. See my analysis of *Triṃśatikā* 1-16 above, pp. 128ff
2. See MV. I.4

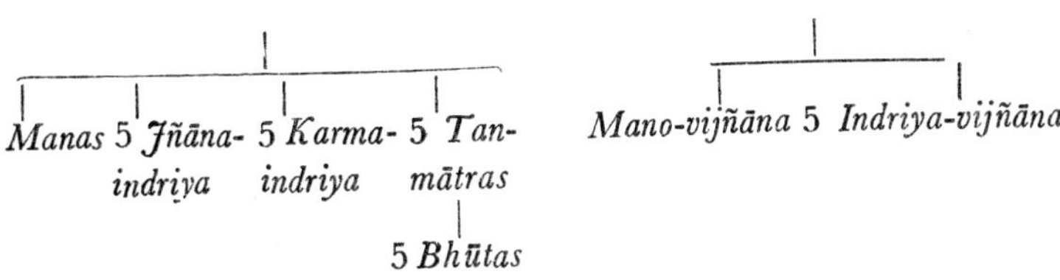

To bring out the comparison still more clearly I may once again reorganize the two schemes as follows:

Sāṅkhya-kārikā (20)	*Triṃśatikā* (1-16)
Prakṛti	*Vijñāna*
Buddhi	*Ālya-vijñāna*
Ahaṅkāra	*Manana-vijñāna*
Manas	*Mano-vijñāna*
Jñāna-indriya	5 *Indriya-vijñāna*
Karma-indriya	
Tanmātras	
Bhūtas	

The points I am making out of the above comparison are the following. The ontological principle of *prakṛti* in the Sāṅkhya system has been replaced by the *psychic* principle of *vijñāna* in the Yogācāra system. *Prakṛti* being a neutral principle, so to speak, could explain the whole phenomena, psychic as well as physical; but *vijñāna* being itself a psychic principle, could explain only the psychic phenomena. Consequently, while the evolution of *prakṛti* stretches right down through the gross physical elements (*bhūta*), the evolution of *vijñāna* stops short at *indriya-vijñāna* (sense-consciousness) where the psychic phenomena ends. Strictly speaking there is a real sense in which the Sāṅkhya system could be called idealism, namely that for it the entire phenomena, psychic as well as physical, derive from the intellect (*buddhi*) through the ego-consciousness (*ahaṅkāra*). Still it is not called idealism. There seem to be two reasons for its not being called idealism : first, it maintains a real distinction between the knowing faculties on the one hand, and the known objects, on the other, although all of them—the knowing faculties as well as the known objects—derive from the same source; second, outside, and totally distinct from, the evolving *prakṛti* there exists a number of real beings called *puruṣas*. If so, there are still greater reasons why Vasubandhu's system should not be called idealism. First of all, the evolving consciousness (*vijñāna*) about which he speaks, does not cover the physical world of *bhūtas* and *bhautikas*, but only the psychic world of *citta* and *caittas*. Secondly, besides the psycho-physical phenomena Vasubandhu does admit the noumenal (*yathā-bhūta*) realities called simply suchness (*tathatā*), which are inexpressible (*anabhilāpya*) even in terms of consciousness. This latter point I have referred to several times,[1] and I will return to it again shortly.[2]

As it is, therefore, Vasubandhu's discussion of consciousness, far from having any idealistic claims, is only an analysis of the psyche, which may be compared to any of the psychological systems of the modern times. It is a depth analysis of the psyche with a view to identifying the dynamics (such as *saṃskāras* and *vāsanās*) of motivation (*tṛṣṇā*), which the Buddha had long ago said to be the root cause (*samudayasatya*) of the human malaise (*duḥkha*). The factors into which the Yogācārins analysed the psyche are not very different from those suggested in the early Buddhism. It was, however, an original contribution on the part of the Yogācārins that they traced all the psychic variations to the unconscious level called *ālaya-vijñāna* (store-consciousness), from where given the opportunities they rise to the conscious level called *pravṛtti-vijñāna* (active consciousness) through the medium of the pre-conscious level called *manana-vijñāna* (thinking consciousness). Here I am obviously suggesting a rough comparison between the Yogācāra and Freudian models of psychoanalysis, without, however, claiming any expert knowledge of the latter.

5. The Imagination of the Unreal (Abhūta-parikalpa)

Another concept that might have led some people to interpret the Yogācāra system in terms of idealism seems to be that of *abhūta-parikalpa* (the imagination of the unreal). That "there

1. See, for example, the analysis of *Viṃśatikā* 10, 21 and 22, above, pp. 172 ff and 194 ff. See also pp. 23 ff.
2. See below p. 224.

exists the imagination of the unreal",[1] is the impeccable declaration of *Madhyāntavibhāga*. It may look only a short step from here to saying that the entire physical phenomena issue from this imagination of the unreal, and that, therefore, they are all imaginary. The fact, however, is that the Yogācārins do not take such a step. What they mean, instead, by the imagination of the unreal, I have already explained above[2] in some detail. Here I need only to recall the central line of their thought. The main point that the theory of the imagination of the unreal makes is that one's experience in the state of *saṃsāra* is largely controlled by the imagination of the unreal. Hence the assertion that "there exists the imagination of the unreal".[3] To be sure, the function of the imagination of the unreal is not to create things, but only to classify them as subjects and objects of experience : "The imagination of the unreal means the discrimination between the graspable and the grasper".[4] That is, graspability and grasperhood (*grāhyatva* and *grāhakatva*) do not belong to the very nature (*svabhāva*) of things as such, but are imposed on them by the imagination (*parikalpa*), and are, therefore, unreal (*abhūta*). Therefore, what the Yogācārins describe as imaginary, and, therefore, unreal, are not the things as such, but the forms of subjectivity and objectivity, and the distinction between them.

The subject-object duality, unreal as it is,[5] is a basic requirement of every piece of experience in the state of *saṃsāra*. Therefore, the saṃsāric experience always invariably involves the imagination of the unreal subject-object duality. What is more, anything that is experienced, either as an object or as a subject, as far as the form in which it is experieneed goes, is an imagination of the unreal. Thus referring to the fourfold appearance of consciousness the text says that "its being the imagination of the unreal remains established",[6] for the four

1. *Abhūta-parikalpo'sti* MVK. I.2.
2. See above, pp. 29 ff.
3. See above note 1.
4. *Abhūta-parikalpo grāhya-grāhaka-vikalpah.* MVKB. I.2.
5. *Dvayam tatra na vidyate* MVK I.2; *Dvayam grāhyam grāhakam ca.* MVKB. I.2. For more details on this point see pp. 32 ff.
6. *Abhūta-parikalpatvam siddham-asya bhavati-ataḥ.* MVK. I.5. *Abhūta-parikalpatvañca teṣām caturṇām vijñānānām siddham* MVKBT. I.5.

appearances of consciousness as living and non-living beings, self and representations of consciousness, are invariably experienced either as subjects or as objects of experience.[1]

So much for the imagination of the unreal as an activity and for what it produces. It can also be considered as a faculty which discriminates between graspable and grasper. Then, the imagination of the unreal becomes the name for the *citta-caitta* complex, collectively or individually : "The imagination of the unreal is *citta* as well as *caittas*, belonging to all three worlds."[2] It implies that any psychic factor presupposes for its existence as well as operation, the distinction between subject and object. Therefore, to discriminate between subjects and objects, and for that matter also to construct the forms of subjectivity and objectivity, is the very inner dynamic of the psyche, and this explains one's persistent idiosyncrasy for the graspable-grasper distinction to which I have already referred.

Thus, in short, the concept of the imagination of the unreal (*abhūta-parikalpa*), neither as an activity, nor as a faculty, nor in its effect, implies idealism. Instead, it amounts to a theory of knowledge arrived at by the analysis of the psyche which the Yogācārins did. They discovered that the basic urge of the psyche was to discriminate between subject and object, an urge so strong that anything that is experienced, is experienced only under the forms of subjectivity and objectivity. In other words, their analysis of the psyche led them to the conclusion that what one experiences in the state of *saṃsāra*, is never the thing as such but the forms of subjectivity and objectivity constructed and projected by the psyche. Here one may recall Kant's theory of categories—categories, which he said, the mind imposes on the sense-data, and under which alone the latter can be understood.

6. The Ineffable (Anabhilāpya)

The distinction between the ineffable and the imagined nature of things seems to have received little attention from those who interpret the Yogācāra system as an idealism. Vasubandhu

1. See above, pp. 45 ff.
2. *Abhūta-parikalpaś-ca citta-caittās-tridhātukāḥ*. MVK. I.9.

refers to the distinction between the ineffable (*anabhilāpya*) and the imagined natures of things twice in *Viṃśatikā-vṛtti*, which I have paraphrased as follows :

> 'The ignorant imagine the *dharmas* to be in the nature of *grāhya*, *grāhaka* etc. Those *dharmas* are non-substantial (*nairātmya*) with reference to that imagined nature (*tena parikalpitena ātmanā*), not with reference to their ineffable nature (*na tu anabhilāpyena ātmanā*), which is object of the knowledge of the enlightened ones alone.'[1]

> 'The ineffable nature of minds is known to the enlightened ones (*buddhānām gocaraḥ*), while the ordinary people are ignorant of it. Therefore, the ordinary people's knowledge of minds has got to be unreal. They can only fancy unreal appearances (*vitatha-pratibhāsatayā*), because their idiosyncrasy for subject-object distinction has not yet been destroyed'.[2]

The first of these two passages distinguishes between the ineffable and imagined natures of *dharmas*, while the second distinguishes between the ineffable and imagined natures of minds. In both cases the imagined nature (*parikalpita-ātma*) is characterised by the subject-object duality, which the ignorant ones impose on things; and the ineffable nature, which is beyond the limit of the ordinary experience, is said to be the object of the enlightened ones. Thus these two passages clearly show that Vasubandhu did recognize a realm of reality, which is not only independent of the thinking mind, but also is beyond the reach of saṃsāric, empirical knowledge. This admission of reality independent of consciousness is one of the strongest cases for my believing that Vasubandhu was not an idealist. The distinction between the ineffable and the imagined natures of things far from sounding idealistic reminds me of Kant's distinction between phenomena and noumena.

The ineffable nature of things is discussed in *Madhyānta-vibhāga* under the title *śūnyatā* (emptiness).[3] *Śūnyatā* has been

1. Viṃś. Vṛ. 10; see above pp. 23-24, and pp. 172 ff
2. Vimś. Vṛ. 21, and see above p. 194
3. MV. I. 14-23

defined as being given when the *abhūta-parikalpa* stops constructing the forms of subjectivity and objectivity.[1] In other words, *śūnyatā* refers to the graspable-grasper distinctionless state of things (*grāhya-grāhaka-bhāvena virahitatā* MVB.I.2). That is, if ever one can perceive things without characterizing them as subjects and objects, there one has *śūnyatā*. But such a vision of the things as such is not possible for one in the state of *saṃsāra*, for there one cannot see anything at all except under the aspects of subjects and objects of experience. Therefore, what one experiences in the state of *saṃsāra* is the imagined nature (*parikalpita-ātma*) of things, while what one experiences in the state of *nirvāṇa* is the ineffable nature (*anabhilāpya-ātma*) of things.

Madhyāntavibhāga I.14-23 is a detailed description of *śūnyatā*. What I found most interesting in that discussion is the fact that there has been no attempt at all to describe, let alone to define, *śūnyatā*, the reality as such, in terms of consciousness. This is once again a proof for the fact that the Yogācārins have not thought of absolutizing consciousness. MVK.I. 15 gives a list of synonyms for *śūnyatā*,[2] which, as I have already pointed out, does not include 'consciousness' nor any such idealistic terms. If the Yogācārins had an idealistic conception of reality, terms like *vijñāna*, *vijñapti* or *citta* should have appeared at the top of their list of synonyms for *śūnyatā*. So the logical conclusion is that they have no conception of reality as consciousness, nor do they believe that consciousness is the absolute mode of reality.

However, Vasubandhu does recognize a higher mode of knowledge, which he calls the supra-mundane knowledge (*lokottara-jñāna*) in contrast with the ordinary man's knowledge of things. Thus,

That indeed is the supramundane knowledge
When one has no mind that knows,
And no object for its support. . .[3]

1. *Śūnyatā tasya-abhūta-parikalpasya grāhya-grāhaka-bhāvena virahitatā*. MVKB. I.2.

2. *Tathatā bhūtakoṭiś-ca-animittam paramārthatā*
Dharmadhātuś-ca paryāyāḥ śūnyatāyāḥ samāsataḥ. MVK. I. 15. See also above, pp. 75-76.

3. *Acitto'nupalambho'sau jñānam lokottaram ca tat*. Triṃś 29.

This reference to supramundane knowledge (*lokottaram jñānam*) should not be mistaken for a reference to belief in consciousness as the absolute mode of existence. The supramundane knowledge on the contrary means the intuitive knowledge (*nirvikalpakam jñānam*) which enables the enlightened ones to see things as such (*yathā-bhūtam*), not under the aspects of subjects and objects[1]. The same intuitive knowledge is again referred to as the unsurpassed enlightenment (*anuttarā bodhiḥ*),[2] to which one will attain at the dawn of *nirvāṇa*. Thus, in short, the supramundane knowledge referred to by Vasubandhu is not a being by itself, but the supreme endowment of the enlightened ones.

7. Pluralism Rather Than Monism

I may now consider the possibility of a pluralistic conception of reality within the Yogācāra system. My arguments for an interpretation of the Yogācāra texts in terms of pluralism are not many, nor quite positive. Therefore, all I am claiming is that there is a clear possibility of such an interpretation. First of all, the traditional understanding that the Yogācāra system is monistic seems to have followed from the assumption that it is idealistic, for, as the history of philosophy has it, monism has been more often than not a corollary of idealism. If so, once the Yogācāra texts are proved to be open to interpretation in terms of realism, it immediately calls for a reviewing of their traditional understanding in terms of monism, too.

As I have already indicated,[3] there is nowhere in the texts a statement to the effect that the Yogācārins believed in monism. On the contrary, there are a few passages which are difficult to understand without presupposing a belief in a plurality of beings. Such is the case, for example, with the passage dealing with the problem of knowing other minds.[4] Moreover, an assumption of pluralism, instead of rendering any part of the text difficult

1. *Evam hi samam-anālambhya-ālambakam nirvikalpakam lokottaram jñānam-utpadyate, grāhya-grāhaka-abhiniveśa-anuśaya prahīyante.* Tr. Bh. 28; . . . *nirvikalpakatvācca lokād-uttīrṇam-iti jñāpanārtham lokottaram ca tad-iti.* Tr. Bh. 29

2. *Prāpnoti-anttarām bodhim dhīmān kāya-traya-ātmikām.* TSN. 38

3. See above p. 23

4. *Viṃśatikā*, 21

to understand, makes the entire text more intelligible. Above all, there are some positive references, however scanty they may be, to a plurality of the enlightened ones (*buddhāḥ*).[1] I am well aware that the plural forms such as *buddhāḥ* and *bhagavantaḥ* in these cases need not necessarily refer to a purality of beings, but that, instead, they may be just a reverential form of addressing an enlightened one. However, it is not impossible that Vasubandhu in using such plural forms was really suggesting a plurality of enlightened ones.

8. Viṃśatikā : Critique of the Correspondence Theory of Knowledge

Viṃśatika, a treatise in twenty stanzas, taken by itself is likely to appear as a plain case for idealism. It will be little surprising if a random reader of this text rushes to the conclusion that Vasubandhu is an idealist. On the contrary, if one reads it in the overall perspective of Vasubandhu's other writings such as *Madhyānta-vıdhāga-bhāṣya*, *Trisvabhāva-nirdeśa* and *Triṃśatikā*, one will easily see that it is only a critique of the correspondence theory of knowledge, which says that every bit of knowledge necessarily refers to an extra-mental object, and that, therefore, a knowledge of something is a valid proof for the extra-mental existence of that thing. Therefore, what I am suggesting, and what I have followed in my study of Vasubandhu, is that in evaluating *Viṃśatikā* one should take into account that

(i) the theory of *vijñapti-mātratā* is only an explanation of one's saṃsāric experience,[2]

(ii) the theory of the transformation of consciousness (*vijñāna-pariṇāma*) covers only the *citta-caitta* complex and that it does not cover the *bhūta-bhautika* complex, too,[3]

1. . . . *anabhilāpyena ātmanā yo buddhānām viṣaya iti*. Viṃś. Vṛ. 10.
nirabhilāpyena ātmanā buddhānām gocaraḥ. Vıṃś. Vṛ. 21
Buddhānām hi sa bhagavatām sarvaprakāram gocaraḥ. Viṃś. Vṛ. 22
2. See above pp. 201 ff.
3. See above pp. 214 ff.

(iii) Vasubandhu's analysis of consciousness provides only a depth analysis of the psyche, not of the entire psycho-physical complex,[1]

(iv) the theory of *abhūta-parikalpa* (imagination of the unreal) is after all only a theory of knowledge,[2]

(v) what is imagined or constructed (*parikalpita*) by the mind is only the graspable-grasper distinction (*grāhya-grāhaka-vikalpa*),[3]

(vi) Vasubandhu clearly recognizes an ineffable (*anabhilāpya*) realm of reality, which for its existence and operation does not at all depend on the thinking mind or consciousness,[4]

(vii) Vasubandhu has never described the absolute mode of existence in terms of consciousness,[5]

(viii) and that an assumption of a plurality of beings does not contradict any part of the texts.[6]

Seen against the above principles, the points *Viṃśatikā* makes are the following, the details of which are found in my analysis of the same text.[7]

(i) Knowledge or experience need not necessarily refer to extra-mental realities. This is confirmed by the dream-experiences, the sufferings of the hell inhabitants, and other illusory experiences.

(ii) Therefore one cannot argue for the existence of extra-mental realities on the basis of knowledge.

(lii) The atomic conception of reality cannot be proved from knowledge : one does not have an experience of atoms, neither collectively, nor singly, nor as a single reality.

1. See above pp. 219 ff.
2. See above pp. 222 ff.
3. See above p. 223.
4. See above pp. 224 ff.
5. See above p. 226.
6. See above pp. 227-228.
7. See above Chapter Five

(iv) The conception of reality in terms of atoms involves many logical contradictions, too. For example, it cannot explain concepts like 'movement', 'relation', 'unity', 'quantity' etc.

(v) Without having recourse to the correspondence theory of knowledge one can meaningfully explain the concepts of social interactions between individuals, moral retribution etc.

(vi) In the ultimate analysis reality as such is inaccessible to ordinary minds, for it is ineffable and is revealed only to the enlightened ones.

(vii) Consequently, saṃsāric experience is comparable to a dream-experience. As the dream-experiences do not refer to extra-mental realities, so neither do the saṃsāric experiences reach extra-mental things as such. What one experiences in the state of *saṃsāra*, are mostly representations of one's own consciousness. *Saṃsāra* is therefore a transcendental dream. To have the vision of things as such one must wake up from this transcendental dream.

Thus *Viṃśatikā* is not a polemic against realism, as many seem to have thought, nor is it a defence of idealism, but is only a polemic against the correspondence theory of knowledge, and a defence of the view that *saṃsāra* experience is comparable to dream experience.

It is remarkable that a recent study of Vasubandhu by Dr. Stefan Anacker, University of Wisconsin, has come up with the same conclusion as mine. His words are worth quoting at length :

> It has been assumed that since the store-consciousness is held responsible for the other consciousnesses and the manner in which they perceive, Vasubandhu's Yogācāra represents a form of idealist philosophy. The peculiar slant of Dharmapāla and Hsuan-tsang, which focused philosophical attention on the store-consciousness, has done much to support this view. However, when one reads the Yogācāra works of Vasubandhu, one can easily see that the notion of a "Yogācāra idealism" is thoroughly misleading in his case. In the *Mahāyānasaṅgrahabhāṣya*,

Vasubandhu makes it clear that the inter-reaction of the store-consciousness and the six consciousnesses needs in addition some sort of external stimulus. When Vasubandhu lambasts the idea of an external object in the *Viṃśatikā*, this seems to mean that the object-of-consciousness, the perceived datum, is internal, and that whether we can infer an object which refers to it exactly is highly dubious. The external stimuli are only inferrable—what we see directly is always our own cognition, coloured by our particular psychic "seeds". What is involved here is that these stimuli may be interpreted by different psychic series in quite different ways.

Rather than pointing towards an idealistic system, the theory of the store-consciousness is used for totally different purposes by Vasubandhu. It is the recognition that one's normal mental and psychic impressions are *constructed* [italicized by the author himself], i.e. altered and seemingly statisized by our consciousness-complexes, that makes the actual main point of the *Triṃśatikā*. "Cognition-only" involves primarily the doctrine of the three natures of reality and their interrelationships. . .[1]

9. The Doctrine of Three Natures (Trisvabhāva-nirdeśa)

Finally I should add a word about Vasubandhu's doctrine of three natures (*svabhāva*), namely the other-dependent nature (*para-tantra-svabhāva*), the imagined nature (*parikalpita-svabhāva*) and the absolutely accomplished nature (*pariniṣpanna-svabhāva*). What each of them stands for should be by now more or less self-evident from my analysis of the concepts of *vijñapti-mātra*, *vijñāna*, *abhūta-parikalpa*, *anabhilāpya* and *śūnyatā*. Roughly speaking, the whole psyche is the other-dependent nature, for it depends for its reality as well as operation on the seeds of habits left by the past deeds. Consequently, the entire *citta-caitta* complex has been described as the other-dependent nature.[2] Similarly, *abhūta-parikalpa* (the imagination of the unreal) has been described as the other-dependent nature, because, as a faculty of discrimination between the graspable and the grasper, it is the same as the

1. Stefan Anacker, *Vasubandhu : Three Aspects : A Study of a Buddhist Philosopher* (Ph. D. Dissertation. University of Wisconsin, 1970). pp. 69-70.
2. See TSN. 6-7, and my analysis of it above pp. 94 ff

citta-caitta complex,[1] and, as an activity it is the very function of the same *citta-caitta* complex. In a way the very mode of the saṃsāric existence, in which one is bound to discriminate between the graspable and the grasper, an activity that depends on seeds of past experiences, is the other-dependent nature.

The imagined nature (*parikalpita-svabhāva*) is what the imagination of the unreal (*abhūta-parikalpa*) produces, namely the false forms of subjectivity and objectivity, and the distinction between them.[2]

The absolutely accomplished nature (*pariniṣpanna-svabhāva*) is the suchness (*tathatā*) of things, perceived neither as subject, nor as object of experience,[3] but intuited (*nirvikalpaka*) through the supramundane knowledge (*lokottara-jñāna*) of the enlightened ones.

I have mentioned above[4] that Vasubandhu's system can be seen as an improvement on the Sāṅkhya system. The improvement is effected through the introduction of the concept of the three natures and their relationship. In Sāṅkhya system, the two principles, *prakṛti* and *puruṣa* are envisaged as mutually independent, excluding, and conradictory principles. Hence it had to leave unanswered the question of how the interaction of these two principles could be explained. Vasubandhu has solved, or rather avoided, this question by suggesting that the *paratantra-svabhāva* and *parikalpita-svabhāva*, which together roughly replace the Sāṅkhyan *prakṛti* are only adventitious functions, so to speak of the *pariniṣpanna-svabhāva*.

10. Idealism or Realism

I may conclude this chapter, and thus the whole of this study, by referring to the latest work of Dr. Walpola Rahula, *Zen and the Taming of the Bull, Towards the Definition of Buddhist Thought* (London : Gordon Fraser, 1978), which has just come out while I was writing these last pages of my thesis. Dr. Rahula's central position is that the Buddhist philosophy all through its history has always remained the same :

1. *Abhūta-parikalpaśca citta-caittās-traidhātukāḥ.* MVK. I.9
2. See for example above p. 91
3. See for example above p. 92
4. See above pp. 219

Some scholars seem to have thought that great Buddhist doctors like Nāgārjuna, Asaṅga or Vasubandhu were expounding their own systems of philosophy in contradiction with each other. This was not so. They were all expounding the teaching with their own new interpretations, explanations, arguments and theories, according to their own genius, ability, knowledge and experience. What is more, they always supported their new theories and interpretations with quotations from Canonical texts. Their contribution to Buddhism lay not in giving a new philosophy, but in providing, in fascinatingly different ways, brilliant new interpretations of the old philosophy.[1]

Secondly, he strongly objects to the view that according to the Yogācārins mind (*citta*) or consciousness (*vijñāna*) is lhe only reality, the ultimate reality :

Some scholars have maintained that, according to the *vijñapti-mātratā* or *cittamātratā* philosophy in the Yogācāra (-Vijñāna-vāda) system, the mind (*citta*) or consciousness (*vijñāna*) is the only reality, the ultimate reality. It must be categorically stated at the very outset that this is wrong, a serious mistake, and that it is against all fundamental teaching, whether Theravāda or Mahāyāna.[2]

Thirdly, according to him both the Mādhyamikas and the Yogācārins were all presenting the same old theories of *nairātmya*, *śūnyatā*, *tathatā*. and *pratītyasamutpāda*, in different terms.

The *śūnyatā* philosophy elaborated by Nāgārjuna and the *citta-mātra* philosophy developed by Asaṅga and Vasubandhu are not contradictory, but complementary to each other. These two systems known as Mādhyamika and Yogācāra or Vijñāna-vāda, explain and expound, in different ways with different arguments, the very same doctrines of *nairātmya*, *śūnyatā*, *tathatā*, *pratītysamutpāda*, but are not a philosophy of their own, which

1. Walpola Rahula, *Zen and the Taming of the Bull, Towards the Definition of Buddhist Thought*, (London : Gordon Fraser, 1978), p. 79.

2. Ibid. p. 79.

can properly be called Nāgārjuna's or Asaṅga's or Vasubandhu's philosophy. It can only be said that they are Nāgārjuna's or Asaṅga's or Vasubandhu's explanations, arguments and theories, postulated to prove and establish the Canonical teaching of *śūnyatā*, *cittamātra* or *nairātmya*. If any difference of opinion existed between them, these arise only with regard to the arguments and theories designed to establish the old fundamental Canonical teaching, but not with regard to the teaching itself.[1]

Consequently he would not consider the Yogācāra system to be an idealism,[2] any more than the early Buddhism is. If so, the answer to the question whether the Yogācāra system is an idealism or realism, would depend upon whether the early Buddhism was an idealism or realism.

1. Walpola Rahula, *Zen and the Taming of the Bull, Towards the Definition of Buddhist Thought*, (London : Gordon Fraser, 1978), pp. 82-83.

2. In fact he has clearly objected to comparing it to Berkeley's idealism. (Ibid. pp. 83-84).

APPENDIX I

THE VERSES ON DISCRIMINATION BETWEEN MIDDLE AND EXTREMES AND VASUBANDHU'S COMMENTARY ON THEM

A CHAPTER ON DEFINITIONS

Having paid homage to the founder of this science,
[27]* Son of the well-gone,
And also to its expositor for people like me,
May I now endeavour to analyse its meaning.

1. The definition,
[28] The coverings,
The truth,
Meditation of the opposite,
Its stages,
Attainment of results,
And the pre-eminence of the path.

These are the seven topics discussed in this science. They are namely the coverings, the truth, meditation of the opposite, stages of that meditation, attainment of results, and, seventhly, the pre-eminence of the path. There, beginning with the definitions, [the text] says :

2. There exists the imagination of the unreal,
[29] There is no pair,
But there is emptiness,
Even in this there is that.

---

*The numbers in square brackets refer to pages above where the respective stanzas and passages are analysed.

There, the imagination of the unreal means the discrimination between the garspable and the grasper. The pair is the graspable and the grasper. Emptiness means that state of the imagination of the unreal which is lacking in the form of being graspable or grasper. Even in this [emptiness] there is that, namely, the imagination of the unreal. Thus, when something is absent in a receptacle, then one, seeing that receptacle as devoid of that thing, perceives that receptacle as it is, and recognizes that receptacle, which is left over, as it is, namely as something truly existing here. Thus, the definition of emptiness is shown to imply no contradiction.

3. Neither void nor non-void :
[41] So is everything described,
That indeed is the middle path,
For there is existence as well as non-existence,
And again existence.

On account of the existence of emptiness, on the one hand, and that of the imagination of the unreal, on the other, it is not void. And on account of the non-existence of the pair of graspable and grasper, it is not non-void, either. This description applies to everything, whether conditioned or unconditioned. The term 'conditioned' goes for what is called the imagination of the unreal, while the term 'unconditioned' goes for what is called the emptiness. That indeed is the middle path, for, on the one hand, there is the existence of emptiness within the imagination of the unreal, and, on the other, the existence of the imagination of the unreal within the emptiness. It is therefore neither exclusively void nor exclusively non-void. This reading is thus in accordance with the scriptures such as *Prajñā-pāramitā*, [where it is said] : "all this is neither void nor non-void".

Thus having stated the positive and negative definition of the imagination of the unreal, now the [author] gives its own-definition :

4. Under the appearance of things inanimate,
[46] Living beings, self and representations of consciousness,
Is born the consciousness.

There is nothing as its [i.e. consciousness's] object,
And thus that object being absent
That [consciousness] , too, is non-existent.

In the form of colour etc. the consciousness appears as inanimate things, and in that of five senses it appears as living beings. These five senses refer to one's own as well as other's streams of existence. The appearance of consciousness as self is the same as defiled thought, because it is associated with self-delusion etc. The representations of consciousness are otherwise called the sixfold consciousness. The appearance of inanimate things as well as of living beings are devoid of form; likewise the appearances of self and representations of consciousness are not in the way they appear to be. This is why it is said that there is indeed nothing as its [i.e. consciousness's] object. That is, the four kinds of graspables—namely, (i) colour etc., (ii) the five senses, (iii) thought, and (iv) the sixfold consciousness—are absent. Thus the graspable being absent, the grasper, namely the consciousness, too, is non-existent.

5. Therefore its being the imagination of the unreal
[55] Remains established,
For it is not so,
It is not altogether absent, either.

For its existence is not the way it appears to be. It is not totally absent, either, because there is the production of illusion only, for

From its cessation results liberation.

For otherwise there would be neither bondage nor liberation, which would imply the denial of the facts of defilement and purity.

Thus having stated the own-definition of the imagination of the unreal, now [the author] states its inclusive definition. It shows how, there being only the imagination of the unreal, there could be the inclusion of the three natures.

6. The imagined, the other-dependent,
[58] And the absolutley accomplished,
Are derived [respectively] from

The objects, the imagination of the unreal,
And the absence of the pair.

The object is the imagined nature, the imagination of the unreal is the other-dependent nature, and the absence of the graspable-grasper duality is the absolutely accomplished nature.

Now is shown a definition which can be used as an instrument in comprehending the negative definition of the same imagination of the unreal :

7. Depending upon perception
[61] There arises non-perception,
And depending upon non-perception
There arises non-perception.

Depending upon the perception that there are only representations of consciousness, there arises the non-perception of knowable things. Depending upon the non-perception of knowable things, there arises the non-perception of the mere representations of consciousness, too. Thus one understands the negative definition of graspable and grasper.

8. Therefore it remains established
[62] That perception has the same nature
As non-perception.

Because, there being no perceivable things, there is no possibility of having perception either.

Therefore the sameness
Of non-perception and perception
Should be recognized.

Bacause perception as such is not obtained. Though not having the own-nature of perception, still it is called perception because there are the appearances of unreal objects.

Now follows the classification-definition of the same imagination of the unreal :

9. The imagination of the unreal
[64] Is *citta* as well as *caittas*,
Belonging to all three worlds.

[The three worlds refer to] the distinction between the worlds of passion, forms, and formless beings.

Now follows the synonym-definition :

> There, perception of objects is consciousness,
> And perception of their qualities is mental factors.

Consciousness is perception of just the objects. The mental factors, namely, feeling etc., are the perception of the qualities of the same objects.

The next verse states the function-definition :

> 10. One is the source-consciousness,
> [66] And the other is the enjoyment-consciousness.
> There, the mental factors are
> Enjoyment, determination and motivation.

The store-consciousness being the source of other consciousnesses is called the source-consciousness. The active consciousness, which has the latter as its source, is called the enjoyment-consciousness. Enjoyment refers to feeling etc., determination to concept, and motivation to the conditioning forces such as volition, attention etc., of consciousness.

[The next two verses] state the defilement-definition :

> 11. The world is oppressed / defiled
> [68] (1) By being concealed,
> (2) By being raised,
> (3) By being led,
> (4) By being seized,
> (5) By being completed,
> (6) By being trebly determined,
> (7) By enjoying,
> (8) By being attracted,

> 12. (9) By being bound,
> [68] (10) By being orientated, and
> (11-12) By being subjected to suffering.

There, (1) 'by being concealed' means 'by being impeded by ignorance from seeing things as they are', (2) 'by being raised' means 'by the installation of the impressions of deeds on consciousness by the conditioning forces', (3) 'by being led' means 'by being taken by consciousness to the place of re-birth', (4) 'by being seized' means '[by being seized] by the *nāma* and *rūpa* of egohood', (5) 'by being completed' means '[by being completed] by the six organs', (6) 'by being trebly determined' means '[by being trebly determined] by contact', (7) 'by enjoying' means 'by feeling', (8) 'by being attracted' means '[by being attracted] by the desire for a new existence, the seeds of which have already been sown by previous deeds', (9) 'by being bound' means '[by being bound] by the inclinations towards sense-pleasure etc., which are conducive to a new birth of the consciousness', (10) 'by being orientated' means 'by making the deeds of former existence tend to manifest their matured fruits in a new existence', (11-12) 'by being subjected to suffering' means '[by being subjected] to birth, old age, and death'. By all these is the world oppressed / defiled.

This [list of]

> The oppressives / defilements,
> All proceeding from the imagination of the unreal,
> Could be classified
> Either into three groups,
> Or into two groups,
> Or into seven groups.

The classification of the oppressives/defilements into three groups is as follows : (1) oppressive oppressors, namely ignorance, desire and inclinations; (2) deed-oppressives, namely conditioning forces and existence/birth; (3) birth oppressives, namely the remaining members.

The classification of the oppressives/defilements into two groups is as follows : (1) causal oppressives/defilements which include the groups of oppressive oppressors, and deed-oppressives; (2) resultant oppressives which are the same as the birth-oppressives.

The classification of the oppressives/defilements into seven groups refer to the seven kinds of causes such as, (1) cause of error, namely ignorance, (2) cause of sowing of seeds, namely conditioning forces, (3) cause of direction, namely consciousness, (4) cause of seizure, namely *nāma* and *rūpa* and the six bases, (5) cause of enjoyment, namely contact and feeling, (6) cause of attraction, namely desire, inclinations and existences/birth, and (7) cause of unrest, namely birth, old age and death.

All these oppressives/defilements operate due to the imagination of the unreal.

The ninefold definition, giving the summary-meaning of the imagination of the unreal, has [now] been explained. Those definitions are, namely, positive definition, negative definition, own-definition, inclusive definition, instrumental definition, classification definition, synonym-definition, activity-definition and defilement-definition.

Thus having explained the imagination of the unreal, the author now shows how the emptiness should be understood :

13. About the emptiness
[72] One should summarily know
Its definition,
Its synonyms along with their meaning,
Its classification,
And the reason for its classification.

How the definition of the emptiness is to be understood ?

14. The negation of the pair
[73] Is indeed the assertion of such negation;
This is the definition of the emptiness.

There is the negation of the pair of the graspable and grasper. The definition of emptiness, then, is the assertion of that negation. Thus, it is shown how the emptiness is to be defined in negative terms. And, what those negative terms are, [is further stated] :

It is neither [total] assertion,
Nor [total] negation.

Why not [total] assertion ? Because there is the negation of the pair of subject and object. Why not [total] negation ? Because there is the assertion of the negation of that pair. This indeed is the definition of the emptiness. Therefore, with reference to the imagination of the unreal, the emptiness is :

> Neither different from the imagination of the unreal,
> Nor identical with the imagination of the unreal.

If different, it would imply that the 'universal' [*dharmatā*] is other than the particular things [*dharmas*], which is unacceptable. For example, 'impermanence' is not other than the impermanent things, and the state of suffering is not other than suffering itself. If identical, there would be no place for purifying knowledge, nor would there be the commonplace knowledge. Thus is shown a definition which states that emptiness is that which is free from being different from thatness.

How is the synonym [of emptiness] to be understood ?

> 15. Suchness, the extreme limit of existence,
> [75] The uncaused, absoluteness,
> The source-reality :
> These are summarily the synonyms of emptiness.

How is the meaning of these synonyms to be understood ?

> 16. The synonyms respectively mean that the emptiness is
> [75] Never otherwise,
> Never falsified,
> Never admitting a cause,
> The object intuited by sages,
> And that it is
> The source of the powers of the sages.

The emptiness is called suchness, in the sense that it is never otherwise, and insofar as it remains ever the same way. It is called the extreme limit of existence in the sense that it is never falsified, because it is never an object of doubt. It is called the uncaused, because it does not admit for itself any cause, for it is far from having any cause whatsoever. It is called the absoluteness/the ultimate object, because it is the object of the knowledge of the sages, meaning that it is the object of the ultimate knowledge. It is called the source-reality, because it is the source of the powers to the sages, meaning that the powers of the sages have their origin depending upon it : here the term *dhātu* is used in the sense of *hetu*, indeed.

How is the classification of the emptiness to be understood ?

[76] 17. It is defiled and purified;

So is its classification. In what condition is it defiled, and in what condition is it purified ?

It is with and without impurities.

When it is with impurities, then it is defiled, and when it is rid of the impurities, then it is purified. Getting rid of the impurities once associated with it, implies that it is changing in character. How is it then that it is still not impermanent ? Because its

Purity is understood
As the purity of elemental water,
Gold and space.

[The purity of the emptiness is recovered] by shaking off the accidental impurities, which does not mean a change in its own-nature.

Here is another classification according to which there are sixteen kinds of emptiness: (1) emptiness of internal [elements], (2) emptiness of external [elements], (3) emptiness of internal as well as external [elements], (4) emptiness of the great, (5) emptiness of emptiness, (6) emptiness of the absolute object, (7) emptiness of the conditioned [elements], (8) emptiness of the unconditioned [elements], (9) emptiness of the ultimate [element], (10) emptiness of the eternal [element], (11) emptiness of the unforsaken [element], (12) emptiness of nature, (13) emptiness of defining marks, (14) emptiness of every power, (15) emptiness of negation, (16) emptiness of negation as own-nature.

All those kinds of emptiness should be briefly understood :

18. There is the emptiness of the enjoyer,
[79] Emptiness of the enjoyed,

Emptiness of the body of the enjoyer and enjoyed,
Emptiness of the basic thing,
Emptiness of that by which it
[i.e. the emptiness of enjoyer etc.] is perceived,
Emptiness of the way in which it is perceived, and
Emptiness of that for which it is perceived.

Here, the emptiness of the enjoyer means the emptiness of the internal senses etc., the emptiness of the enjoyed means the emptiness of the external elements, the emptiness of their bodies, namely the *śarīras* which are the basis of both the enjoyer and the enjoyed, means the emptiness of the internal and the external elements. The basic thing means the universe which is the basis of the enjoyer, the enjoyed and their bodies. Its emptiness is called the emptiness of the great because of the vastness of the universe. The emptiness of the internal senses etc., is perceived by the knowledge of emptiness, whose emptiness is called the emptiness of emptiness. The emptiness of internal senses is perceived as the absolute object, whose emptiness is called the emptiness of the absolute object. The emptiness of that for which the Bodhisattva attains the emptiness of the internal senses etc., is the final kind of emptiness.

For what, indeed, is the emptiness of the internal senses etc. attained ?

[80] 19. For the attainment of the twofold prosperity,
[namely], the conditioned as well as the unconditioned fortune,
For the everlasting benefit of the living beings,
[namely], for the ultimate benefit of the living beings,
And for not leaving the *saṃsāra*,

[that is, otherwise], not seeing the emptiness of the eternal *saṃsāra*, one, being depressed, would rather leave the world.

For the non-cessation of fortune,

Even in the absolute state of *nirvāṇa* there is something that one does not give up, the emptiness of which is called the emptiness of the unforsaken.

[81] 20. For the purity of the lineage,
Lineage means nature, for it belongs to one's own nature.
For attaining the defining marks,

[that is], for attaining the marks that are characteristic of great men.

And, for the purity of the powers of enlightenment,
Does the Bodhisattva attain the emptiness of internal senses etc.

[namely], for the purity of the powers such as strength, fearlessness, special endowments etc. Thus, indeed, the fact of the fourteen kinds of emptiness should be known.

What other kinds of emptiness are still there ?

21. The negation of *pudgala* and *dharmas*
[82] Is indeed one kind of emptiness there,
The existence of that negation in it [i.e. in the enjoyer etc.]
Is another kind of emptiness.

The negation of *pudgala* and *dharmas* is one emptiness. Another kind of emptiness is the existence of that negation in the above said enjoyer etc. These two kinds of emptiness are explained at the end in order to make the definition of the emptiness clear : in order to avoid the exaggeration of *pudgala* and *dharmas* the emptiness is explained, on the one hand, as the negation of *pudgala* and *dharmas*, and in order to avoid the underestimation of their negation the emptiness is explained, on the other hand, as having the negation of *pudgala* and *dharmas* for its own-nature. This is how the classification of emptiness is to be understood.

How is the reason [for such a classification] to be understood ?

22. If it were not ever defiled,
[84] Then all living beings would be ever liberated;
If it were not ever purified,
Then all efforts for liberation would be futile.

If the emptiness of elements would not be defiled by the accidental and secondary defilements, even when no remedy is applied, then, since there are no defilements whatsoever, all living beings would become liberated without any effort at all. Again, if it would not become purified, even when some remedy is applied, then the efforts towards liberation would prove fruitless.

However,

23. It is neither defiled nor undefiled,

[85] Also, it is neither purified nor unpurified;

How is it that it is neither defiled nor unpurified ? It is so by its very nature,

Because of the shining nature of *citta*;

How is it neither undefiled nor purified :

Because of the accidental character of the defilements.

Thus, the above-mentioned classification of emptiness into defiled and purified is justified.

There, the summary-meaning of emptiness is to be understood under two heads : one, the definition [of emptiness], and the other, the establishment [of the same definition]. There, definition is again, twofold : positive and negative. The positive definition is likewise twofold : one, [the assertion that emptiness is] neither assertion nor negation; two, [the assertion that emptiness is] that which is free from being different from thatness. By the establishment [of definition] is to be understood the establishment of synonyms of emptiness etc. There, by the fourfold introduction of the emptiness the following four definitions of it are intended: its own-definition, operative-definition, defilement-purity-definition and rationality-definition; these definitions help one respectively to get rid of uncertainly, fear, indolence and doubt.

Appendix II

A TREATISE ON THE THREE NATURES

1. The imagined,
[92] The other-dependent,
The absolutely accomplished:
These are the three natures,
Which should be thoroughly known by the wise.

2. That which appears is the other-dependent,
[93] For it depends on causal conditions;
The form in which it appears is the imagined,
For it is merely an imagination.

3. The perpetual absence of the form
[93] In which the other-dependent appears,
Is to be understood as
The absolutely accomplished nature,
For it is never otherwise.

4. What is it that appears?
[93] It is the imagination of the non-existent.
How does it appear?
In the form of duality.
What will result from its non-existence?
There will be the state of non-duality.

5. What is meant by the imagination of the non-existent?
[93] It is thought,
For by it [the subject-object duality] is imagined.
The form in which it imagines a thing
Never at all exists as such.

6. The *citta* takes on two modes, as cause and effect,
[94] It is then respectively called
The store-consciousness and the active consciousness,
The latter being seven-fold.

7. The first is called *citta,* meaning 'collected',
[94] Because in it are collected the seeds
Of defilements and habits;
The second, however, is called *citta,*
Because it acts in diverse ways.

8. Collectively [i.e. as a collection of store-consciousness and seven active consciousnesses]
[95] It is the imagination of the unreal forms [of subjectivity and objectivity];
That, too, is said to be three-fold:
Maturing, caused and phenomenal.

9. Of them, the first, [namely the maturing one],
[95] Is the basic consciousness,
Because its nature is to become matured;
The others, [namely the caused and the phenomenal ones],
Are the active consciousness,
For, the latter for its reality, depends
On the knowledge of the perceived-perceiver distinction.

10. The profundity of the three natures
[98] Is indeed recognized, because
The defiled and the pure are each
Existent as well as non-existent,
Dual as well as unitary;
Also because
The three natures are not mutually different
In definition.

11. The imagined nature is said
[99] To be defined both as existent and as non-existent,
For on the one hand it is grasped as existent,
While, on the other,
It is totally non-existent.

12. The other-dependent nature is said
[99] To be defined both as existent and as non-existent,
For, it exists as an illusion,
It does not exist, though, in the form in which it appears.

13. The absolutely accomplished nature is said
[100] To be defined both as existent and as non-existent,
For, it exists as a state of non-duality,
It is also the non-existence of duality.

14. The nature that is imagined by the ignorant is said
[100] To be both dual and unitary,
For, as it is imagined
A thing has two forms,
But as those two forms do not exist,
It is unitary.

15. The other-dependent nature is said
[101] To be dual as well as unitary,
For, it appears in dual form,
While it has an illusory unity as well.

16. The absolutely accomplished nature is said
[101] To be dual as well as unitary,
For, on the one hand,
It is by nature the absence of duality,
And, on the other hand,
It is in the nature of unity without duality.

17. What is to be known as being defined
[102] As defilement are the imagined and the other-dependent natures,
While the absolutely accomplished nature
Is recognized as the definition of purity.

18. The absolutely accomplished nature
[104] Is to be understood
As not different in definition from the imagined nature,
For, the latter being in the nature of unreal duality,
Is by nature the absence of that duality.

19. The imagined nature, too,
[105] Is to be understood
As not different in definition from the absolutely accomplished one,
For, the latter being in the nature of non-duality,
Is by nature the absence of duality.

20. The absolutely accomplished nature
[105] Is to be understood
As not different in definition from the other-dependent nature,
For, the latter being non-existent in the form in which it appears,
Is by nature the non-existence of that form.

21. The other-dependent nature, too,
[106] Is to be understood
As not different in definition from the absolutely accomplished one,
For, the former being in the nature of non-existent duality,
Is by nature non-existent in the form in which it appears.

22. For the sake of proficiency
[107] A particular order of the natures
Is recommended, which takes into account

The conventions [about them], and
How one understands them.

23. The imagined nature is essentially of conventional values,
[108] The other, [namely the other-dependent nature],
Is essentially that which brings about such conventional values,
And the third, [namely the absolutely accomplished nature],
Is the nature freed of all conventional values.

24. First, the other-dependent nature,
[109] Which is essentially the absence of duality
Is understood;
Then, the unreal duality,
Namely the duality that is mere imagination,
Is understood.

25. Then is understood
[110] The absolutely accomplished nature,
Which is positively the absence of duality,
For, that very nature is then said
To be both existing and non-existing.

26. All these three natures
[111] Depend for their definition
On [the concept of] non-duality;
For, [with reference to the imagined nature],
There is the unreality of duality,
[With reference to the other-dependent nature],
It is not in the dual form in which it appears,
And, [with reference to the absolutely accomplished nature],
It is by its very nature the absence of that duality.

27. It is like the magical power,
[112] Which by the working of incantations
Appears in the nature of an elephant;

There is altogether no elephant at all
But only its form.

28. The elephant stands for the imagined nature,
[113] Its form for the other-dependent nature,
And, that which remains when the elephant has been negated,
Stands for the absolutely accomplished nature.

29. So, the imagination of the unreal
[113] By the working of the basic thought
Appears in the nature of duality;
There is altogether no duality at all,
But only its form.

30. The basic consciousness is like the incantations,
[114] Suchness is like the piece of wood,
The [subect-object] discrimination is like the form of the elephant
And the duality is like the elephant.

31. In comprehending the truth of things
[119] All three definitions have to be taken together,
[Although methods of] knowledge, rejection and attainment
Are to be employed respectively.

32. There, knowledge is non-perception,
[120] Rejection/destruction is non-appearance,
Attainment, effected by perception,
Is direct realization.

33. By the non-perception of duality
[121] The form of duality disappears;
The non-duality resulting from its disappearance
Is then attained.

34. It is just as the case of magic,
[122] In which the non-perception of the elephant,

The disappearance of its form, and the perception
of the piece of wood,
Take place all at once.

35. The attainment of liberation becomes effortless
[123] By getting rid of misunderstanding,
Intellectually seeing the meaninglessness,
And following the threefold knowledge.

36. Through the perception
[124] That there is only thought,
There arises the non-perception of knowable
things;
Through the non-perception of knowable things,
There arises the non-perception of thought, too.

37. From the non-perception of duality
[125] There arises the perception of the essence of
reality;
From the perception of the essence of reality
There arises the perception of unlimitedness.

38. The wise man, having perceived the unlimitedness,
[125] And seeing the meaning of oneself and others,
Attains the unsurpassed elightenment,
Which is in the nature of the three bodies.

Appendix III

A TREATISE IN THIRTY STANZAS

1. Various indeed are the usages
[128] Of the terms *ātman* and *dharma* :
They [all] refer
To the transformations of consciousness;
Threefold is such transformation :

2. They are, namely,
[134] Maturing, thinking, and representation of consciousness of object.
There the maturing [consciousness]
Is otherwise called the store-consciousness,
Which carries the seeds of all [past experiences].

3. It has [within itself]
[135] The representations of consciousness
Of unknown objects and places;
It is always associated with
Touch, attentiveness, knowledge,
Conception and volition.

4. The feeling therein is that of indifference;
[135] It [i.e. the store-consciousness] is unobscured and undefined;
Similarly indifferent are touch etc.,
And it [i.e. the store-consciousness] is like a torrent of water;

5. And it ceases to exist at the attainment of *arhattva*.
[135] The consciousness called *manas*
Has the store-consciousness for its support and object.
It is essentially an act of thinking.

6. It is always associated with four defilements,
[136] Which are themselves obscured and undefined;
Those four defilements are, namely,
Belief in self, ignorance about self,
Pride in self, and love of self.

7. It [i.e. the consciousness called *manas*] is associated
[136] Also with others like touch etc.,
Which are all of the same nature
As the region in which one is born.
It does not belong to one in the state of arhatship;
Nor does it operate
In the state of suppressed consciousness,
Nor in the supra-mundane path.

8. It [i.e. the above described] is the second
[137] transformation [of consciousness].
The third transformation of consciousness
Is the same as the perception of the sixfold object;
It could be good or bad or indifferent in character.

9. It is associated with three kinds of mental factors:
[138] Universal, specific and good;
It is associated, similarly,
With primary as well as secondary defilements;
It is subject to three kinds of feelings, too.

10. Of those associates the first, [namely the universal.]
[138] ones,
Are touch etc.,
[The second, namely] the specific ones,
Are desire, resolve and memory.
Together with concentration and knowledge.
Faith, sense of shame, fear of censure,

11. The triad of non-covetousness etc., courage,
[138] Composure, equanimity along with alertness,

And harmlessness are [the third, namely] the good ones.
The defilements are passionate attachment,
Grudge, stupidity,

12. Pride, [false] views, and doubt.
[139] Anger, hatred,
Hypocrisy, envy, jealousy, spite along with deceit,

13. Dishonesty, arrogance,
[139] Harmfulness, shamelessness, defiance of censure,
Sluggishness, conceit, unbelief, indolence,
Carelessness, bad memory,

14. Distraction of mind,
[139] Thoughtlessness, remorse, sleepiness,
Reasoning and deliberation,
Are the secondary defilements.
The latter two couples, [namely
Remorse and sleepinesss, reasoning and deliberation],
Can be of two kinds, [namely defiled and undefiled] .

15. Depending on the conditions available
[139] The five sense-consciousnesses,
Together or separately,
Originate on the root-consciousness,
Just as waves originate on water.

16. The thought-consciousness, however,
[139] Manifests itself at all times,
Except for those [i] who are born
Into the region where the beings are in a state of unconsciousness,
[ii] Who have entered either of the two trances,
In which there is no operation of consciousness,
[iii] Who are unconscious by reason
Of sleepiness or faint.

17. This [threefold] transformation of consciousness
[146] Is just the distinction [between subject and object];
What is thus distinguished,
Does not exist as [subject and object].
Therefore this is all mere representation of consciousness.

18. The consciousness contains all seeds;
[147] Its such and such transformations
Proceed by mutual influence,
On account of which such and such [subject-object] discriminations arise.

19. Once the previous stage of maturation
[150] Has been exhausted,
The impressions of deeds
Along with those of the two-fold grasping
Engender the next stage of maturation.

20. The subject-matter that is liable
[151] To subject-object distinction
By whatsoever sort of subject-object discrimination,
Is all just imagined nature;
It does not exist.

21. The other-dependent nature, however,
[153] Is the act of graspable-grasper discrimination;
It depends for its origin on conditions.
The absolutely accomplished nature
Is the latter's [i.e. the other-dependent nature's]
Perpetual devoidness of the former [i.e. the imagined nature].

22. For that reason, indeed,
[155] It is said to be neither different,
Nor non-different
From the other-dependent nature.
It is like impermanence etc.

As long as this absolutely accomplished nature
Is not seen,
That other-dependent nature, too,
Is not seen.

23. Corresponding to the three-fold nature
[157] There is also a three-fold naturelessness;
Referring to this fact it has been said
That there is the naturelessness of all elements.

24. The first nature is natureless by its very
[157] definition,
The second nature, again, does not come into being by itself,
And this constitutes the second kind of naturelessness.

25. That from which all elements have their ultimate
[157] reality,
Is the third naturelessness,
It is also called suchness,
Because it remains always as such;
That is itself the state in which one realizes the meaning
Of mere representation of consciousness, too.

26. As long as consciousness does not abide
[158] In the realization [that the subject-object designations]
Are mere representations of consciousness,
The attachment to the twofold grasping
Will not cease to operate.

27. One does not abide in the realization
[159] Of mere representations of consciousness
Just on account of the [theoretical] perception
That all this is mere representation of consciousness,
If one places [= sees] something before oneself.

28. One does abide in the realization
[159] Of mere [representation of] consciousness

When one does not perceive also a supporting consciousness,
For, the graspable objects being absent,
There cannot either be the grasping of that,
[Namely, the grasping of the supporting consciousness].

29. That indeed is the supramundane knowledge
[160] When one has no mind that knows,
And no object for its support;
It follows the revulsion of basis
Through the twofold removal of wickedness;

30. That itself is the pure source-reality,
[160] Incomprehensible, auspicious, and unchangeable;
Being delightful, it is the emancipated body,
Which is also called the truth [-body] of the great sage.

IV

A TREATISE IN TWENTY STANZAS AND ITS EXPLANATION

In the Mahāyāna system it has been established that those belonging to the three worlds are mere representations of consciousness. This is clear from the aphorism, 'Oh ! Jinaputra, those belonging to the three worlds are mere mind'. The terms mind [*citta*], thought-consciousness, [*mano-vijñāna*] and representation of consciousness [*vijñapti*] are synonyms. Here mind should be understood along with its associates [*samprayoga*]. The term 'mere' indicates the exclusion of the [external] objects.

1. It is all mere representation of consciousness,
[166] Because there is the appearance of non-existent objects.
Just as a man with a cataract
Sees hairs, moons etc.,
Which do not exist in reality.

Here it is asked,

2. If the representations of consciousness
[167] Are without [extra-mental] objects,
Then there would be no determination [of experience] with regard to space and time,
Nor would there be indeterminacy of it with regard to streams [i.e. individuals]
Nor would there be determination of actions prompted [by a particular experience].

What is being said ? If a representation of colour etc. arises without the corresponding external objects like colour etc., then the former is not determined by the latter. Why is it, then, that a representation of colour etc. does not arise everywhere, but only in some particular places ? Even then it does not always occur, but only sometimes. Again, it occurs to the streams of all present in those places and at those times, not just to the stream of a single person .The latter, for example, is the case with regard to the appearance of hair etc., which occurs only to the streams of the cataract-ridden people, not of others. Why is it, again, that the hairs, flies, etc. seen by the cataract-ridden people do not function as hair etc., while those seen by others do ? Food, drink, clothes, poison, weapons etc., seen in a dream do not function as food etc., while those seen in a waking state do. The city of Gandharva does not function as a city, while other [cities] do. Therefore in the absence of [external] objects it does not make any sense to speak of the spatio-temporal determination [of experience], the indeterminacy of streams [to which their representations of consciousness occur], and the fixed ways of their functioning. This objection does not hold, because

3. Determination of space etc., is obtained
[167] Just as [in] the case of a dream;

The term *svapna-vat* in the stanza means *svapna iva*, both meaning "just as [in] the case of a dream". How ? In a dream, without [corresponding external] objects, things like flies, gardens, ladies and men, are seen. They are not seen everywhere, but only in some particular places [for example where the dreamer sleeps]; even in those places they are not seen always, but only sometimes [for example, only when one dreams]. Thus the spatio-temporal determinations are obtained even when there are no corresponding external objects.

Again, indeterminacy [of experience] with regards to streams [i.e. individuals] is obtained
Just as [in] the case [of the experience] of ghosts :

In this line, the term "obtained" [*siddha*] is understood [from the previous line]; and the term *preta-vat* means *preta-iva*, [both meaning "just as in the case of the experience of ghosts"]. How is the analogy obtained ?

All of them [i.e. the ghosts] have the same vision
of pus-river etc.

'Pus-river' means 'a river full of pus', just as 'ghee-jug' would mean 'a jug full of ghee'. The ghosts having the same kind of matured [seeds of] deeds see, all of them, the pus-river, and not just one of them. "Etc." means that, similar to the river full of pus, there are also rivers full of urine, excrement etc., and places inhabited by people carrying spears and swords, all of which are seen by the ghosts. Thus, the indeterminacy of streams to which the representations of consciousness occur is obtained even when there are not [corresponding external] objects.

4. Determined actions [resulting from experience]
[168] Are obtained as those [obtained] by a dreamer.

The term 'obtained' [*siddha*] is understood from the previous stanza. For instance, a dreamer experiences the discharge of semen, although in a dream there is no [sexual] union of two persons. Thus, indeed, the fourfold factor, namely the spatio-temporal determination etc., is obtained in different instances.

Again, all those [four factors are obtained]
As in the case of hells;

The term 'obtained' [*siddha*] is understood from the previous line. *Naraka-vat* means *narakeṣu iva,* [both meaning "as in the case of hells"]. How are [the four factors] obtained [in the case of hells] ?

There all [its inhabitants without exception]
Behold the infernal guards etc.,
And experience the torments by them.

The sight of the infernal guards in hells experienced by the hell-inhabitants is obtained with spatio-temporal determinations, indeed. "Etc." includes similar sights of dogs, birds, iron-balls and mountains coming in and going out. They are the experiences equally of all the inhabitants of hells, not merely of one. Similarly, the torments [inflicted] by the infernal guards are also experienced by all the inhabitants. All these experiences are obtained inspite of the fact that in reality there are no infernal guards etc. [If, therefore, all the inhabitants of hells have similar experiences], it is owing to their own matured [seeds of] deeds of the same kind. Thus in places other than hells, too, the four factors, namely spatio-temporal determinations etc., should be understood as obtained.

Why is it, again, that the beings like the infernal guards, dogs, and birds, are said to be non-existent [in hells]? [This is] because they do not fit in with the context. They cannot possibly be some of the hell-inhabitants, [who are condemned to hell], for it would mean that they, too, are experiencing the sufferings of hell. It cannot also be the case that the beings in hells torture each other, for then it will be impossible to determine which of them are hell-inhabitants, and which are infernal guards. Nor is it possible for them to torture each other, because being of equal strength of action, stature and valour they cannot frighten each other. [If the infernal guards etc. were real beings in hell], they would themselves be unable to bear the heat of the flaming iron-like ground. How then would they torture others ? Or supposing that they are not some of those hell-inhabitants, [who are condemned to hell], why should they, then, be born there ?

How indeed are the animals born in heaven ? The animals, ghosts, infernal guards etc. are also born in hells, in the same manner.

5. Animals are born in heaven;
[169] However, they are not similarly born in hell,
Nor are the infernal guards born in hell,
For they do not experience the sufferings of hell.

The animals born in heaven enjoy there the pleasures accruing from the deeds due to which they are born there. Thus they are enjoyers of the pleasure of that world. But as for the infernal guards etc., they do not experience the infernal sufferings. Therefore, neither the birth of animals nor of infernal guards in hell does make sense.

[It may then be argued that] due to the deeds of the hell-inhabitants, some special beings are born there—beings which are endowed with such colour, figure, size and strength that they get the title of infernal guards etc. In order to generate fear in others these beings transform themselves so that they seem to perform actions such as [extraordinary] manual gestures etc. They also take on the appearances of ram-mountains rushing in and out, and of thorns turning up and down in an iron forest.

It is not that they [i.e. the infernal guards etc.] are not born at all [in the manner described above]. [However],

6. If the birth of [special] beings
[169] Can be thus recognized [as issuing]
From their [i.e. the hell-inhabitants'] deeds,
Why not then recognize
The transformation of their consciousness ?

That is, why not recognize the transformation of consciousness itself as issuing from their deeds ? Why should again [special] beings be imagined to be born ? Moreover,

7. An impression of deed is imagined to be in one place,
[170] And its fruit in another place !
Why not instead recognize [the fruit]
In the same place as the impression ?

The birth of [special] beings, and their transformation, is imagined [to take place] due to the deed of the hell-inhabitants. The impression of [that] deed is embedded in their stream of consciousness, not elsewhere. Why not then recognize that its [i.e. the impression's] fruit being a similar transformation of consciousness, is in the same place as the impression [itself]?

[It may be argued that] the fruit has been [rightly] imagined to exist where the impression does not. For what reason ? For reason of the Scriptures. If it were consciousness itself that appears as colour etc., then there would not be things like colour etc. In that case the existence of the bases [of knowledge] such as colour etc., would not have been stated by the Lord. This is no reason. Because,

8. It was with a hidden meaning
[171] That the existence of the bases of knowledge

Such as colour etc. was stated
[By the Buddha] to his disciples,
Just as [the existence of] beings
[Apparently] born by metamorphosis
[Was stated by him].

It has been stated by the Lord to the effect that there are beings apparently born by metamorphosis. However, his hidden meaning is that there is an unbroken continuity of the stream of mind. This is confirmed by the saying, "'There is no being, neither *ātman* nor *dharmas*; they are all caused [i.e. accidental]." Similarly, what has been stated by the Lord to his disciples, who were listening to his instructions, about the existence of the bases [of knowledge] such as colour etc., also has rather a hidden meaning. What is that hidden meaning?

9. What the sage spoke of as the two bases of knowledge
[171] Are (i) the own-seed
From which a representation of consciousness develops,
And (ii) the form in which that representation appears.

What is being said? A representation of consciousness appears as colour. [This representation of consciousness] arises from its own duly matured seed. This seed, and the form in which it appears [namely the form of colour], are respectively what the Lord spoke of as the [two] bases, namely, eye and colour, of the same representation of consciousness. Similarly indeed, [another] representation of consciousness appears as an object of touch. [This representation of consciousness] arises from its own duly matured seed. This seed, and the form in which it appears, are respectively what the Lord spoke of as the [two] bases, namely sense of touch, and object of touch. This is the hidden meaning [mentioned in this stanza]. What, again, is the use of thus instructing with a hidden meaning?

10. By this one is definitely initiated
[172] Into the theory of the non-substantiality of self [*pudgala*],

Being thus instructed, the disciples get initiated into the theory of the non-substantiality of self [*pudgala-nairātmya*]. The eightfold consciousness works on the assumption of the pair of subject and object. But, knowing that there is neither a perceiver, nor a thinker, the disciples come to understand the instruction about the non-substantiality of self, and thus they get initiated into the theory of the non-substantiality of self.

> On the other hand, again,
> By this instruction one is initiated
> Into the non-substantiality of objects [*dharmas*] :

Starting with the phrase "on the other hand [*anyathā*]," the stanza further says how, by the instruction about mere representation of consciousness, one is initiated into the theory of the non-substantiality of objects [*dharmas*]. How ? Namely, knowing that mere representations of consciousness produce the appearance of objects like colour etc., and that there are no objects like colour etc. as such. If, therefore, there is no object at all, then there would not be even that mere representation of consciousness. Therefore, how could [the theory of mere representation of consciousness itself] be established ? The initiation into the theory of the non-substantiality of *dharmas* does not at all mean that there are no *dharmas* altogether. On the contrary

> [The self and the objects are non-substantial]
> With regard to their imagined nature.

The ignorant people imagine that *dharmas* are in the nature of being graspable and grasper etc. The non-substantiality of the *dharmas* is with regard to this imagined nature, not with regard to the ineffable nature, which is the object [of the knowledge] of the enlightened ones. Similarly, a representation of consciousness is non-substantial with regard to the nature imagined by another representation of consciousness. This is how one is initiated into the theory of the non-substantiality of the representation of consciousness; and it is through this initiation, which establishes the doctrine of mere representation of consciousness, that one is initiated into the theory of the non-substantiality of all *dharmas*, not through the denial of their [i.e. *dharmas*'] existence.

Otherwise a representation of consciousness would have an object which would be other than the representation of consciousness itself, and thus, the representation of consciousness having objects, the theory of mere representation would not be obtained.

How again is one to understand that the existence of the bases, [of knowledge] such as colour etc., was stated by the Lord with this hidden meaning, and that there are no such things that would become separate objects of the representations of consciousness of colour etc.? Because,

11. The object is experienced
[175] Neither as a single entity,
Nor as many discrete atoms,
Nor as an aggregate of atoms,
Because not a single atom is obtained in experience at all.

What is being said ? The bases of knowledge like colour etc. supposedly become separately, the objects of the representations of consciousness of colour etc. Do they do so as one single entity, like the colour-whole suggested by the Vaiśeṣikas ? or as many atomic entities ? or as aggregated atoms ? As objects [of knowledge] they are not a single entity, because never does one grasp [=know] a colour-whole as different from [its] parts. Nor are they many atomic entities, because one does not ever grasp the atoms separately. Nor are they an aggregated object of [knowledge], because not even a single atom is obtained [in experience]. Why ?

12. One atom joined at once to six other atoms
[176] Must have six parts,

If six sides of an atom are joined at once by six [other] atoms, then it is proved that an atom has six parts, because one atom's place cannot be another's.

On the other hand, if they are said
To occupy the same place,

Then their aggregate would mean
Nothing more than a single atom.

[Let one suppose] that the place of a single atom becomes the place of six atoms [at once]. Then all of them having the same place, the whole aggregate [of them] would be nothing more than a single atom, and there being no mutual distinction [between those seven atoms] there would not be any aggregate [of them], either, to be seen. In fact the atoms do not join [to each other] at all, for they have no parts. The Kāśmīra Vaibhāṣikas [say] that there is no problem of atoms joining [to each other], because it is the aggregates [of atoms] that join to each other. To them it should be said, namely, that an aggregate of atoms is not something different from them [i.e. from the constituent atoms].

13. As there is no joining of atoms,
[177] Whose joining can be attributed on their aggregates ?
The term 'joining' [*saṃyoga*] is understood [from the context].
There can be no joining of atoms,
Not because they have no parts.

Otherwise the aggregates [of atoms] would join [to each other]. Therefore it should not be said that, it is because they [=atoms] do not have parts that there is no joining of them. For, there is no joining of even the aggregates of atoms, which do have parts. Therefore, not even a single atom is obtained [in experience]. Whether the joining of an atom is recognized or not,

14. That which has different parts
[178] Cannot make a unity,

[This is] another [problem] indeed. If an atom has different parts such as an upper part and a lower part, then how can such an atom still have unity ?

[On the contrary, if it has no parts,]
How come it is subject to shadow and concealment?

If each atom did not have different parts, then how is it that at sunrise there is shadow in one place, and sunshine in another place ? For, it [i.e. an atom] does not have an 'other' side where there would not be any sunshine. If, again, difference of sides is not recognized, how can there be concealment of one atom by another? No single atom has indeed an other side where the arrival of one [atom] would cause the obscuration of another. It amounts to saying that there being no obscuration [of any atom], an aggregate of atoms would not be anything more than a single atom, because all atoms would occupy the same place at once.

Why not, then, recognize that the shadow and concealment belong to the aggregate [of atoms], rather than to an atom. Is then the aggregate of atoms, to which they [i.e. shadow and concealment] would belong, recognized as different from those atoms ? It is said,

It cannot be argued that they [i.e. shadow
  and concealment]
Belong to the aggregate of atoms,
Unless the aggregate is admitted to be
Different from atoms.

If the aggregate of atoms is not recognized as different from the atoms, they [i.e. shadow and concealment] cannot be obtained as belonging to the aggregate. No matter whether it is an atom or an aggregate, it is an induced imagination. What use, then, is this thought, if what is defined as colour etc. is not obtained? What indeed is their definition ? It is, on the one hand, their being the object of eye etc., and, on the other, their being blue. That precisely is the [problem] to be solved. 'Blue', 'white' etc. are recognized as an object of eye etc. Is that [object] a single entity, or many entities ? The impossibility of its being many entities has already been said.

15. [If it is assumed that the earth is] a single unit
[179] Then there would be no progressive movement,
Nor simultaneous grasping and non-grasping,

Nor would there be discrete states of many [beings],
Nor would there be subtle and invisible [beings].

If the object of the eye etc. is imagined to be a single entity, rather than many discrete entities, then there would be no progressive walking, which means movement, on earth, for with just one step one will have covered the whole [earth]. Nor would there be the simultaneous grasping [= perception] of the front side [of one thing] and the non-grasping [non-perception] of [its] hind side. Nor would there be the occupation of different places by many discrete elephants, horses etc.; instead where one [animal] is, there can be also another. How then can their discreteness be recognized ? How can there be one place reached by those two animals and yet another not reached by them—[or rather how can one establish it] on the basis of the perception of an empty space between those [two places, because there can be no such empty space].

If two things are distinguished only on the basis of definition, and not otherwise, then the tiny aquatic bacteria being equal in size with the huge animals, would not be invisible. Therefore, of necessity, the difference between atoms should be recognized. [But it has already been stated that] not a single [atom] is obtained in experience. That being unobtained, it becomes proved that colour etc. are not obtained as object of the eye etc., and that there is mere representation of consciousness.

Existence or non-existence [of something] is proved using the means of knowledge [*pramāṇa-vaśāt*]. Of all the means of knowledge sense-perception is the strongest one. If so, there being no object, how does one get the awareness such as 'this thing is being perceived by me' ?

16. Perception [can occur without extra-mental object],
[182] Just as it happens in a dream etc.

The phrase 'without extra-mental object' [*vinā-api-arthena*] is understood from the above discussion.

At the time when that perception occurs,
The [corresponding external] object is not found;
How can then one speak of its perception ?

At the time when in a dream one has the awareness that 'this is being perceived by me', that object is not really seen by one; because, on the one hand, that awareness is determined solely by the thought-consciousness, and on the other hand, at that time the eye-consciousness is obstructed; therefore how can that awareness be recognized as sense-perception at all ? What is more, the respective colour or taste of a momentary object is definitely obstructed at that time.

Something not experienced before is not remembered by the thought-consciousness. Therefore, that vision [i.e. memory] should be traced to an experience. Thus, it is admitted that colour etc., become its [i.e. memory's] object.

It is not proved that a memory is of previously experienced object. Because,

17. It has [already] been said
[185] That there is a representation of consciousness,
Which appears as that, namely the respective object;

It has already been said that even without a corresponding object, there arises a representation of consciousness, such as eye-consciousness etc., which appears as the respective object.

From it [i.e. from a representation of consciousness]
Does the memory arise.

From a representation of consciousness arises a thought-representation of consciousness, which discriminates between the object such as colour etc., and the subject. The same thought-representation of consciousness, which has with it the memory associate, appears as memory. So an experience of an external object is not proved from the fact that a memory arises.

If in a waking state also a representation of consciousness were of an unreal object, as it is in a dream, then the common man would naturally realize the absence of it [i.e. of an object]. But it is not so [i.e. the common man does not realize the absence of an object]. Therefore, all perceptions are not without objects, as a dream-perception is.

This argument does not make any point. Because,

> Those who are not awake
> Do not realize that the objects they see in a dream
> Do not exist.

Similarly, the common man fast asleep by the sleep of the habit of vainly discriminating between subject and object, as long as he is not awoken, sees, as if in a dream, unreal objects, and does not properly realize their absence. When, however, he is awoken through the acquisition of the supramundane knowledge, which, being non-discriminative, acts as a remedy to the habit of discriminating between subject and object, then, the previously acquired impure, mundane, knowledge being put down, he properly realizes the absence of object. Thus the dream-experience and the waking experience are similar.

If, therefore, the representations of consciousness, which appear as objects, arise out of the particular transformations of the stream of the respective beings, and not out of the particular external objects, then how is it obtained that a representation of consciousness is determined by contacts with bad or good friends, or by listening to right or wrong teachings, for there would be neither contacts with good or bad friends, nor their teaching.

> 18. The representations of consciousness
> [189] Are determined by mutual influence
> Of one individual on another.

The determination of a representation of consciousness of all beings is due to the mutual influence of the representations of consciousness of one individual on another's, as the case may be. The term *mithaḥ* means *paraspara*, both meaning 'mutual'. Therefore, due to a particular representation of consciousness of one stream [i.e. individual] there arises a particular representation of consciousness on another stream, not due to a particular external object.

If, a representation of consciousness in a waking state also were without an external object, as it is in a dream, why is it then that the good and bad actions of a dreamer and non-dreamer, do not have similar desirable or undesirable fruits in the future ? Because

> In a dream mind is overpowered by sleepiness,
> And, therefore, fruits of the actions done in a dream
> Are not on a par with the fruits of those done in a waking state.

This is the reason, not the presence of the external objects.

If it were all mere representation of consciousness, there would be no one's body nor word. How then could death happen to sheep etc. at the hands of butchers who have no body to move about ? If it is said that the death of sheep etc. does not happen at their [i.e. the butchers'] hands, why are the butchers blamed for committing the sin of murder ?

> 19. Death is a change of course caused by
> [192] A particular mental representation of another being,
> Just as the loss of memory etc. of other beings
> Are caused by the thought-power of demons etc.

Due to the thought-power of demons etc., changes like loss of memory, dream-vision and possession of evil spirits, occur in other beings; by the thought-power of a magician there occurs an increase of things; the king Sarana had dream-vision by the influence of Arya Mahakalyana; and, again, the defeat of Vemacitra was caused by the distress induced by the thought of the forest-sages. Similarly, by the influence of a particular representation of consciousness of some beings, there arises in other beings a certain change, which will stop the functioning of their vital organ. By this does death, which means the cutting off of the continuous stream of existence, take place.

20. Otherwise how can it be said that
[192] The Daṇḍaka-forest was destroyed by the anger of the sages ?

'Otherwise' means 'if death of other beings is not recognized as being caused by the influence of others' representation of consciousness'.

The householder Upala was asked by the Lord, who wanted to prove that mental torture is a great punishment, "Have you heard, householder, how the Daṇḍaka-forest and the Kaliṅga-forest were evacuated, and made fit for sacrificial rites ?". It was then said by him in reply, "Oh ! Gautama, I have heard that it was by the mental rage of the sages."

Or, how could mental torture be considered
To be a great punishment ?

If it is imagined that the creatures living in those forests were destroyed by the suprahuman beings, who were pleased by the sages, and that therefore those creatures were killed not by the sages' mental rage, then how by that incident could it be proved that the mental torture is a punishment greater than bodily as well as oral tortures ? On the contrary it can be proved, by maintaining that the death of so many creatures happened solely due to the mental rage of the sages.

If it is all mere representation of consciousness, then do the knowers of other minds [really] know other minds or not ? [Whether they really know or not], what of it ? If they [really] do not know, how are they called knowers of other minds ? Therefore, they do know.

21. Knowledge of those,
[194] [Who claim] to know other minds,
Is unreal,
Just as one's knowledge of one's own mind
[Is unreal].

How that [i.e. knowledge of one's own mind] even is unreal ?

For, in the manner in which [the mind] is known
To the enlightened ones,
It is unknown [to ordinary men].

A mind is known to the enlightened ones in its ineffable nature. A mind, both [other's and one's own], is not known as it is to the ordinary men, because [for them], as [their habit of] discriminating between graspable and grasper is not yet destroyed, there is the false appearance [of subject-object distinction].

The theory of mere representation of consciousness being infinite, with incalculable divisions, deep and subtle,

22. This treatise on the theory
[195] Of mere representation of consciousness
Has been composed by me
According to my ability;
It is not possible, however, to discuss
This [theory] in all its aspects,

This [theory] cannot be discussed in all its implications by people like me, because it is beyond the limits of logic. To whom it is known in all its aspects, is being said,

It is known [only] to the enlightened ones.

It is indeed known in all its aspects to the enlightened Lords, for they no longer have any kind of impediment to the [real knowledge] of all knowable objects.

A Treatise in Twenty Stanzas on the Theory of
Mere Representation of Consciousness
Written by Master Vasubandhu

SELECT BIBLIOGRAPHY

Anacker, S. "Vasubandhu : Three Aspects, A Study of a Buddhist Philosopher." Ph. D. Dissertation, University of Wisconsin, 1970.

Annambhaṭṭa *Tarka-saṅgraha*, with the Commentary called *Dīpikā*, and the Hindi Translation called *Indumatī*. Banaras : The Chowkhamba Sanskrit Series, 1966.

Bhandarkar, D. R. "Who was the Patron of Vasubandhu ?" *The Indian Antiquary*, vol. XLI (January, 1912) : pp. 1-3.

Chatterjee, A. K. *Readings on Yogācāra Buddhism*, Banaras : Banaras Hindu University, 1970.

,, *The Yogācāra Idealism*, 2nd rev. ed. Delhi, Varanasi, Patna : Motilal Banarsidass, 1975.

Conze, E. *Thirty Years of Buddhist Studies : Selected Essays*, Oxford : Bruno Cassirer, 1957.

Dasgupta, S. *Indian Idealism*, New York : The Syndics of the Cambridge University Press, 1962.

De Silva, M. W. *Buddhist and Freudian Psychology*, with a Foreword by Robert H. Thouless. Colombo : Lake House Investments Ltd. Publishers, 1973.

Dharmakīrti, *Nyāya-bindu*, with a Sanskrit Commentary by Dharmottara. Edited with notes, introduction and Hindi translation, by Acharya Chandrashekhara Shastri. Banaras : The Chowkhamba Sanskrit Series, 1954.

Edgerton, F. *Buddhist Hybrid Sanskrit Grammar and Dictionary*, 2 vols. New Haven : Yale University Press, 1953; reprint ed. Delhi, Varanasi, Patna : Motilal Banarsidass, 1972.

Frauwallner, E. "Landmarks in the History of Indian Logic." *Wiener Zeitschrift Für die kunde Süd-und Ostasiens und Archiv Für Indische Philosophie* vol. V (1961) : pp. 125-148.

,, *On the Date of the Buddhist Master of the Law Vasubandhu*. Rome : Serie Orientale Roma, III, 1951.

Gokhale, V. V. "The Pañcaskandhaka by Vasubandhu and its Commentary by Sthiramati." *Annals of the Bhandarkar Oriental Research Institute*, vol. XII (1936-37), pp. 276-86.

Hamilton, C. H. "Buddhist Idealism in Wei Shih Er Shih Lwen." In *Essays in Philosophy*, pp. 99-115. Edited by T. V. Smith and W. K. Wright. Chicago : The Open Court Publishing Co., 1929.

,, *Wei Shih Er Shih Lun Or the Treatise in Twenty Stanzas on Representation-only*. New Haven : American Oriental Society, 1938.

Hamlyn, D. W. *The Theory of Knowledge*, Modern Introduction to Philosophy, General ed., D. J. O'Connor, London and Basingstoke : The Macmillan Press Ltd., 1971.

Hoernle, A. F. R. "Correspondence on 'Kumāragupta, the Patron of Vasubandhu'." *The Indian Antiquiary*, vol. XL (September, 1911) : p. 264.

Hsüan-tsang *The Doctrine of Mere-Consciousness*. Translated by Wei Tat. Hong Kong : 1973.

Īśvarakriṣṇa *Sāṅkhya-kārikā*, with the Commentary by Gaudapada, and Hindi Translation and notes by Sri Dhundhiraja Shastri. Banaras : The Chowkhamba Sanskrit Series, 1963.

Jaini, P. S. "On the Theory of Two Vasubandhus." *Bulletin of the School of Oriental and African Studies*, vol. XXI (1958), pp. 48-53.

Kajiyama, Y. "Bhavaviveka, Sthiramati and Dharmapāla." In *Beitrage zur Geistesgeschichte Indiens*: Festschrift für Erich Frauwallner (Aus Anlass seines 70. Geburtstages), edited by G. Oberhammer, (wien 1968) : pp. 194-203.

Kimura, T. "The Date of Vasubandhu Seen from the Abhidharmakośa. The Four Texts." In *Indian Studies in Honour of Charles Rockwell Lanman*, (Cambridge, Mass., 1929) : pp 89-92.

Kochumuttam, T. "A Study of the Buddhist Epistemology according to Dharmakīrti's *Nyāya-bindu*." M. A. Dissertation, University of Poona, 1974.

Macleod, D. N. G. "A Study of Yogācāra Thought : The

Integral Philosophy of Buddhism." Ph.D. Dissertation, University of Dundee, 1978.

Murti, T. R. V. *The Central Philosophy of Buddhism*. London : George Allen and Unwin Ltd., 1955; 2nd ed., 1960.

Narasimhachar, R. "On Correspondence by A.F.R. Hoernle," *The Indian Antiquary*, vol. XL (December, 1911) : p.312.

Nyanatiloka *Buddhist Dictionary* : *Manual of Buddhist Terms and Doctrines*. Colombo : Frewin & Co., Ltd. 1952; 3rd rev. and enl. ed., 1972.

O'Brien, P.W. "A Chapter on Reality from the Madhyānta-vibhāgaśāstra : Translated and Annotated." *Monumenta Nipponica* vol.IX (1953) : pp. 277-303, and vol. X (1954) pp.227-269.

Ono, G. "The Date of Vasubandhu Seen from the History of Buddhist History." In *Indian Studies in Honour of Charles Rockwell Lanman*, (Cambridge, Mass , 1929) : pp. 93-94.

Pandeya, R.C. ed. *Madhyānta-vibhāga-śāstra* Containing the *Kārikā*-s by Maitreya, *Bhāṣya* by Vasubandhu and *Tīkā* by Sthiramati. Delhi, Varanasi and Panta : Motilal Banarsidass. 1971.

Pathak, K.B. "Kumaragupta, the Patron of Vasubandhu." *The Indian Antiquary*, vol.XL (June 1911), pp. 170-171.

" "On Buddhamitra, the Teacher of Vasubandhu." *The Indian Antiquary*, vol XLI (October, 1912): p.244.

Rahula, W. *Zen and the Taming of the Bull* : *Towards the Definition of Buddhist Thought*. London : Gordon Fraser, 1978.

Raju, P.T. *Idealistic Thought of India*. George Allen & Unwin Ltd., 1953; reprint ed., with the subtitle "Vedanta and Buddhism in the Light of Western Idealism", New York : Johnson Reprint Corporation, 1973.

Sharma, C.D. *A Critical Survey of Indian Philosophy*. Delhi, Varanasi, Patna : Motial Banarsidass, 1964.

Smart, N. *Doctrine and Argument in Indian Philosophy*. London : George Allen and Unwin Ltd., 1964; second impression 1969.

Suzuki, D.T. *On Indian Mahāyāna Buddhism*, ed. with an

an Introduction by Edward Conze. New York : Harper Torchbooks, 1968.

Suzuki, D.T. *Outlines of Mahayana Buddhism*, with an Introduction by Alan Watts. New York : Schocken Books, 1907 Fifth printing 1973.

" *Studies in the Laṅkāvatāra Sūtra* : One of the most important texts of Mahāyāna Buddhism, in which almost all its principal tenets are presented, including the teaching of Zen. London and Boston : Routledge & Kegan Paul Ltd., 1972.

Stcherbatsky, Th. *Buddhist Logic*, 2 vols. New York : Dover Publications, 1962.

" *The Central Conception of Buddhism and the Meaning of the Word "Dharma"*. London : Royal Asiatic Society of Great Britain and Ireland, 1923; 2nd ed., Calcutta: Susil Gupta (India) Ltd., 1956.

" *The Conception of Buddhist Nirvāṇa*. Leningrad : The Academy of Sciences of the USSR, 1927; reprint ed., The Hague, Mouton & Co., 1965.

" trans. *Madhyānta-vibhāga : Discourse on Discrimination Between Middle and Extremes*. Bibliotheca Buddhica XXX, 1936; reprint, Calcutta : Indian Studies, Past and Present, 1971.

Takakasu, J. "A Study of Paramārtha's Life of Vasubandhu; and the Date of Vasubandhu." *Journal of the Royal Asiatic Society* (1935): pp. 33-53.

" "The Date of Vasubandhu, the Great Buddhist Philosopher." In *Indian Studies in Honour of Charles Rockwell Lanman*, (Cambridge, Mass., 1929): pp. 79-88.

" "K'uei-Chi's Version of a Controversy between the Buddhist and the Sāṅkhya Philosophers: An Appendix to the Translation of Paramārtha's 'Life of Vasubandhu'." *T'oung Pao*, Serie II, vol. V (1904) : pp. 461-466.

" The Life of Vasubandhu by Paramārtha (A.D. 499-569)." *T'oung Pao*, Serie II, vol. V. (1904) : pp. 269-296 & 620.

Tatia, N. and A. Thakur, deciphered and edited. *Madhyānta-vibhāga-bhāṣya.* Tibetan Sanskrit Works Series Vol. X. Patna : K.P. Jayaswal Research Institute, 1967.

Thomas, E.J. *The History of Buddhist Thought.* London : Routledge & Kegan Paul Ltd., 1933, 2nd ed., 1951.

Ui, H. "Maitreya as an Historical Personage." In *Indian Studies in Honour of Charles Rockwell Lanman,* (Cambridge, Mass., 1929) : pp. 96-101.

Vasubandhu *Vijñapti-mātratā-siddhiḥ* (including *Viṃśatikā, Viṃśatikā-vṛtti, Triṃśatikā,* and Sthiramati's *Triṃśatikā-bhāṣya*). Edited by Swami Maheswarananda. Varanasi : Gitadharma Karyalaya, 1962.

" *Trisvabhāvanirdeśa,* Sanskrit Text and Tibetan Versions. Edited with an English translation, introduction, and vocabularies by Sujitkumar Mukhopadhyaya. Calcutta : Visvabharati, 1939.

Yamada, I. "*Vijñaptimātratā* of Vasubandhu." *Journal of the Royal Asiatic Society* 2 (1977) : pp. 158-176

INDEX OF SANSKRIT EXPRESSIONS